MARK WHITACRE
AGAINST ALL ODDS

To Joe,

Wishing you
the best,
Mark Whitacre

Mark Whitacre

Against All Odds

How "The Informant" and his Family Turned Defeat into Triumph

Floyd Perrry

To order additional copies of this book, contact:
Xlibris Corporation
1-888-795-4274
www.Xlibris.com
Orders@Xlibris.com
63777

CONTENTS

To Hannah

Dr. Mark E. Whitacre
May 2009
Chief Operating Officer
Cypress Systems, Inc.

FOREWORD

BY

PAUL A. WILLIS

FOUNDER & CEO, CYPRESS SYSTEMS INC.
AND
FORMER VOLUNTEER,
MATCH-TWO PRISONER OUTREACH PROGRAM

THE RIGHT MAN

Exactly twenty-four hours after Mark Whitacre was released from federal prison, I hired him to join the executive management team at Cypress Systems, Inc. I did so without reservation and in full knowledge of his circumstances and prior criminal conviction. One year after hiring him, I appointed him Chief Operating Officer and President of Operations at Cypress.

I believe in a God that guides those who seek His purpose. When it came to bringing Mark and me together, I believe that God was guiding us from the beginning. God always has a plan, as foretold by the prophet Jeremiah when God spoke through him in the Old Testament: *"For I know the plans I have for you, says the Lord. They are plans for good and not for evil, to give you a future and a hope."*

> "For I know the plans I have for you,
> says the Lord. They are plans for good
> and not for evil, to give you a future and
> a hope."
>
> Jeremiah 29:11

When I first hired Mark, my hopes for Cypress were many:

- That he would play a strategic role in advancing our corporate mission in the prevention of cancer;

- That he would leverage his broad-based executive management skills in biotechnology and industrial fermentation; and

- That he would energize our overall efforts with the same drive and passion that he had exhibited in leadership positions at previous companies.

Based strictly on business results, Mark's contribution to Cypress has exceeded my wildest expectations. Thanks to his contribution across all levels of the company, I am more excited now about the future of the business and our shared vision for the prevention of cancer than I have been since founding Cypress in 1995.

Mark's contribution has, however, gone beyond mere business accomplishments. Through mutual respect, close personal interaction, and a strongly shared commitment to God, we have formed a deeply fulfilling human relationship more rewarding than our business relationship. An acquaintanceship that began eight years ago has grown deeper through trust, a shared vision, and a shared faith in a great and loving God. Our God is glorified when we unite to fulfill His higher purpose.

Thus, through God's infinite wisdom, I had found the right man. And God's infinite wisdom brought together not just Mark and me, but our spouses and each and every individual who comprises the Cypress team. Our goal at Cypress is not simply to pursue profit; it is to fulfill a larger purpose. That purpose is to serve God in alleviating the suffering of mankind. When the Spirit of God infuses every aspect of one's life, when one's purpose in work is identical to one's purpose in life, one experiences the true and lasting joy of being part of God's grand purpose. There is no greater spiritual pleasure than to integrate work goals with life goals and thus be able to live and act at all times in perfect harmony with God's will.

Earlier in Jeremiah, the Lord said, *"Behold, like clay in the potter's hand, so are you in my hands."* God has shaped each of us in accordance with His plan. As we walk with Him in fellowship and unity, each of us is molded into His image. We feel His joy, and, in consequence, our own joy overflows.

———————

I first met Mark, Ginger, and their children in April of 2001 at the Federal Prison Camp in Edgefield, South Carolina, a minimum-security federal facility. At the time, Mark still had five-and-a-half years left on his sentence. Yet I knew in a heartbeat that he was the right man. I knew he would be worth the wait. His background in selenium research was important, but so was his right thinking regarding taking full responsibility for his past actions and looking to the future.

———————

I also knew well the prison visiting-room setting, the security check-in process, the institutional look and feel, the ever-present prison guard, and, of course, the vending machines full of every known junk food—including my favorite, the Big Texan Cinnamon Bun. One prison visiting room is like any other, so Edgefield held no surprises for me.

My familiarity with these aspects of prison life comes from my volunteer work with the California based Match-Two Prisoner Outreach program, where I had spent considerable time in prison visiting rooms seeing inmates in Avenal and Corcoran State Prisons in California.

Upon seeing Mark for the first time, I was not surprised by his outward appearance. I had seen pictures of him from media coverage of the case, including one of him in his prison greens. What surprised me—and remains vivid in my memory today—was seeing from a distance (since I was still being processed through visitor admissions) Mark's ear-to-ear smile and Ginger's warm, accepting expression as she sat next to him and lovingly held his arm. I detected from afar their collective radiance and a positive energy that melted those prison walls.

It touched my heart. As I cleared security and arrived at the circle of chairs where they were sitting, I looked at them with such joy and a sense of the familiar that we could have been meeting for the first time at the local diner for the blue plate special (meat loaf, mashed potatoes, green beans, and coconut-cream pie).

———————

I had read the earlier books on Mark's case, yet what I saw that first visit was not a couple that was still in the midst of suffering and had just been through years of whistleblower and legal hell. By normal standards, this couple had every right to be mad at the world. Yet they were not. What made the difference? Why, in spite of all that had happened were they able to sit in a prison and radiate such positive energy, arm-in-arm, so graceful in manner and so positive in tone? Because they understood, in God's hands, all things work together for good.

Things don't just happen by chance, devoid of inter-connected meaning. God always has a Master Plan. Often we can only see and understand that Plan much later. I am truly grateful to be part of God's great plan and to be a small part of this amazing Whitacre family story. It is a story of overcoming failure, finding redemption, and renewing faith. It is a story of receiving a second chance in life by being worthy of a second chance in life.

The great founder of the Protestant Reformation, Martin Luther, said

I do not fear failure, but rather I fear succeeding at something that does not really matter.

Like him, I believe we should learn from failure applied to the right purpose. A failure in pursuit of a worthwhile endeavor is worth far more than a success in an endeavor not worthwhile. Failure teaches us far more than success ever will. Failure gives us the opportunity to dig deep within our souls and, in broken humility, touch the hand of God and know that He has unconditional love for each of us.

We all have two choices in times of personal failure: We can examine ourselves, assume full responsibility for our mistakes, seek forgiveness, take corrective action, and, with our heads held high, look to the future one day at a time with a drive to become *better*. Or we can succumb to the situation, blame others, dodge responsibility, wish things were different, count all that has been lost, and allow the weight of the problem to give way to a resentment that eats our lives away. In a word, we can become *bitter*. The difference between the words b*etter* and *bitter* are one letter, the letter "i."

> "Each person has the choice to get better or bitter. The difference is the letter "i."
>
> PAUL A. WILLIS
> CYPRESS SYSTEMS, INC.

Mark and Ginger cannot change the past. They can only change the future by focusing on building better lives in knowledge of Christ. They refused to let Mark's long prison sentence destroy them.

It did not take long to understand the positive basis for their lives, marriage, family, and experience of prison. It was, first, their foundational faith in Jesus Christ, and, second, their conscious decision that they—for the good of their marriage and family, and despite all that had happened—were going to focus on getting *better* and not *bitter*.

There was a young and humble missionary named Jim Elliot, who gave his life in the jungles of Ecuador. He once prayed, *"Lord make my way prosperous, not that I achieve high station, but that my life may be an exhibit to the value of knowing God."* In this story about Mark and Ginger you will see no better example of the value of truly knowing God. Are Mark and Ginger perfect? No. Were mistakes made? Yes. Extensive information about Mark, his whistle blowing story, and the complex legal case that ensued are in the public domain. Most of it is accurate; some of it is not. Yet despite mistakes and a lack of perfection, Mark and Ginger return again and again to that bedrock faith. They are now emerging from their suffering. They take no credit themselves for it. They give God all the praise.

This true-to-life book by Floyd Perry stands out from the rest as an accurate and compelling story of how Mark and Ginger did it. How, through years of suffering and separation, they held each other together and made themselves and their children stronger; how they repeatedly dug deep inside to find the faith and determination to hold on.

I also hope that, through this book, you will find a new perspective yourself. I hope that Perry's story of the Whitacres inspires you as it has inspired me. Perhaps it will cause you to re-evaluate your own lives and thereby increase your commitment to God.

Perhaps then you will come, like Mark and Ginger Whitacre, to see your problems not as problems at all, but as opportunities to grow, as occasions to become better not bitter. In the process, perhaps you will also come to know and deeply experience the unconditional love that a gracious God has for you and for all of us.

Paul A. Willis
May 2009
Fresno, California

INTRODUCTION

THE ARRIVAL

"It is a good maxim to trust a person entirely or not at all."

HENRY FIELDING

Rumors had swirled around the compound for over a week: a high-profile transfer prisoner was due any day now. Nuke walked by and yelled, "Hey Wall Street," using my prison nickname.

I strolled his way, "What's up, Nuke?"

"Know anything about the new guy s'pozed to be comin' in?"

"Not a clue," I shot back.

I returned to my cube and got quizzed again, this time from Donny and Shane, two of the younger but savvier inmates on the compound.

"Hey Perry, heard anything about the new guy due to arrive? Wasn't he, like, in your business or something?" asked Donny.

"I have no idea guys," I said with a shrug. "I'm clueless."

"Perry, you're always clueless!" Shane laughed.

It was true. Information had a way of spreading fast around the compound, but I was usually the last to know. Eventually, I learned that a highly publicized white-collar prisoner, someone who had been down (in prison) for years already, was in transit to the Pensacola camp. Whoever the guy was, he had the place abuzz. I had no idea who was coming, where he caught his case (jurisdiction where he was convicted), or what he did. And I certainly didn't know his name.

Then on May 2nd, 2003 at eight o'clock in the morning, a Yellow Taxi Cab, with *First Minute Only $1.70* stamped in black letters on the outside of the cab driver's door, pulled up slowly in front of the red brick building standing at a right angle to the chow hall just across the staff parking lot. The building was known simply as *R&D*. When you do a tour of duty with the United States Bureau of Prisons, you quickly learn that *R&D* doesn't stand for *Research & Development*. It stands for *Receiving & Discharge*—as in prisoners.

Out of the taxi hopped a smiling, well-tanned, energetic man with a perfectly shaved head and a relaxed yet alert manner. Mark Edward Whitacre had arrived at the Federal Prison Camp in Pensacola, Florida. He looked to be about forty-five. He was extremely fit. He wore tassel loafers, khakis, and a golf shirt and could have passed for a lost visitor who had stumbled onto the prison compound area of the Saufley Naval Air Base in Pensacola, Florida.

As he emerged from the cab, Whitacre pulled out a wad of ones, fives, and tens left over from the eighty dollars he started with in South Carolina. He gave the cabbie every last dollar, however much it was. *Always remember the little guy.*

Then Whitacre quickly disappeared into R&D. He had been through R&D Intake many times before, so the humiliation process was no process at all and did not faze him in the slightest. He had been shuffled around by the system so many times that he was now one heads-up inmate. He knew the little things to look out for, the things that can trip you up. He knew how to stay out of trouble because trouble was something he had trained himself to see before it came around the corner.

Whitacre wasn't about to let anything go wrong now. The Pensacola camp was the best in the system, and he and his wife Ginger were so confident this would be his last stop that she took a house off Scenic Highway on the east side of Pensacola, not too far from the beach. The BOP—more formally known as the United States Bureau of Prisons—had granted Whitacre a transfer furlough from a minimum-security federal prison camp in Edgefield, South Carolina, to Pensacola—a minimum-security prison camp widely considered the best in a federal prison system made up of more than one hundred facilities.

Transfer furloughs are granted to low-risk, non-violent inmates who are on the move to a new prison from either a low to a minimum, or from one minimum to another. They have no history of disciplinary problems and must not have had a gun charge as part of their conviction. A day earlier in Edgefield—on Whitacre's forty-sixth birthday—an assistant warden handed him a one-way Greyhound bus ticket and eighty dollars. The bus ticket was courtesy of the U.S. taxpayer. The eighty dollars came out of his own pocket, more precisely from his commissary account.

Whitacre had exactly sixteen hours to get by bus from Edgefield to Pensacola. That's not a lot of wiggle room for most of us, but for a prisoner, a transfer furlough of any duration is an eternity of pure bliss, a walk among the free. Had Whitacre taken sixteen hours and ten minutes instead of sixteen hours exactly, the Bureau would have declared him a fugitive from justice and issued a bench warrant for his arrest.

But Whitacre never made mistakes in prison. Even if the bus had had a flat tire, he would have found a way to get to Pensy on time. He was precise and played by the rules. In fact, the entire time Whitacre was down he never got one Shot (disciplinary action). That's unheard of in the BOP system. Inmates get shots just for walking past the wrong cube at the wrong time.

Mark Whitacre is the former Archer Daniels Midland (ADM) executive who came to prominence in the 1990s as the sole cooperating witness for the FBI in a landmark antitrust case involving commodities price-fixing. He worked undercover for the FBI for nearly three very long years. Somewhere during that journey, he stumbled badly and embezzled nine and a half million dollars from the company, keeping the money in an off-shore account.

When I first met Whitacre that day in May in 2003, I was myself five months into an eighteen-month prison sentence. I had owned and operated a money management operation first for many years in Boston, then briefly in Kansas City, and ran afoul of the Securities and Exchange Commission. The SEC came down hard on me, and rightly so. I did things no fiduciary in his right mind would do.

By the time I bumped into Whitacre, he had already been down nearly five years, with another four to go. He paid a much heavier price than I did, but his case and transgressions were larger and more complicated than mine. My eighteen-month sentence was child's play compared to his, which was 128-months (10-years-and-8-months)—an almost ten-fold difference. To him and so many of the other long timers on the compound who had been down a long time, Nuke included, I was the ultimate short timer.

I had read about Mark's case long before we connected at Pensacola. I quickly realized that the man standing in front of me, fit and smiling but now, like myself, in prison greens, was a far cry from the man portrayed in the books and articles written about him years earlier. They had cast him as unstable and naïve. At certain moments in the heat of battle, perhaps he had been, but I found him by May of 2003 to be grounded and mature.

The day after his arrival, Mark and I began a daily ritual of walking and talking—in a circle on the jogging track, back and forth on the air base's landing tarmac, or up and down the access road—often for two to three hours at a stretch. There's a lot of downtime when you're in prison, a lot of time to walk and talk, and Mark and I took full advantage of it.

This book is the result of those countless hours together in prison and many more with him and his family since then. This is the story of a man who survived character assassination, emotional meltdown, suicide attempts, lengthy incarceration, and disgrace. It is also an account of how one man, his wife, and their three children somehow managed to come out on the other side with few wounds that haven't healed. Even the most skeptical reader will have to say such an outcome is extraordinary.

FPC Pensacola is a work camp. The inmate population's primary job is grounds-maintenance for the United States Navy. The pay is twelve cents an hour, and the heat and humidity are brutal. At the time of our mutual incarceration, Pensacola was an open, loosely regulated, non-severe minimum-security facility operated for male prisoners by the United States Bureau of Prisons. The compound is located on the northeast corner of Saufley Naval Air Field, an outlying base of the huge Pensacola Naval Air Station complex located one hundred and eighty miles west of Tallahassee and fifty miles east of Mobile, Alabama. It's an easy stop off the I-10, a vast stretch of interstate highway that runs continuously from the Atlantic Ocean in northern Florida to the Pacific Ocean in southern California.

———————

During one of our early walk-and-talks, Mark talked about what a flawed man he was. "Flawed?" I asked. "So you were the business variation of Mae West?"

"What's *that* mean?" he asked.

"When some guy asked her about her moral standards, she said, 'I was Snow White, but I drifted.'"

Whitacre laughed.

"Yeah, I drifted all right. I did a good thing helping the end-consumer recover more than a billion dollars by working undercover for the FBI, but I was embezzling on the side big time. No matter how you slice or dice it, Bud, I was wrong."

"Why'd you do it?"

"Why'd I do what? Go undercover? Or embezzle?"

"Embezzle. Did you really need that much extra money? You had assets to fall back on. You had that monster Moweaqua estate. You had income-producing rental properties. You had a hefty 401-K, a good salary, perks galore, and other savings. So unless you were spending more than you were taking in, I don't see the motive."

Whitacre grew pensive. Fearing he was about to clam up, I threw him a quick prompt, "When did it start?

That brought him back. "It actually started before the FBI ever came on the scene. In hindsight, my behavior was pathetic. Inexcusable."

"Was the process cumulative? Did you embezzle all at once? How'd you start?"

He continued, "I started small."

I could sense the story was about to get real juicy, so not wanting him to stop, I adopted that controlled matter-of-fact nothing-surprises-me voice that Cardinal Lamberto used in *Godfather III* when the sick and aging Don Michael Corleone confessed that he had ordered his brother Fredo killed years earlier for going against the family.

"Go on . . ." I said, almost adding in a priestly tone "my son."

"I was *just* high enough in the organization," he continued. "I had *just* enough check-signing authority and was living *just* enough beyond my means and had *just* enough contempt for some of the things I saw going on around me that I could justify it in my mind."

"So just when did you pull the trigger?"

"The first embezzlement was in 1991. Two hundred kay. Believe it or not, I fell for that Nigerian scam, blinded by the promise of a very large payback on a relatively modest outlay. Not to defend my own stupidity or anything, but in those days, the Nigerian scams were new at the time. They arrived by fax, not e-mail, and there was no "scam alert" cover page that came with it."

"You actually fell for one of those 4-1-9 schemes?"

"Not only did I fall for it, I got two of my VPs to go in on it with me. We threw about two hundred grand combined down that black hole before we finally realized it was an elaborate, clever scam."

"But that's not embezzling. I presume you all were using your own money. When did you embezzle?"

"It started really because after that happened I felt bad about getting my colleagues, two really good guys with families, involved. They were out a lot of money because of me. Of course, I was out the most money, but I made more than they did. The only way I could get that kind of money back and reimburse them was to put in place a phony invoicing scheme and bill the company for business that didn't occur."

"I see, so you started out by rationalizing to yourself that you felt morally obligated to pay back your friends and recover for them, and yourself, the two hundred grand that you had thrown down a black hole like an idiot."

"Exactly."

"That's only human nature. I understand. But that only justifies two hundred k. What about the bigger sums? What caused you to ramp up the amounts you were stealing?"

"Once I saw how easy it was, I came up with all kinds of reasons why I deserved more. For example, I was putting in ninety to one-hundred-hour work weeks, yet getting paid far less than some of the guys above me who didn't work nearly as hard as I did. They were often out playing golf or off somewhere on vacation boondoggles. So that was another thing. Then, once I went undercover for the FBI, my justification was that I needed the money as a backstop, and that's where the bulk of the transfers occurred. I had the system down. I wasn't getting caught. And I had the justification I needed—needing a financial insurance policy for Ginger and the kids in case I ever got caught as the mole."

"Whatever happened to your request of the FBI that they make some sort of *legal* provision for you in the event ADM found out and gave you the boot?"

"They were working on it, but I didn't believe it. Or else I didn't want to believe it. Turns out that FBI Headquarters in D.C. were all signed off on it until, ironically, they found out that I was embezzling."

Given what I was in prison for, I thought to myself, judge not, lest ye be judged. A long silence ensued. Neither of us was there voluntarily, but we knew why we were there, Mark more completely than me.

Given the full embezzlement story, I understood better why Whitacre wanted to be unequivocal about accepting responsibility. When he reached his ethical fork in the road, he took the wrong one, then built the requisite internal justifications for doing so.

Yet his mitigating circumstances were vastly greater than mine. *Could this be what long prison sentences do?* I thought. *Wear you down until you admit guilt even when others are calling you a national hero?*

It took Mark more courage to blow the whistle knowing he was dirty than it takes if you're as pure as the driven snow. In my view, Whitacre was given excessive jail time for what he'd done wrong and no credit at all for what he'd done right. But that is precisely what this book is about, how Mark transcends that view and goes beyond the accepted wisdom that he got a "raw deal."

In 2000, two very good books were published about Mark and the ADM trial. One became the basis for a major motion picture. The other became a reliable source for information on the complex case and the consequences for U.S. antitrust law. Because of these books and the extensive media coverage they helped generate, the moniker "The Informant" became synonymous with "Mark Whitacre" in the public's mind.

Both books, however, are now nearly a decade old. Both focus primarily on Mark's role as the mole and the subsequent cases, hearings, and trial. Neither devotes more than passing reference to Mark and Ginger's early years, neither covers his long prison years or the post-prison years, and neither chronicles his protracted efforts to obtain a presidential pardon. Most importantly, neither explores in depth how Whitacre and his family survived the ordeal, came to a place of total acceptance, and have gone on to lead productive and flourishing lives.

Mark has made an impressive comeback as a business leader since his release in December of 2006: He was recently appointed chief operating officer and president of operations of a respected California-based biotechnology company, Cypress Systems Inc.

As a private citizen, he's made an even greater comeback. His former FBI supervisors now call him a national hero. A Discovery Channel documentary about Mark aired in March of 2009, called *Undercover: Operation Harvest King*. And October of 2009 brings with it the release of *The Informant*, a Steven Soderbergh film with Matt Damon starring as Whitacre. Requests for interviews continue to escalate, and visitor-numbers to Mark's website, established at the urging of friends and colleagues, have been coming in at the rate of several thousand per day.

The ADM years were years of crisis for Mark Whitacre. His character may have been very much on display during that crisis, but it certainly was not made by that crisis. Having spent a good deal of time with Whitacre examining his character, I can say he is a complex, but not a complicated, man. This book strives to explain that. It attempts to describe what motivates him and how he has achieved what so few achieve after release from prison: near-total restoration of reputation.

Until now, the source and nature of Whitacre's character have remained unexamined, as have the roles played by his wife Ginger and their children. Until now, few individuals outside the immediate family have appreciated the profound and complementary faith-based character traits that Ginger and the kids demonstrated over a span of more than fifteen years.

Thus, this book aims to distinguish itself from the two previous Whitacre books by describing and interpreting events, not from some lofty or objective distance, but from close proximity to the man while both of us were still in prison, and, later, after he got out. It attempts to give readers both an accurate and up-to-date understanding of his journey and an experience of that journey from an internal perspective, from "inside his head."

On one level, this book simply fills gaps by answering questions about important events that occurred before, during, and after the Archer Daniels ordeal. On another, however, it covers aspects of the man and his family that would otherwise go unexplained. People want to know what happened from *his* point of view, from *his family's* perspective.

I am uniquely positioned and privileged to give that perspective. Accordingly, this book makes no claim of neutrality. Knowing what I know about the man and his family, and knowing—arguably better than anyone outside the family—what they have been through, I am biased *in favor* of Mark, Ginger, and their children.

The Whitacre family has arrived on the opposite shore of a river that few families are able to navigate without drowning. Today, Mark Whitacre—businessman, scientist, ex-mole, convicted felon, former inmate, devoted husband, and much-loved father—is not just surviving; he is thriving.

PART ONE

THE EARLY YEARS

Mark & Ginger, Homecoming King & Queen (1975)

PART ONE—THE EARLY YEARS

CHAPTER ONE

Two Good Kids

**"Youth is a circumstance you can't do anything about.
The trick is to grow up without getting old."**

FRANK LLOYD WRIGHT

Mark Edward Whitacre hails from Morrow, Ohio, a small village thirty miles northeast of Cincinnati calmly nestled in the hills between I-71 and the Little Miami River. Its population in the nineteen-sixties was about a thousand if you counted the herd of prize-winning rabbits Mark raised as a teen.

Ginger Lynn Gilbert, his future band mate, girlfriend, prom queen, best friend, wife, rock of Gibraltar, family anchor, and lifelong partner, hails from Maineville, Ohio, an even smaller village just seven miles down the road from Morrow. Maineville's population in the nineteen-sixties was all of five hundred—if you rounded up every horse, cat, and dog in Warren County and included them.

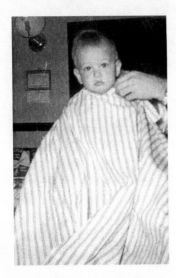 

Mark Whitacre Age 3 (1960)   **Ginger Gilbert Age 2 (1960)**

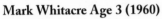

Maineville, where Ginger grew up, got its name from early settlers who came from the state of Maine to work the fertile soil on the banks of the Little Miami River. The only Maineville native of note over the past century has been Bill Butterworth who married into the Deere tractor and equipment family and became President and Chairman of John Deere for nearly thirty years, from 1907 until his death in 1936.

Morrow, where Mark grew up, got its name from The Honorable Jeremiah Morrow, a governor who ran Ohio in the 1800s. Governor Morrow was not *from* Morrow, so the village has no notable natives, unless we consider our protagonist. Judging from local headlines at the time of the Archer Daniels scandal, Mark never lost his good reputation among the local townspeople and is today revered as Morrow's most famous hometown boy.

Prior to the huge news splash engendered by the national revelation in 1995 that their own Mark Whitacre blew the whistle on a real big company, Morrow was known for only two things: (a) wine, and (b) a Kingston Trio folk song that is a pun. Vineyards Estate Winery has been producing award-winning wines in Morrow for many decades, and the folk song recorded in 1960 by the Kingston Trio is called "To Morrow." It is musically equivalent to the Abbott and Costello comedy routine, "who's on first" since the lyrics to the song go, "For the train today to Morrow, if the schedule is right, today it goes to Morrow and returns tomorrow night."

These two good kids were born into the baby-boomer generation, the one that evolved from "aw gee, Wally" to "ask not what your country can do for you . . ." to "don't trust anyone over thirty" to today, which after all they've been through has more of a tinge of "don't trust anyone at all."

The two came into this world a little more than a year apart, Mark in May 1957 and Ginger in August 1958. As boomers went at the time, they were straight-arrows, not Vietnam War protesters, not long-haired hippies, not rejecters of their parents' values, and definitely not experimenters with mind-altering drugs. They did, however, think of themselves as part of a large and affluent generation that could change the world forever. Eventually, the two of them would change the world forever and themselves in the process.

When I asked them to recall the major traumas of their youth, they looked at each other quizzically, turned back, and said, almost simultaneously, "there weren't any." They were too young to remember the biggest national trauma of that era, the November of 1963 assassination of President Kennedy: Mark was only six at the time and Ginger five.

Mark Age Four (1961)

Mark and Ginger's upbringing calls more to mind the innocent fifties than the rebellious sixties or the socially progressive seventies. As teens in the small-town slice of southwestern Ohio, they weren't entirely geographically isolated. After all, there was radio, black and white television, cars, and buses. They got mail. And, as the Kingston Trio song reminds us, trains came in and out of Morrow all the time.

Yet Mark and Ginger lived unhurried, protected lives in a two-township area where everyone knew everyone else, where no one locked their doors at night, and where drugs didn't exist. Crime was rare, and, on the rare occasions when one did occur, the local sheriff figured out who did it within hours. In the Morrow of the nineteen sixties, you were conservative, patriotic, and diligent—or you moved somewhere else.

For some individuals, place or location is the dominant aspect of character development. For others, it's people, authority figures: a teacher, minister, rabbi, or coach. For Mark and Ginger, it was each other. No person or place had a greater influence on their attitudes, habits, and character development than each other.

They met young, grew up together, seldom separated, and kept no secrets. They discussed anything and everything with each other rather than with the world beyond. They influenced each other's thinking far more than environment or role models influenced their thinking. They were more emotionally rooted in their complementary personalities than in their physical environment.

It is undeniable that growing up in such a supportive small-town environment as Morrow helped shape Mark and Ginger. The community and its institutions and individuals imbued in them solid core values, and certainly this conservative, Christian-values-oriented upbringing in America's heartland stood them in good stead when things got rough years later, but the real glue was each other.

Mark and Ginger have been as one from an early age. They remain so today. It is safe to say that, had Mark had to bear the pain of the lonely prison years with a less loyal partner, he would not have made it. Together, they got through it with grace and dignity thanks to their vast reservoir of trust and goodwill that started in junior high school.

While it is undeniable that growing up in a supportive, low-stress, small-town environment helped shape Mark and Ginger, what really shaped them was the constant presence of the other. While it is undeniable that the community imbued them with strong core values, where they really adopted and tested their values was with each other. And while their prototypically middle-America upbringing held them in good stead when things got rough years later, what really held them together were each other.

Sometimes it would reach extremes. I recall a particular mail call in Dorm A at Pensacola. It was a Monday and I was hoping for mail after the week-end hiatus. I hustled over to get in line at the mail door, an open side door in the front hall of the dorm. When the dorm hack was good and ready, when you got to the head of the line, you gave him your name and reg number (no matter how well he knew you).

When I got there, I saw Mark.

"How long you been standing here?" I asked.

"I don't know, maybe twenty minutes" he replied sheepishly.

"Didn't you just spend the whole weekend with Ginger and the kids over in the visitors' center?"

"Yeah, it was great."

"Then you must be expecting legal mail or something?"

"Nah, nothin' special. Just never know if I might have a letter from Ging."

Invariably he did. Despite having just spent the past Friday evening, Saturday all day, and Sunday all day with his family, Mark would get a stack of family mail with maybe a postcard from one son, a letter from another, a letter with a photo from his daughter, and two long letters from Ginger herself. This after just spending the whole weekend together.

Later I discovered they had boxes of correspondence between them from the prison years. The sheer volume of their letter and card exchange defies imagination. When asked how she found time to write Mark so often, given that she spent almost three days a week with him in the prison visitors' center, then went home, raised kids, did laundry, taught school, worked on his pardon, and generally lived a busy life, Ginger shrugged in a cheerful, matter-of-fact way, "it was easy, he's my husband."

Ginger and Mark simply built this level of commitment and complete devotion to each other into their connected DNA from an early age.

Some letters stand out more than others. On their twenty-first wedding anniversary—June 16th of 2000—Mark was in the early years of his lengthy prison term. He had been down two years and three months. Ginger was living in Aiken, South Carolina at the time; he was incarcerated in the Edgefield camp twenty miles up the road. Ginger sent Mark a letter, reflecting on their more than two decades together.

In prison, there's no such thing as getting *too many* expressions of love or support from the outside. Words that may sound trite when viewed from the free-world perspective never sound trite to any prisoner, period. Any letter, card, or photograph you get means so much more when received by someone on the inside from someone on the outside.

Ginger's anniversary letter stands out for its sincerity, steadfastness, and simplicity:

> **Dear Corky,**
> **What I have learned most is that my love for you is endless. It will never die, never be replaced, and will always be cherished. You have the promise of my love forever, my faithfulness, my desires, hopes, and dreams for us in the future and the hope that you know truly how much I love you and cherish you.**
>
> > **Your Wife Always,**
> > **Ginger**

With letters like that and the clockwork-like visits every weekend, rain or shine, prison life becomes but a backdrop for the more loving internal environment. It is no wonder the Whitacre family bears fewer scars than most families who lose the primary breadwinner to a long prison sentence. Had I gotten but one such letter my entire fifteen months of incarceration, I would have whistled and danced around the complex for the duration of my stay.

How and where did this extraordinary couple meet? What made their relationship work so well so long?

Mark and Ginger attended different but nearby elementary schools. Morrow and Maineville were so small that the two townships merged school systems after the sixth grade into one consolidated junior-senior high school known as the Little Miami District High School, named after that river that meanders not far out the back door of Farmer and Evelyn Whitacre's four-acre lot in Morrow. Ginger and Mark first met in 1970 on the school band bus.

Mark in Band Uniform Age Thirteen (1970)

Ginger was thirteen and in seventh grade; Mark fourteen and in eighth. She played bells. He played sousaphone and trumpet. Their relationship sprung forth from nature having its way, like tulips popping up from the ground in spring.

Mark recalled to me vividly the effect Ginger had on him on first sighting:

She was stunning, Bud, absolutely stunning! I remember well when I first saw her. It was a late afternoon and the Junior High band was loading up for an away game. Rays of soft twilight shone through the bus window at just the right time of day and just the right angle. There she was sitting, the light illuminating her beautiful face. It was as if, at that moment, God threw a spotlight on her just for me to notice.

Even though it was late fall, she still had her summer tan. Her skin's still like that: one day in the sun and she's bronzed up for the season. She had long curly hair, down well past her shoulders, so curly and full. I loved those curls.

I sat down beside her, all smiles. We rode together from that day on. We never held hands. She never put her head on my shoulder. We never hugged in the dark. *Not even a touch.* She was a shy 7th grader. I was a loquacious 8th grader, so I talked and she listened. She hung on every word. It made me feel fantastic, and she listened, really listened. Everything around us was just a blur, not important. Nothing else mattered—just her, just me. I was hooked! I think back to that first moment often.

After that first meeting, the once-long bus rides between their school and a rival's became totally different, always too short and never long enough.

Mark had a sensitivity in those early years that he showed only to Ginger. She may have seemed shy on the outside, but inwardly she was secure and intuitive and thus an important confidant for Mark. She fully understood the meaning and value of his openness. Mark had no problem talking while she listened, but he also focused intently on her reactions while he talked.

Emotionally mature at an early age, the two were able to set aside what each was feeling in order to find out what the other was feeling and identify with it. Because they related to each other so well and so early, their tools of communication today as adults are exceptionally well-developed. As Deepak Chopra wrote in *The Path to Love*, " . . . to communicate with another person isn't to pass on information. It is to draw another into union with yourself." (Chopra 1997, 129).

Ginger understood already at thirteen that important emotional bonding was going on between her and Mark, even though she hardly said a word. He, like most boys, was so busy competing for her affection—long after he "had her at hello"—that he was less conscious of the union they were forming. He got it later, and, once he did, it was for life.

They developed on those many band bus rides not just an understanding of how their differing styles of communication worked; they also developed equality. Not equality in the sense of talent, skills, intelligence, and the like. Citing Chopra again, "Equality isn't based upon external factors or images. We all have an equal right to be appreciated, respected, and understood . . . . to accept another person means accepting her emotions. There is nothing more basic or intrinsic." (Chopra 1997, 127) He always made the right moves. Without that, the shy, sun-bronzed girl from tiny Maineville would have pushed away the eager-to-please courtier. He was sufficiently in love with her to communicate in his own way the depth of his feelings, and he did it at an early age and a time when both girls and boys were taught not to expose their true feelings. Accepting Ginger didn't mean just sitting on the band bus with her and engaging in monologue. It meant understanding and accepting her emotions at an age when she was shy about verbalizing them.

Mark was one year ahead of Ginger in school, so they saw much less of each other once he started ninth grade and had to move to the school building that housed the ninth-through-twelfth graders. Ginger remained in the junior high building to complete her eighth grade, but once she hit ninth and migrated over to the other building, the two re-connected and soon became inseparable.

This meant they were a single unit at every dance, prom, and social gathering of any kind. In the spring of 1973, when Mark turned sixteen and got his driver's license, he bought a car off his dad's lot at cost. Suddenly Mark and Ginger were free to roam.

Having a car gave them mobility, range, freedom. They grew accustomed to driving over to Lebanon—the "big" town in the area with a population that was all of 17,000. Lebanon had then and still has today, in the same location, a burger joint called Frisch's, where Mark and Ginger routinely went after school for a double-decker Big Boy and coke.

They were inseparable through his high-school graduation. Their stability and traditional views led many a distraught classmates to their door. Others respected Mark and Ginger and often approached them to discuss their love-life problems.

Both had religious upbringings, Ginger more so. She was involved with the Maineville Methodist Church from an early age and later enjoyed being a Rainbow Girl, the youth service organization that teaches charity and community service to girls ages eleven-to-twenty. As she matured, she became treasurer of her junior class and homecoming queen.

Generally, however, the two established a pattern early on that placed Ginger in the quiet background and Mark in the talkative foreground. It fit their personalities, but there was never any question that Ginger was the calming influence, a quiet ballast to Mark's more extroverted nature. She was not merely a submissive or meek partner to her Energizer Bunny partner. She was almost always in the right, and Mark more often than not deferred to her good judgment. They never outgrew each other. Their mutual affection, support, and above all loyalty were the bedrock qualities that got them through the later years.

There was some question as to how Mark got the nickname Corky. Some have suggested that he popped off like the cork of a champagne bottle. Mark's mother, Evelyn Whitacre, always referred to him as a "real corker" because as a baby he laughed a lot and seldom cried.

Both Ginger's parents worked in factories the whole time she was growing up, her mother for Procter & Gamble in nearby Cincinnati, and her father in the Ford plant for thirty years. Donnie Gilbert, as her father was known, farmed on the side to bring in extra money. A principal farming activity, until prices declined in 2005, was breeding, growing, and selling fish—the kind used for fish bait.

Donnie has since retired from both farming and Ford, so Ginger's younger brother, Mike, is running things. Mike still raises crops of corn, hay, and other feed stocks for the family's beef cattle operation.

Ginger's maternal grandmother lived with Ginger from the time she was seven, making it clear from an early age that the Gilbert family pulled together and family came first.

Ginger's parents got divorced but not until she was grown and gone. Even though thirty when it happened, Ginger was devastated. Yet everything seems to work, and the entire family remains on good terms, including her father Donnie and his second wife Joyce and her mother Sandi and Sandi's second husband Ron.

Mark's parents—like Mark and Ginger themselves years later—married young, stayed together through thick and thin, and are still happily married today. They live in the same house on the same four-acre lot where Mark grew up. Mark's father, now eighty-one, still mows all four acres himself. When I met Mark's parents, the elder Whitacres were in their mid and late seventies; yet both looked to be in their early sixties. They loved and supported all their children, but they showed particularly strong loyalty to Mark when he needed it most, the prison years. At no time did either Mark or Ginger see his parents argue, not even during the prison years or the years of Mark's pre-prison meltdown.

It is somewhat ironic that Ginger's father did the farming while it was Mark's father who got the nickname "Farmer" somewhere along the way. Farmer Whitacre was a strong role model. He seldom drank and never smoked, and his own father died of goiter, a disease caused by a lack of iodine rarely seen today, at the age of 45. Farmer was only thirteen at the time and had four younger sisters. He asserted his authority and, in order to care for his mother and all those baby sisters, went to the Ohio Registry of Motor Vehicles, obtained a special hardship driver's license, and began driving trucks commercially at the age of thirteen.

As he grew older, Farmer stayed in the "transportation" business by buying and managing two automobile dealerships for many decades in nearby Blanchester, Ohio. Both his BuickPontiac dealership and, directly across the street, his ChevyOlds dealership allowed Farmer Whitacre to prosper. He was, by all accounts, a born salesman who combined hard work and honesty to make a good living for the Whitacre family. If his BuickPontiac lot didn't have the car a customer wanted, Farmer would walk with the customer to the ChevyOlds lot across the street and see if there was anything there that they might like.

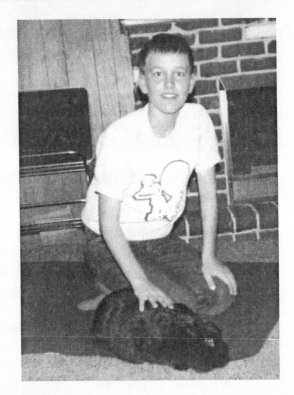

Mark Age Ten with 3ʳᵈ Prize Winning Rabbit "Fluffy" (1967)

Mark played Little League baseball and joined the Boy Scouts; Ginger stayed busy with the Rainbow Girls. When his favorite hobby, raising rabbits, demanded increasing amounts of his spare time, Mark quit the Boy Scouts to raise rabbits competitively for the county 4-H Club. He had a booming little enterprise that consumed his every evening and week-end. At his peak, Mark was raising over twenty prize rabbits. The capstone of all this came in 1972 when he won the rabbit competition at the Warren County, Ohio, Fair with his prize New Zealand Red Rabbit, fondly known as Big Red.

Instead of studying, Mark spent his after-school time raising his champion rabbits and hanging out with Ginger. He was popular enough to have been elected senior class president and homecoming king his senior year, the same year Ginger became homecoming queen alongside him, even though she was only a junior and the queen's crown should rightfully have gone to a senior. Not only was she beautiful and deserving of the award for that reason alone, but the two were such an item by then that not a soul at Little Miami High could imagine anyone but Ginger sharing the throne with him.

The relationship they enjoyed from an early age created favorable emotional dynamics. Ginger was fortunate enough not to have to go through the experience of getting love wrong and suffering the pain that follows. Her classmates were not so lucky. Mark and Ginger were among the fortunate few who knew from an early age with no ambiguity that they were right for each other.

Their stability at such an early age helped them help others. They became role models and confidantes in matters of the heart to their more confused teenage counterparts. They also maintained a more formal dress code in high school than their blue-jeans-wearing classmates; she wore dresses frequently or pants suits when her female peers sported blue jeans. Mark wore leisure suits and loafers, not jeans and cowboy boots.

After Mark had gotten his driver's license, they both took summer jobs at the King's Island Amusement Park, part of the Cedar Fair group of amusement parks and located in Mason, Ohio, just a few miles west of Morrow.

They regaled me with visually rich descriptions of pulling up in front of a crowd of friends or park attendees in his new pride-and-joy, a red 1968 Pontiac GTO, decked out with fire flames on the hood and sides, Magnum chrome wheels, and cherry-bomb, dual-exhaust mufflers.

This GTO was straight out of the film *American Graffiti*.

Mark's 1968 GTO Sixteenth Birthday Gift (1973)

PART TWO—THE EARLY YEARS
CHAPTER TWO

WHIZ KID

**"The test of a first-rate intelligence is the ability to hold
two opposed ideas in mind at the same time and still
retain the ability to function."**

F. Scott Fitzgerald
(The Crack-Up, 1936)

Mark finished comfortably, if unspectacularly, in the upper third of
his June 1975 high school graduating class at Little Miami High. Once he
matriculated at Ohio State, however, he got intensely serious about academics.
When asked what took so long, he said it was a combination of factors: one,
he was physically separated from Ginger, which gave him more time than
he knew what to do with, so he applied it to his studies, and, two, he was
finally being challenged intellectually for the first time. For whatever reason,
he turned on the after-burners starting his freshman year at Ohio State, and
that began a pattern of academic and scientific excellence that continued
for many years. In total, Mark attained nine post-high-school degrees.

Ginger graduated from Little Miami High one year later and ranked
much higher than Mark in her class standing. She wasted no time enrolling
at Ohio State herself and joining him in Columbus. Shortly after her
arrival there, he scuttled his original plan to pursue a traditional four-year

bachelor's degree in Pre-Veterinary Sciences and applied instead for a joint-bachelors-and masters-degree Honors Program in Animal Nutrition. Ohio State's renowned College of Agriculture was well known for its world-class Animal Sciences Department and at the time accepted fewer than twenty students into this program from a university enrollment of more than fifty thousand. Mark was studying with the cream of the crop.

In December of 1979 he finished both the bachelor's and master's programs in four years, graduating *cum laude* with a 3.65 GPA for the BS and, for the MS, "with distinction" and a 3.9 GPA.

Ginger, majoring in agricultural economics, moved through the Ohio State academic matrix in a more relaxed, less ambitious, way. The two of them matured in tandem in Columbus, but Mark's academic program was much more challenging. Nonetheless, the maturity process was parallel for both of them. They became even more stable and reliable than they had been in high school. Unlike many young adults who go off to college, they did not start skipping out on going to church; rather, they deepened even further their commitment to God and their Christian faith and a more mature extension of their totally-committed, no-holds-barred, mutual love and support. They were more stable as a couple at the tender ages of 22 (his age of graduation with his BS and MS) and 21, respectively, than your average forty-five-year-old couple. As such, they put down a strong foundation early in their lives that served them well when decades later they would have to go through the ordeal of being an informant and nine miserable prison years.

Ginger Freshman at Ohio State, Mark Sophomore (1976)

Fully six months before completing his joint-degree program at Ohio State, Mark, who likes to leave nothing to chance, decided there was only one way to stand out from the other applicants for Cornell University's prestigious PhD program in Nutritional Biochemistry: go there and make himself known, in person, to one of the leading academic authorities on the subject that Mark had chosen for his dissertation project. That authority was Dr. Gerald Combs Jr., and the subject-matter was a trace element called selenium.

So, during Ohio State's summer break in August of 1979, with nothing but confidence and gumption—no appointments, no advance calls—Mark and his favorite companion took turns driving nonstop from Columbus to Ithaca, twelve hours straight, with the express purpose of meeting Dr. Combs. He was at the time and remains today a world-renowned scientist in selenium research. When Mark first met him that summer of 1979, Combs was one of the stars in the acclaimed Nutritional Sciences Division at Cornell University.

Mark and Ginger and his parents holed up in an Ithaca motel so cheap and grungy that Ginger had to wear flip flops in the shower to avoid strange and dangerous looking plant growth on the floor tile. Mark succeeded in his goal to be more than just a name on an application. He found Dr. Combs in his office, politely introduced himself, and explained his academic background and interest in selenium research. After listening carefully, Dr. Combs looked at Mark's transcript and GRE scores, and then told him he would provisionally accept him assuming Mark met all the formal and procedural requirements of applying.

Before he and Ginger had left town the next day, Mark dropped his completed application in a local Ithaca mailbox. It was a done deal: Mark was in. He just hit a home run.

Acceptance at Cornell was a life-altering event for both of them. Both Combs and his division were world-renowned for their nutritional biochemistry expertise. The young couple knew that garnering a PhD in that discipline from that university would open many lucrative doors in the multi-billion dollar life sciences industry.

Once Mark got accepted at Cornell, Ginger blew off her senior year at Ohio State and headed north with her man. Her decision to do so was reinforced by the fact that they had gotten married just months earlier while both were still at Ohio State.

Mark & Ginger Wedding Photo (June 16, 1979)

Between the ages of eighteen and twenty two, Mark went into acceleration mode and never looked back. He moved through major rites of passage at warp speed and like a knife through butter: marriage to Ginger in June of 1979, graduation with double honors from Ohio State in December, and matriculation into Cornell's rigorous PhD program only a month after that, in January of 1980.

A week before he was to start at Cornell, a Whitacre family motorcade lit out for Ithaca, New York. The wagon-train consisted of the young marrieds in their used Chevy Impala that was packed floor-to-ceiling and Mark's proud parents in their truck pulling a horse trailer, also packed floor-to-ceiling. Every worldly possession the young couple had was in those vehicles, while every non-worldly hope and dream for the future was in their hearts and heads.

As soon as they got to Ithaca and the beautiful Finger Lake region of New York south of Syracuse, they found a great apartment not far from campus. Unfortunately, it was a leaky sieve because their first month's electric bill nearly exceeded the rent itself. Their utility bill was so high in fact—$350 in 1980—that, if they wanted to both stay warm *and* eat they would have to find a cheaper place. With luck and some good timing, they happened on to a nice duplex even closer to campus.

To pay the rent at their new place and still have something left over for the rare pizza and a movie, Ginger held two jobs, working seven days a week. She worked these double jobs gladly because she knew that his PhD would ultimately lead to a high-paying job in industry. Given their completely selfless team effort, neither thought anything of it. She let him devote full attention, guilt-free, to his research and dissertation: endless hours working in the lab, pouring over scientific tomes in the library, and sitting at the kitchen table in their cramped little duplex, studying intensely.

One of Ginger's two jobs was as a secretary in the Astrophysics Department of Cornell, where famed astronomer Carl Sagan was a tenured professor. Her second job, working in retail on weekends at the Ithaca shopping mall, lacked any glamour whatsoever, but both jobs helped bring home the bacon while Mark focused on his lab work and thesis. Ginger didn't merely subordinate her personal goals and ambitions during the Cornell days; she energetically managed all non-academic, work-a-day matters to ensure that Mark was distraction-free at all times.

Ginger, like all girls from good Midwestern stock, was early-to-bed and early-to-rise. Her routine in Ithaca was to be asleep by 8:30 pm and up at 5:00 am. Mark, by contrast, did not get to bed most nights until well past midnight—but still got up with her at 5:00 am. He was averaging five hours of sleep a night to her nine, but he had no choice. His academic program was so demanding and the combination of class prep and lab work so time-consuming—and his ambition already so boundless—that, as a graduate student, sleep was a luxury he simply couldn't afford. His dissertation focused on the biochemical role of selenium at the cellular level, research which required that he collect, organize, and conduct thousands of enzyme lab analyses and interpret several years of detailed, painstaking research on the subject. He had thousands of lab animals to catalogue and tend to. He funded his research through a grant from the National Institute of Health. It paid his hefty tuition, all his lab costs, all selenium-related research expenses, plus a stipend of $456 per month.

For a man who understands nutrition so well, Mark was a hard-core junk-food junkie. He loved the greasy meals at the Ithaca Diner; Ginger, lacking his iron stomach, was less enthusiastic. After a hearty, greasy meal there, they often drove to Buttermilk Falls a couple miles down the road, where they would sit on the hood of their Impala and stare up at the sky or out at the water as they'd launch into wide-ranging conversations about their dreams and aspirations. On hot summer evenings, they would drive to Lake Cayuga, one of the Finger Lakes just a few miles from campus. Sometimes, when he emerged from the lab bleary-eyed and starving at the end of a long and intense academic day, she would surprise him by bringing a blanket, a picnic basket, and their world-champion four-legged Frisbee-catcher, Sheba, onto the campus quad and have a nice picnic dinner all laid out on the grass. These shared hours of idyllic timelessness were their primary decompression ritual. They had friends at Cornell, but any free time they could carve out was spent with no one but each other. They were a unit unto themselves and, since they were barely scraping by financially, had little time to socialize. During one of our walk-and-talks, I expressed skepticism that "all of this"—waving my arms around the prison compound—was easier than passing your time in the groves of academe. Mark cleared the matter up with one short sentence: "Prison is a cakewalk compared to the Cornell years."

Mark & Ginger Cornell Graduation (May 1983)

For Mark and Ginger, time is measured more by meaning and intensity than months on a calendar, which is why three short Cornell years loom larger in their minds than nearly nine tedious prison years. Those were the foundation years, the maturation years, the years that deepened the ties that bind.

Mark has the happy talent of being at ease with almost anyone, from the most hardened, drug-dealing, and callous long timer to the softest, most conceited, once-rich white-collar criminal, from nasty young rogues to the gentle older bridge players on the compound. Since high school he had developed the notable trait of personal magnetism. Everyone he met liked him and wanted to help further his goals. Mark, always eager to win friends, and never shy, exploited his talent to charm people, but he did so, not just to further his own ends, but to help others.

If he pursued a goal, he got it. In high school, for example, he became prom king, senior class president—and valued confidant to other classmates. To get into Cornell, for example, he used his personal magnetism and ability to convey his commitment to Dr. Combs. In prison, for example, he never got a single "shot" (disciplinary action) during nearly a decade of being down. That's almost unheard of in prison.

How did he do this? Through a mixture of charm and strong interpersonal skills, he could defuse any potential conflict with another inmate looking for trouble (of which there are always plenty in any prison).

Mark and Ginger are generous with not only their time, but also their money. Even during the tight financial years in Ithaca from 1980 to 1983, if someone they knew had a truly serious problem, they would find a way to help. As Benjamin Franklin observed in his *Autobiography*, "A man [is] sometimes more generous when he has little money than when he has plenty."

From an early age, Mark cared about both appearance and reality. Many inmates in prison tend to boast about not caring what other people think of them. Mark was more the opposite. He nurtured his reputation, whether in prison, high school, at Evonik, or at Archer Daniels Midland, as a matter of both dignity and effectiveness, and even today he is his own best unabashed public relations expert.

Mark takes care not only to *be* friendly, frugal, and hardworking, but also to avoid any appearance to the contrary. Mark understands that the best of intentions can get misconstrued if they don't also *appear* to be the best of intentions to the other person. This is a rare quality in a human being because it requires high moral standards in a person not to use their personal magnetism to pursue strictly selfish ends.

Mark Whitacre is a self-created and self-willed man who, as we will see as this story unfolds, may have been a late bloomer, someone whose single-mindedness of purpose did not kick in until Ohio State, but who since then has moved through life at a calculated pace toward calculated ends. And his calculated ends are truly laudatory: to reduce the incidence of cancer and serve God. As we will see in Chapter Sixteen, *Vocation Becomes Avocation,* he works tirelessly, in tandem with his boss Paul A. Willis, to help *reduce the incidence* of cancer. They don't want to just find, for example, a better method to treat cancer after it hits; they want to use research findings that prove selenium's role as a free-radical scavenger to greatly reduce the incidence of cancer.

In that regard, he is returning to his roots laid down in graduate school. It is a testament to Willis that he saw in Mark a rare blend of charm, high ethical and religious standards, solid scientific knowledge of selenium, and practical business skills to hire him right out of prison.

Ultimately it is unclear whether Mark was a late bloomer or just a whiz kid who was bored until he got to college. It is also ultimately unclear whether Mark developed the ability to win arguments without antagonizing opponents from Ginger, his father, or his own self-awareness. But what is clear is that Ginger was key, no matter what. Although those years in Ithaca from 1980 to 1983 were financially tight, the two were so mutually supportive that the tighter the situation got financially, the more certain they became that they were on the threshold of a successful and fulfilling life together.

Ginger helped Mark learn lessons about rivalry and resentment, pride and modesty. Throughout his subsequent life and career, he may have made a few enemies, although none comes to mind other than his superiors at Archer Daniels, and there may be some jealous rivals out there somewhere, although in researching this book I have never met nor heard of any. Mark has far fewer rivals and enemies than most men, especially men so accomplished in their field.

Mark had learned one law about human nature that would serve him well as he went on to become a rising star in the business world: that people are far more likely to help you realize your ambitions if you're able to keep them from becoming jealous or competitive with you. Given his excellent interpersonal skills, and given his newly minted PhD from Cornell, the only limitation in 1983 on Mark and Ginger's future was their imaginations.

PART ONE—THE EARLY YEARS
CHAPTER THREE

RISING STAR

"There may be luck in getting a good job, but there's no luck in keeping it."

J. OGDEN ARMOUR

Mark was twenty-two when he started the Cornell PhD and twenty-five when he finished. He was offered several jobs in the "ag-biz" (food products and agricultural industry) even before he completed his PhD. There was no question in either of their minds: he would apply his knowledge in the financially remunerative world of mega-agribusiness and maximize his earnings power. He wanted nothing more than to make a good living so that he and Ginger could raise a family, build toward financial independence, and satisfy some pent-up consumption demand as well.

Ralston Purina began a full-court recruitment of Mark fully half a year before he finished Cornell. To receive a job offer so far in advance of the award of the PhD was not the norm. Ralston was headquartered in St. Louis. Working there would fit their needs nicely. Ralston offered Mark an attractive compensation package, and the idea of returning to the Midwest appealed to them both. Mark and Ginger are not East Coast people. They wanted to avoid a life that would be too fast, too busy, and too stressful. Part of Ralston's courtship involved flying the couple from Ithaca to St. Louis to visit Checkerboard Square (world headquarters) in St. Louis and showing them around town. They loved the company, the city, the pace of life there. Within days, Mark had negotiated aggregate compensation favorable enough for them to afford to buy a beautiful house on Frederick Lane in Glendale, Missouri, a middle-class suburb of St. Louis. This was their first real home. It was also the place where, for the first time in years, Mark didn't have to stay up until midnight studying.

85 Frederick, Glendale MO 63122

Mark & Ginger's First House Suburb of St. Louis (1983)

Mark's initial assignment at Ralston was in Research & Development. However, this Rising Star had no intention of contenting himself with the typical duties of a Ralston scientist, a man in a white lab coat buried deep in the bowels of research. Charging ahead, he began actively assisting sales personnel in using the scientific underpinnings in the lab as a sales tool in the field. Here his cross-over sales & science skills first emerged. His flair for selling, inherited from his father, was informed by his detailed knowledge of the scientific and nutritional benefits of Purina's products.

Mark became as involved in the sales side of the company as he was in the research side. He always carried his checkerboard-logo briefcase. He often wore their checkerboard-emblem ties. Whatever sold product. His enthusiasm was contagious, and his science-cum-salesmanship ability became a powerful combination that benefited Ralston greatly.

Meanwhile, those eighteen months at Ralston working both sides of the aisle became the blueprint for what would accelerate his rapid climb up three different corporate ladders. He delivered high-impact results under demanding competitive business conditions by using a two-pronged approach.

Good sales professionals in that business knew that if you were selling animal feed and other agri-products into the food chain, the main factor that could derail the sale was not knowing your ingredients or what they did nutritionally. He could handle any customer's objection at any point in the sale by taking off one hat and donning another. He may have been hired as a scientist, but he loved the art of the sale. And he had no problem picking up the phone. A typical call from Mark went like so:

Kevin? Hi, it's Mark Whitacre from R&D over at Purina. Hey listen, I'm a research scientist, not a salesman, so I don't usually call on customers, and I sure don't want to bother you, but I know you're the top poultry nutritionist there at Schnuck's, so I thought I'd give you a call. I just want to talk scientist-to-scientist, know what I mean? You got just a minute? Good.

Our salesman covering your account told me about your frustration. He said your egg-laying hens are producing small, light eggs, and nothing is working for you. He said production in your flocks is declining too fast as they age.

Now strictly from the scientific perspective, I can help you address that issue, and I'll tell you flat out, I'm not tryin' to sell you anything; I'm a scientist. But I studied at Cornell under the son of the man who created the concept of phase feeding of laying hens, Dr. Gerald Combs. I did my PhD thesis under Dr. Gerald Combs Jr., himself a scientist.

I know you guys at Schnuck's are already into phase feeding, and I also know you're one of our most important customers here at Purina. You're already buyin' tons and tons a year of Accu-line™ from us now, and you're ramping up to increase your number of laying hens. Bud, you guys are the BEST.

Now hear me out. All I think you need to do is just tweak your feed formula a little bit and check to make sure your phase feeding program is reducing your costs and not increasing them. I'm willing to personally come over to your lab in Cincinnati and work with you until we get your feed formula right. If we can maybe, you know, check your percentages of Accu-line™ in the formula and check the selenium levels too, and then you and I together can get it to the point where every single Schnuck laying hen is producing the heaviest and greatest number of eggs per bird.

Think you'd be willing to work with me on that before you switch from our Accu-line brand to one of our competitors?

You would? You sure? Great Kevin!

Why don't I drop by tomorrow? I have an errand to run not far from your office anyhow. Check your calendar and let me know what time is good for you. No obligation. I'm not trying to sell you anything. I just want to do right by you, make you look good. You get all the credit. You're one of our most important customers, Kevin, and we want your business.

Two PM? Sounds good. OK, I'll be there at two tomorrow Kevin. Thanks for holding off on this. We're gonna get this thing straightened out, the sooner the better, OK? See you tomorrow . . .

Mark was a scientist, but, like all consummate salesmen, he hated to lose a sale. He knew how to keep a customer from defecting. His enthusiasm, hustle, and detailed product knowledge earned customers' trust and helped improve sales. He was in research, not sales, but he was a quick study and learned lots from the account reps to combine what they had with what he had. If he moved beyond his job description when he made that call, who can fault him? He just saved an account, got the salesman a fat commission, and built goodwill with a major Purina customer. Mark had a knack for connecting with the decision-maker at any organization, building trust, and closing the sale based on high credibility due to product knowledge and a cheerful persistence that never spilled over into obnoxiousness.

Meanwhile, his main function at Ralston was analyzing the difference between two suppliers' methionine, an amino acid added as an ingredient to livestock feed. One supplier was Degussa (now called Evonik), the huge German agricultural and chemical company; the other, Monsanto, the U.S. agricultural giant.

Since Ralston purchased large quantities of this important food additive, it was vital to know which supplier's was better, Evonik's DL-methionine or Monsanto's version, called *Alimet™*. He accomplished such research at Purina's mammoth animal research farm in Gray Summit, Missouri, forty minutes southwest of St. Louis.

Once Evonik and Monsanto realized he was Ralston's research point man for methionine and thus a major factor in influencing their buying decisions, both companies lobbied him heavily. Legally, but heavily. Like any ethical scientist, however, Mark followed the data and let the facts and test results guide him. After exhaustive testing, he found that Evonik's methionine was more effective than Monsanto's *Alimet™*. As far as he was concerned, that ended the debate right there. Monsanto could have dangled four 50-yard-line Super Bowl tickets under his nose, and he wouldn't have budged. Once he learned that Monsanto's was only sixty-five percent as effective as Evonik's, he took great pains to explain that to the Ralston purchasing agents. Monsanto's product might have been cheaper, but not when compared on a potency basis.

Mark was a cross between Thomas Edison, the scientist-inventor, and Ross Perot, the super-salesman who became a legend at IBM for filling his *yearly* sales quota in two weeks. Mark's unbiased research and ability to explain his results to the purchasing agents in a way they could understand weren't lost on senior managers at Evonik. They appreciated that he chose their product over Monsanto's and noticed, in the course of their work with the Ralston purchasing agents, that Mark didn't merely analyze products with scientific rigor; he also had the mindset, conversational flow, and self-confidence of a truly great salesman. Unable to find that combination of talents anywhere in the agricultural industry, Evonik launched an all-out campaign to lure Mark away from Ralston. The job offer was more than a *quid pro quo* for choosing Evonik's methionine over Monsanto's; it was recognizing the importance of achieving higher sales based on a thorough scientific understanding of each product's merits, not just aggressive sales tactics.

Ultimately Evonik made him an offer he couldn't refuse: they wanted him to be *the* prime mover in their USA's marketing department and were prepared to pay him extremely well for it. No matter how generous the offer, any decision to change companies would be made only after lengthy discussion with Ginger. In the same way they vetted all major decisions since high school, they canvassed all their options, non-financial as well as financial, before accepting the Evonik offer in March of 1984. A month later they were living in New Jersey. Evonik's USA division was based in Teterboro, New Jersey at the time, just across the Hudson River from Manhattan.

Evonik, picking up the entire tab, moved Mark and Ginger from their suburban home in Glendale, Missouri to a new one in West Milford, New Jersey, some forty minutes north of Teterboro headquarters. Evonik not only packed all of their belongings and transported everything seamlessly from the Midwest home to the New Jersey house; in a highly unusual move, the company also bought the Whitacres' Glendale house from them to eliminate any possible distractions for Mark.

Once he joined Evonik, his higher salary allowed Ginger, for the first time, to be a full-time homemaker. Mark was all of twenty-seven, and Ginger, twenty-six. It only made sense that their thoughts would turn to starting a family.

After several months, however, nothing was happening. They consulted a specialist who tested them and found that they had less than a ten-percent chance of getting pregnant.

This was not a problem for Ginger and Mark. If they couldn't have biological children, they would simply adopt. They contacted the Lutheran Adoption Services, which has a long and stable history of providing adoption services that focuses on the needs of children, and passed a series of preliminary qualifications. In December of 1984 Mark and Ginger adopted two biological siblings. They considered this a great blessing. Tanya was seven at the time of adoption; Bill five. Both had been living in a foster home near Albany, New York, for two years. Ginger and Mark became their legal parents just two weeks before Christmas 1984.

Since Tanya and Bill were not babies or toddlers when they were adopted, and since it was right before Christmas, Mark and Ginger gave this little seven-year-old girl and five-year-old boy one Christmas to remember! It was Tanya's first Barbie doll and Bill's first G.I. Joe, among many other wonderful gifts that children that age would love.

What happened next was completely serendipitous. Just four months after adopting Tanya and Bill and with medical proof in hand that the possibility of ever getting pregnant was close to nil, Ginger became pregnant with Alex. Almost overnight, the Whitacres went from just the two of them to a full-blown instant family of five. On top of this, while Ginger was pregnant with Alex, Mark couldn't resist the urge to notch their now-suddenly complicated lives one degree further: he took an offer to rotate into a four-year stint in Germany at Evonik's world headquarters in Hanau.

Such a move offered substantial financial benefits, including the foreign-earned-income exclusion from taxation on a U.S. taxpayer's first $75,000 of income (in 1985) and a favorable currency exchange rate where one dollar was worth three marks forty pfennigs at the time, a liberal housing and food allowance, and a company car.

There would be one big trade-off, however: Mark was expected to travel extensively, including a full month in the Far East once every quarter plus heavy travel within Europe in between, putting him on the road some hundred-and-eighty to two-hundred days per year, or fifty percent of the time.

But the caveat of heavy travel was no deterrent for the ambitious executive and rising star, especially considering the financial offsets and Ginger's preoccupation with the new family. He accepted the promotion to *Leiter, Kundeberatung* (head of customer service) and a newly enlarged Whitacre family moved to Hanau, Germany, which is just 25 kilometers west of Frankfurt, in August of 1985.

Ginger, Mark, & Kids in Front of House at Schanzenstrasse 3,
Hanau, Germany (1986)

Ginger was five months pregnant with Alex, who started hearing and learning German while still in the womb.

Mark's travel workload was indeed grueling, but he was now a forward-propelled junior executive at Evonik who wanted to get ahead fast. For that reason he gladly travelled to virtually every English-speaking city in the world: Johannesburg, Bombay (now Mumbai), Hong Kong, Singapore, Kuala Lumpur, Manila, and even the Down Under cities of Sydney, Australia and Auckland, New Zealand. When added to the European Community cities he had to cover, Mark covered most of the world but the Americas.

Mark's ambition knew no bounds, and Ginger, pregnant with Alex, was comfortably ensconced in their beautiful new home at *Schanzenstrasse 3*, in Hanau, Wolfgang, Germany, a quaint little *Dörfchen* (village). Mark went from a forty-minute drive to work in New Jersey to a five-minute walk to the office in Hanau. German labor laws and a different work ethic in Germany meant that even management, including Mark, had to conform to Germany's pro-labor work hours; that meant you got home by 5 PM every night, when he wasn't on the road. This schedule was in sharp contrast to his New Jersey workload, where he had typically left home at six in the morning and returned at eight in the evening.

Mark's only concern during those years was the management practices prevalent in German industry in the 1980s. Evonik had a highly structured and centralized organization and heavily emphasized the then-prevalent business method called management by objective ("MBO"). Nothing was left to chance at Evonik, everything was done by committee. Managerial risk-taking was not part of the corporate culture. Managers were not merely discouraged from experimentation or "shooting from the hip;" they could get fired for it.

As such, MBO was a double-edged sword. On the one hand, Evonik's disciplined budget process and MBO mindset frustrated him. On the other, Evonik cultivated a highly ethical business environment. Mark thrived in and took for granted thereafter high ethics as an essential component of doing good business.

Back in the nineteen eighties, when Mark was at Evonik, a major difference between American companies and those outside the United States was degree of enforcement of the laws of business competition. In fact, what we in the United States call *antitrust law*, most other countries call *competition law*. Between 1984 and 1989, the years Mark was at Evonik, it is safe to say that competition laws had not yet been internationalized along the lines of the U.S. model. While competition laws were codified into law in both Asian and European countries at the time, their enforcement was highly variable from country to country.

The substance of antitrust or competition laws is that the interests of consumers must be protected and entrepreneurs must have an opportunity to compete in an open market economy where they have access to markets. U.S. business law was quite clear on the matter and had been for nearly a hundred years. Senator Sherman gave his name to the Sherman Antitrust Act as far back as 1890. Lieber's *Rats in the Grain* and Eichenwald's *The Informant* both contain excellent discussions of the history of American antitrust law. While he was traveling on business to Asia and countries within Europe for Evonik, Mark never was conscious of specific activity that might have involved price-fixing, nor did he see that other countries' competition laws were being broken. He was involved in the scientific and technical-sales side of the business. This is important because years later, after he exposed ADM's price fixing cartels, he would be accused of having learned how to price fix while working in foreign countries.

Because he was an outgoing, ebullient American in the Hanau office, he became popular with his fellow Evonik workers. Predictably, Mark threw himself into learning German; he mastered rapid, idiomatic spoken German and specialized business terms in short order. Germans always appreciate any Americans who take the time to learn their language, because so few do. This led Mark's co-workers to nickname him Deutsche Mark.

As his German proficiency improved, his technical sales ability also improved, and the results were demonstrable. By the autumn of 1988, it became clear that he would be moving up the Evonik corporate ladder soon. The only question for him and Ginger was, up the ladder in what geographical location? Geographical division competition for Mark's blend of selling skills and technical knowledge exploded into internecine war. Evonik-Asia was enjoying rapid growth in sales, in no small measure due to Mark's frequent trips there. The Singapore office wanted him badly. However, Evonik-USA continued its own robust rate of growth and was clearly one of Evonik's most important markets. So Evonik-USA wanted him back at their Ridgefield Park headquarters just as badly.

Meanwhile, the Whitacre family was getting restless in tiny Hanau. Ginger enjoyed living there, and the children integrated well into the local school and community. But there comes a time in any foreign country when you feel like there's still nothing like home. It was not enough, so their status as American expatriates had begun wearing thin, and Mark's heavy travel schedule exhausted Ginger and the children more than it did him. Tanya was by then ten, Bill eight and little Alex now three. Everyone was ready for a move back to the familiar, so it took little to persuade them that the assignment in the States was the better of the two options.

Mark and Ginger purchased a home in Warwick, New York, about forty-five minutes northwest of Manhattan. Mark commuted again, but this time to Evonik's Allendale, New Jersey, facility, where he became Director of the Applied Technology Center. He oversaw some fifty employees across all Evonik product lines. It was an important position, and the rising young business star enjoyed the honor of being the first non-German national to hold that position. He also used his bilingual and considerable other skills to take Evonik's technical sales and service staff to a significantly higher platform.

Nine short months after being charged with running the Allendale facility, Evonik promoted Mark again, this time to head an entire division at their new U.S. headquarters in Ridgefield Park, New Jersey, just a stone's throw from the Teterboro Airport. Barely thirty, Mark leapfrogged into his most important managerial position in his relatively brief business career to date. As vice president and head of an entire U.S. division, the Organic Chemicals and Feed Additives Division, he was thrust into improving Evonik's research and revitalizing its sales for two important products in Evonik's lineup, methionine and sodium cyanide. Little did Mark realize at the time that the groundwork he was laying at Evonik USA—improving management skills and enhancing scientific knowledge—would position him to accept a bigger job at a different firm, one that would compromise his ethics and, ultimately, be his undoing.

The new Whitacre home in Warwick was a five-acre spread with rolling hills, a large pond and a big red barn. The house itself was a newly built plantation-style delight that included a wrap-around porch and large rooms. Warwick is in Orange County not far from Greenwood Lake where today baseball Yankees great Derek Jeter owns a home. It is also horse country, so their daughter's love of riding and dressage blossomed. Tanya grew proficient at riding English-style and entered dressage competitions. Mark and Ginger were present at one of her competitions when her horse suddenly ran into the center of the arena and headed directly for the judge, who barely managed to dive out of danger's way. Needless to say, Tanya didn't score well at that competition.

Ginger was disappointed but not surprised when Mark reverted to keeping long business hours. The five-minute walk to work in Hanau had morphed into an hour drive each way to and from Evonik USA's Ridgefield Park operation, and if there was rain, the commute turned into two hours each way.

Mark and Ginger were pleased that the three children took after Mark in one important respect: All three took up the hobby of raising and showing rabbits in 4-H Club shows as Mark had with his Grand Champion New Zealand Rabbit, Big Red. Each had his or her own rabbits—and the accompanying responsibility for the care, feeding, and training of their particular brood. Mark's 1972 trophy sits on the mantel at home, beside the *eight* trophies that their youngest son won in rabbit-showing competitions.

In the spring of 1989, only nine months into his return to Evonik USA, Mark was instrumental in a strategic decision by Evonik to explore a joint venture with the Archer Daniels Midland Company of Decatur, Illinois in a specific, and lucrative, product: lysine. Mark was aware that no other company in the world produced both methionine and lysine under one roof. Yet, given how amino acids tend to interact, one without the other was useless. Evonik USA's thinking was that, if it planned to continue selling to Tyson Foods, Frank Perdue, and Cargill, and if it knew these companies needed both amino acids in their animal feed, why not create a combined production facility?

Mark headed negotiations for the Evonik USA side, while long-time Archer Daniels senior executive Terry Wilson did the same on their side. This potential joint venture was important enough for Mark to bring Evonik's top divisional man from the home office in Germany, Dr. Fritz Hahn, to the meetings. He was president of Evonik Chemicals Division worldwide, so he was a serious player. Knowing that a substantial capital investment would be required, Hahn attended the negotiation and gave it top priority. He also knew that ADM possessed the raw material essential to lysine production, dextrose, which Evonik simply did not have. One of Mark's first observations as talks between the two companies got underway was how streamlined and non-bureaucratic ADM's decision-making process was compared to Evonik's. Hahn, as the one with ultimate decision-making authority, was limited in his decision-making independence. He had to run everything by his executive board back in Germany and get a majority vote on it before he could move on to the next stage of negotiation.

After six years of doing business the Evonik way—the tediously slow, consensus-building, reams-of-red-tape way—Mark saw first-hand that ADM's faster decision-making process was a competitive advantage for them. *Here is a company that can turn on a dime*, he thought. *Look at how much latitude they give their managers to run their own divisions.* He learned that ADM's managers established their own budgets, set their own goals, and were held individually accountable. If they hit their targets, they received liberal performance-based stock options. This struck Mark as a powerful motivator and a practice that contrasted sharply with Evonik's. The latter dispersed accountability across such a broad number of people that, ultimately, no one was accountable and no one took risks. ADM managers, by comparison, worked harder and took full responsibility for their division's success or failure.

Mark also noticed that ADM was not afraid to let new ideas bubble to the surface, where they would then try them out. ADM seemed to invite failure rather than attempt to manage it away. In business, there is no such thing as certainty, but Evonik always sought it. They over-analyzed and over-meeting'ed every project and invariably came up with false certainty as to its likely success or failure.

Mark quickly realized that the Evonik bureaucracy would take four years to get a lysine plant in operation, whereas ADM's streamlined management and execution structure could have the world's largest lysine plant up and running within eighteen months. What ADM understood that Evonik did not was that the right decision, if made too late, can become the wrong decision.

On one of his trips to Decatur to discuss the lysine joint venture, Mark met ADM's president, Jim Randall. Randall impressed Mark because Randall intuitively understood, in contrast to Hahn, that the agri-and chemical businesses were constantly changing. Randall, for example, was easily able to proceed with less than a hundred percent certainty. If he didn't have all the facts, he relied on instincts built on years of experience. Randall had no problem committing ADM to a $300 million capital-investment in lysine, or other new products in the emerging biochemicals sector, based as much on his intuitive sense about the market potential as on statistical evidence and spreadsheets. By contrast, Evonik tried to reduce every business decision to a gradual and incremental risk-free activity. As they strategized endlessly, the market opportunity would pass them by.

By the end of the second day of negotiations, Randall was fed up with Evonik's plodding *modus operandi*. He also perceived that Mark was not cut from the same tedious cloth that characterized Hahn and his board back in Germany. He saw—and liked—Mark for the impatient, hard-charging young manager he was. He saw a young executive with a can-do attitude who was growing increasingly frustrated. Whenever Hahn and his team left the room for a private huddle to re-assess some minute change in the negotiation, Randall joked with Mark, in Hahn's absence, which Evonik executive would come back to request yet another month to crunch just a few more numbers or run yet another matrix-scenario analysis on the lysine joint-venture deal.

In the midst of these negotiations, Mark had a sudden realization. He called Ginger one night from Decatur and said that while he was sitting across the table earlier that day from Randall and his executives at ADM, he realized he was on the wrong side of the table. ADM was a risk-taker; Evonik was a risk-eliminator. ADM was nimble; Evonik was plodding. Hahn was someone who, on a bright sunny day, wouldn't leave home without an umbrella, "just in case."

Later, at home, he remarked to Ginger that the ADMers understood that market opportunities don't wait for you while you try to anticipate every potential loss scenario. His efforts to persuade Hahn and others at Evonik that sometimes you have to just move forward despite incomplete information fell on deaf ears. When he said, "Let's take a calculated risk here and make mid-course corrections and strategy adjustments as we go along," he might as well have been talking to a wall.

Randall summed up the two companies' differences when he responded to Hahn's remark, proudly made, that Evonik had over 4,000

PhD's working at the company with the response, "that would be my worst nightmare."

Seeing Mark's frustration with the Evonik bureaucracy, Randall put out a not-so-subtle feeler one day when the two were alone. "You know, Whitacre, I think we oughta joint venture this lysine plant, but *without* Evonik." That remark constituted a clear job offer. Our rising young business exec at Evonik began thinking that his star could rise a lot faster at ADM.

Little did the young couple know what fate had in store for them.

PART TWO

THE ADM YEARS

Mark Age 35 ADM Corporate Officer (October 1992)

Chapter Two

PART TWO—THE ADM YEARS

CHAPTER FOUR

Auspicious Beginnings

**"When the ancients said a work well begun was half
done, they meant to impress the importance of always
endeavoring to make a good beginning."**

POLYBIUS (ca. 203-120 BC)
Greek Historian of the Hellenistic Period

When Randall dangled the thinly veiled job offer under Mark's nose during one of Hahn's many breaks from the conference room negotiating table, Mark just smiled silently. It took every ounce of self-control not to stand up and walk out of the room with Randall and say, "sorry, Dr. Hahn, I'm going with the other guys." Instead, he held his counsel because vetting any such offer with Ginger would have to come first.

The couple debated the pros and cons of a move to ADM at length. While admitting that neither she nor Mark felt at ease in the greater metropolitan population of the East Coast, Ginger raised legitimate concerns about uprooting the family and Mark's putting himself in a situation where even longer work hours would be expected. Her husband's intense frustration with Evonik's plodding ways was so palpable, however, that, by week's end, they were both ready to pack the bags and go.

Mark immediately followed up on Randall's exploratory probe. From the privacy of his Warwick, New York home, he called Decatur headquarters in the second week of September, 1989. Randall was out of town, so he asked the ADM operator to connect him to Terry Wilson. Mark knew that Wilson, the other senior ADM executive involved in the Evonik joint-venture discussions, would be intimately involved in any decision to hire him.

After a few preliminaries, he told Terry that after four years in Germany with Evonik and three more in New York, the family might be interested in returning to their Midwestern roots. Upon hearing that, Wilson had an ADM corporate jet waiting for him in less than twenty-four hours at the Teterboro airport. He and Randall wanted Mark to see and hear at ADM headquarters where they thought the lysine-production discussions should be going but weren't. At that meeting, Mark and Randall got to know each other better. Even though Randall was twice Mark's age—in his mid-60s to Mark's barely thirty-two—they clicked. Age didn't matter; common mindset did: Both were technical by nature yet shared a hands-on approach to sales. Randall had a degree in engineering; Mark, in nutritional biochemistry.

At this recruiting meeting, Mark first met Michael "Mick" Andreas, son of ADM's all-powerful Chairman Dwayne Andreas, and liked him. Mick was hands-on and results-oriented. Everyone at Archer Daniels was results-oriented; the more Mark learned, the more he liked it. Randall made Mark an offer on the spot. It was substantial: ADM would double his base salary (in a part of the country where the cost of living was half New York's). They would name him President of the BioProducts Division, the fastest-growing division within the company. They would buy the Whitacres' Warwick house.

Perhaps most convincing, Randall said they would deploy between $500 million and $1 billion into BioProducts, "in size and with speed." In less than five years. No red tape, no lengthy approval process. Mark's mandate would be to make ADM the leader in lysine and other biotechnology businesses: build them, buy them, or joint-venture them.

The decision was a no-brainer, and the company lived up to its promise: Within eighteen months of Mark's arrival, ADM built a multi-hundred-million dollar lysine plant from scratch and had it running. While the plant was under construction, Mark simultaneously went on a buying and joint-venture binge that would have an enormous positive impact on ADM's strategic direction for more than a decade.

From the day he joined ADM in 1989, Mark took the BioProducts Division from a standing start to the largest biochemical production complex in the world. He did it in less than six years by prudently deploying more than a billion dollars of capital. Since his division was the fastest growing within the company, he became a focal point for analysts trying to project future growth prospects for the company. Mark responded by assisting the company's public relations with food analysts. When analysts came to Decatur to speak with ADM management about the company's progress, he always made time for them.

Mark's remarkable run from new division head in 1989 to corporate vice president in 1992 did not go unnoticed by analysts. A consensus was growing among them that this bright, young, hard-working manager may be in line for one of the top general management positions at a Fortune 100 company that had delivered average annual returns to its shareholders of greater than twenty percent.

Within a week of becoming a corporate vice president, Mark would be asked to do something that would turn him against the very company that just placed so much faith in him.

Mark and Ginger were so confident in the fit and permanency of his new position that one of their first actions after he accepted the high-paying job as division head was to purchase as their home the large compound just twenty minutes south of Decatur that for many years had been called The Old Homestead. The Chairman had lived there for years, as did the chairman before him, John Daniels, the "Daniels" of Archer Daniels Midland. The 1846-built estate was located in the little town of Moweaqua, Illinois.

These were indeed auspicious beginnings for the fledgling Whitacre family.

Whitacre Family's Moweaqua House Where They Lived From 1989-1995

Whitacre Family Moweaqua Horse Stables Across From Main House

PART TWO—THE ADM YEARS

CHAPTER FIVE

GOING UNDERCOVER

"No man does anything from a single motive."

SAMUEL TAYLOR COLERIDGE (1772-1834)
Author, *Rime of the Ancient Mariner*

The Archer Daniels Midland Company of Decatur, Illinois, known far and wide as "ADM" and "Supermarket to the World" to millions of Americans who listen to *Marketplace* on National Public Radio or watch *Meet the Press* on NBC, was large and profitable the year Mark went undercover against the company and several of its senior managers, specifically Michael "Mick" Andreas, vice chairman of the company, and Terrance "Terry" Wilson, president of the corn division. That year, 1992, Archer Daniels ranked 60th on the Fortune 100 list, with $8.5 billion in revenues and a market capitalization of almost $9 billion. The stock price reflected the prior decade's excellent operating results and generated an average annual return over the prior 10 years of 21%.

Archer Daniels had hired Mark three years earlier to run its up-and-coming new BioProducts Division; it was a perfect fit. He was smart, ambitious, and hard-working, and the company was eager to continue deploying substantial sums of capital to his division to continue its growth trend. Mick Andreas's father, Dwayne Andreas, ran the show at Archer Daniels Midland and had done so for decades. A self-made man, Dwayne was the son of a farmer and a college dropout, and a veteran of more than half a century in the agricultural commodities processing business who had vast reach. By the time Mark got there, the wily and hard-working Chairman was already in his mid-seventies, yet he had the energy of a man half his age; he was hands-on and strictly results-oriented; he had no time for excuses, and Mark liked that. Dwayne Andreas deserves much respect, and I will simply call him "The Chairman" throughout the rest of this narrative.

The Chairman was a shaker and mover on the larger stage, with high-level contacts in Washington DC, in Moscow, in all important grain-producing countries. These contacts and the importance of commodity processing to the creation of food for the world, gave The Chairman vast political influence. The Chairman left little doubt in anyone's mind, least of all his son Mick's or that of the young head of the BioProducts Division, who was in charge. Unless you were The Chairman, other titles, such as vice chairman for Mick or corporate vice president for Mark, meant little. Results meant everything.

Mick's father may have been The Chairman, but Mick was no slouch. He knew the business and played a number of important roles at ADM, the most productive of which was as head of the commodities trading desk. In his own right, Mick was a smart, heads-up commodities trader. He knew grains. He knew the Chicago Board of Trade and the Chicago Merc (Chicago Mercantile Exchange). And he knew how to trade the spot and futures markets in just about any commodity with a deft hand.

One cold morning in November of 1992, Mark was in his office and, as usual, multi-tasking, when his boss Michael "Mick" Andreas, hauled him into the executive conference room on the second floor.

Mick had about ten years on Mark. He was forty-five in October of 1992 to Mark's more tender thirty-five. Mick had just been named Vice Chairman of ADM; simultaneously Mark was named Corporate Vice President of ADM.

These two promotions clarified a lingering problem ADM had with Wall Street analysts: concern about succession planning. Wall Street had for years criticized the Board for their failure to name a successor. The

Chairman was already seventy-four in 1992, and his number two, ADM President Jim Randall, sixty-eight, so analyst concerns were legitimate.

The boards of most major public corporations consider succession planning one of their most important jobs. Witness GE and the way it groomed Jeff Immelt before he took over from Jack Welch. Not so at ADM. Only after years of vocal analyst concerns did The Chairman finally admit that he might be mortal. Mostly, however, he was concerned about ADM's flat stock price and was convinced it would improve if he named a credible succession team.

And so he did. With the appointment of Mick as Vice Chairman and Mark as corporate Vice President, the signal was sent to the Street that, in time, Mick would become chairman and Mark operating head for all of ADM. The announcement was also a diplomatic way of acknowledging that, with the passing of the old guard, Mick's role would be less on the operating side—with the exception of trading commodities, which was his forté—and more on the oversight side, whereas Mark's role would be as the hands-on head of operations, especially in the newer, value-added products.

Mark's ADM Business Card, Corporate Officer Age 35 (1992)

Chinese Version, Mark's ADM Business Card (1992)

"M & M," as Mick and Mark were called, may have been only ten years apart in age, but the two were light years apart in virtually every other category. Mick was more balanced and enjoyed the non-business life as much as he did life at ADM. By contrast, Mark was all business and all ADM. Mark also had youth on his side, as well as strong credentials as a scientist. He was a decisive young manager and a super-salesman. In the eyes of Wall Street, the Board had made the right pick.

At the time of the appointments, an analyst at Dain Bosworth (now Dain Rauscher) came out with a brokerage report identifying Mark as the best choice to run the operations and new-products side of the sprawling entity. In the Board's eyes, this analyst got the story so right that they sent the independent analyst report to all shareholders as an enclosure with the 1992 annual report.

When Mark was first hired at Archer Daniels in 1989, he had no clue that a policy of pre-arranging price and volume allocations with their competitors, mostly non-U.S. processors of the same agricultural products, was already an established way of doing business by some of the senior executives at the firm. The whole notion of agreeing secretly with your competitors to maintain certain target levels of volume and pricing was totally alien to him.

It wasn't long, however, before he began to hear unsettling remarks. For example, a vice president over in lactic acid had told him repeatedly that Terry Wilson, president of the corn division, was a price-fixing *hombre* par excellence, a savvy manager and experienced global coordinator who knew how to get all the players in line and make it happen with volumes and prices. Word was that Terry had already made it happen in citric acid, corn refining, and sodium gluconate and, in the process, made ADM hundreds of millions of dollars. Who could complain?

That particular November morning in 1992, however, as Mark was heading for the executive conference room to meet with Mick, little did anyone know it was the first step that would blow the company, numerous senior managers, and Mark himself, to smithereens.

As he walked toward the conference room, he scratched his head and wondered, *why the executive conference room? Why not just swing by my office informally, per usual?* M & M both had offices on the second floor of the ADM building that overlooked a huge, noisy trading operation. Their offices were close, giving them easy access to each other, and Mick typically just popped his head into Mark's office when he had something on his mind.

A little red flag went up in his mind that something wasn't quite right. As he walked into the conference room, a second red flag went up because Mick wasn't alone. The head of ADM security, a Chairman loyalist, was also there. A highly competent security director, he did whatever The Chairman said needed to be done that was in the interest of the company, and he did it well. The guy was not to be trifled with.

Mark took one look at the scene and knew there was Big Trouble. Mick was pale and shaken, sheet-white. The head of security was even grimmer than his usual self, which was plenty grim. Mick wordlessly motioned for Mark to sit down and then grunted with a mixture of fear and scorn that Mark was not going to believe what his father, The Chairman, had done.

His first thought was, *oh I'm not? Well let me tell you Mick, I could in fact think of a thousand over-the-top, heavy-handed things that your imperious, strong-willed father could have done.* But holding his counsel, Mark just sat there, silently waiting to be enlightened by The Chairman's own son.

Mick told Mark that his father had gotten the FBI involved in the sabotage thing. Mark groaned inwardly and got a sinking feeling in the pit of his stomach.

The "sabotage thing" referred to the problems Mark's division was having with the company's new $300 million dollar lysine plant. Lysine is an amino-acid component of protein and an important additive in animal feed. Among other things, lysine helps chickens and pigs bulk up.

The lysine business was no little sidebar for ADM. It was a huge and growing half-billion-dollar market with major customers like Tyson and Perdue. Global demand was guaranteed to grow as the world population grew. Under Mark's guidance, ADM had built the largest, most technologically advanced lysine plant in the world.

From the start of the new plant's operation, however, he had a contamination problem. Producing lysine requires the use of a single, specific bacterium known as the Brevi bacterium. To produce pure lysine, there can be no other bacteria in the fermentation process. The waste that a Brevi bacterium eliminates is lysine. These Brevi bacteria reproduce rapidly, excrete, and die, leaving the valuable excrement. If the process gets contaminated, other, unwanted viruses introduce their own rapid reproduction cycle and interfere with the lysine excretion process. This causes something other than pure lysine to come out of the fermentation vats. When that happens, you have to throw out the whole batch.

His lysine yields were low due to this recurring contamination problem. Each batch that had to be thrown out cost the firm hundreds of thousands of dollars, so ADM's—Mark's—lysine operation was losing about $7 million per month, and the responsibility for that rested squarely on his shoulders.

He and his team had been trying for months to solve the contamination problem every which way possible. He hired new engineers from competitor firms. He brought in outside consultants. He re-trained plant operators. He tried everything, but nothing worked. He had two choices: either fix the problem, or leave ADM in disgrace.

Having just been named operating heir apparent at the company-wide level, and knowing that the company's potential for growth in the biotech sphere was exponential, Mark told himself that failure was not an option. But he needed time.

———

At one point, he and ADM's then-president, Jim Randall, had talked about the possibility of plant sabotage. While sabotage could not be ruled out, Mark thought there was a greater likelihood that Randall's hand-picked managers and laborers who had come over from the corn-processing division were simply not maintaining strict sanitary standards. Randall was in denial about it because they were "his" men, but these good 'ole Decatur boys didn't fully understand the need for absolute scrubbed conditions. You had to be pure when handling absolutely anything at any phase of the lysine-creation process. No exceptions.

Mark's suspicion pointed to a vast cultural clash between these untrained "corn grinders" as upper management called the long timers from ADM's mammoth corn operation, and his own hand-picked biotech scientists in their white lab jackets. The scientists were carefully-trained professionals who took every precaution and used strict sanitary protocol at every step in the process to insure that the Brevi bacterium and *only* the Brevi bacterium got into the fermentation process.

To Mark's credit, his advancing the sabotage theory gained traction because recent events gave an air of plausibility to the theory. Just a few months earlier, in late summer of 1992, ADM gave a tour of its new lysine plant to representatives from its two Japanese competitors. The Japanese had spent two decades building their own processing plants, so they could hardly believe that ADM was able to build a plant in just eighteen months that was capable of producing fully half the total world demand for lysine. Drawing on the motto, "seeing is believing," ADM invited their Japanese counterparts to Decatur to see the new plant with their own eyes.

Shortly after the Japanese contingent left, suspicious things started happening in lysine. The people at Ajinomoto, ADM's largest lysine competitor, somehow gained detailed knowledge of ADM's contamination problem. In fact, at times, the Japanese became aware of the existence of ADM's specific process problems before ADM itself knew. This gave some minor credibility to the theory that ADM's Japanese competitors were sabotaging the lysine operation.

From that small base of suspicion, however, Mark had built a bigger story around the sabotage theory. Being desperate, he did this to buy more time. He falsely told Mick some months earlier he had received an unusual call from someone at the Ajinomoto Company, who "whispered" to him that Ajinomoto was paying an ADM employee to insert a contaminating virus into the lysine vats. Mark presented this concocted story to Mick strictly to win some breathing space and time so he could once and for all clean up the contamination problem.

Mick was already angling and maneuvering, and he took Mark's fabricated story in an unanticipated direction by asking at the time, "Can we flip this guy?" In other words, Mick wanted to know if the saboteur—a person who did not actually exist—would take money from ADM instead of from his current paymaster to not only stop adding the bad virus, but also reverse the tables and actually steal for ADM the hardier, more disease-resistant strain of the Brevi bacterium that Ajinomoto had. The Japanese had developed over many years a stronger, more evolved micro-organism than ADM had.

He was at a loss as to how to respond to Mick's thought process because, of course, he had made the whole story up to begin with. Mick went further and took that made-up story about a "Japanese extorter/saboteur" to The Chairman. The Chairman did what The Chairman knows best: Launch a massive, high-level power play by contacting his "DC people." With the prospect of sabotage and extortion coming from foreign interests, The Chairman went through his back-channel contacts at the CIA to advise him.

CIA is foreign, not domestic, so they determined quickly that this was a domestic law-enforcement matter and tossed the case over to the FBI in Washington. The chain of hand-offs went from CIA Headquarters at Langley to CIA in Chicago to FBI Chicago to FBI Springfield, Illinois. FBI Springfield contacted their one and only Special Agent in Decatur, and it was that Decatur agent who had just met with Mick that morning.

Mick made it clear that the company did *not* want the FBI nosing around in any of their businesses. Mark understood.

The agent that Mick had just met with wanted to debrief Mark as well, in an effort to find out just what was going on. Mick knew that federal agents could start snooping around and get wind of other unusual activity. The company had more than its share of skeletons in the closet. If the FBI were to find out that Mick and Terry were talking to the Japanese about fixing the price of lysine or discover how they had obtained their technology for citric acid, or that they had obtained their bacitracin technology by hiring someone to bring it from the competition, it would not be up to a kosher meal.

The FBI agent wanted to meet with Mark as soon as possible. Mark began to feel a suffocating noose wrap itself around his neck. He knew the FBI would want everything Mark had concerning possible sabotage of the lysine plant via deliberate contamination. Names, conversations, phone logs, the whole bit. Mick handed Mark a business card that said *FBI Special Agent Brian Shepard* on it.

The Archer Daniels outside attorney wanted Mark to meet the FBI agent downtown, in the attorney's office, discreetly and as far away from Archer Daniels headquarters as possible. If word leaked out, the entire city of Decatur would know in a milli-second. Decatur was then a small town that was all about the Archer Daniels Midland Company.

Mark was by now totally panicked. He rubbed his eyes, thought the situation through, and realized he could either tell Mick now that he had made the sabotage story up to buy time or see the entire charade through.

Mark was being coached to tell the FBI two lies, one about who approached whom for an illegal transfer of the lysine microbe, and another about which phone line was the one they should tap. This was not looking good for Mark.

Yet at 3 PM that afternoon, he was dutifully sitting in the company lawyer's office in a downtown Decatur Citizen's Bank building. His face was flush; his heart pounding. The fight-or-flight impulse was fully present. On the drive down, he had mentally dismissed Mick's advice. He knew hiding was no longer possible, so he was determined to just fess up, tell this agent the truth. He didn't owe it to The Chairman or Mick or ADM to lie to the government about anything.

When he was ushered into the attorney's conference room, however, he got the shock of his life. Two men, not one, were there. One was the FBI agent, a total stranger at that point. The other was an all-too-familiar face. Standing to shake Mark's hand, the agent said "Brian Shepard, FBI Decatur." The other man neither stood up nor greeted Mark. In fact, he made absolutely zero eye contact.

"What are you doing here?" Mark asked ADM's head of security.

"Mick just wanted to make sure this meeting goes OK for you, so he asked me to be here in case any points needed clarification," the Enforcer replied, sounding like all of rationality and calm were on his side.

Mark screamed internally, *yeah right!* while glaring back at him and saying nothing. He turned to the agent and tried to convey his alarm with his eyes.

Get this creep outta here! the eyes were screaming to Shepard, *he's head of ADM security! He's not here to let the truth be known. He's here to make sure I lie the way I was coached to lie. If he stays, I'm on my way to criminal conduct, and then the company will own me!* The FBI agent was either too preoccupied or simply too ingenuous to pick up on Mark's silent screams.

What's wrong with this agent? He kept thinking. *Why would he let such an interview be conducted in this manner, with the Enforcer present?*

Shepard remained clueless. *Is this guy already in the company's pocket? Doesn't he realize I can't possibly speak truthfully or confidentially with the Enforcer right beside him? Doesn't the Enforcer's mere presence violate FBI*

interviewing protocol? Does this agent not realize he's about to become just
another unwitting pawn as the company manipulates the truth to serve its
own nefarious ends?

The meeting played out even worse than Mark could have imagined. Shepard naively went about his questioning and remained clueless as to what the Enforcer was doing behind his back. As Mark sat, answering the agent's questions, the Enforcer stood behind the agent, gesturing and making faces at Mark. If he started offering too much information in response to an open-ended question, or got too "free-form" in his answers, the Enforcer would quickly move a hand up to his neck and make the cutting motion, as in "Cut! Cut! Stop what you're saying immediately!" If it looked like Mark was close to revealing a detail of ADM's price fixing activities, the Enforcer'd give Mark the most menacing look he could muster. If on the other hand he gave the agent useless verbal filler, the Enforcer would nod his head approvingly and make a forward-rolling motion with his hands, as in, "that's it, just keep the crap rolling."

The outcome of that meeting was the exact opposite of what Mark had wanted going into it. He had been coerced, by virtue of the Enforcer's presence, into telling the story the way he had been coached. Mark's bosses imposed on him the same thing it imposed on its entire work force, all the time: blind loyalty, mixed with thinly-veiled threats of retaliation if you didn't play ball.

Fortunately, Shepard left one small window of opportunity open for Mark.

"Mr. Whitacre, we'll need to install a recording device on your home OPX line ASAP. I'll get the necessary approvals and contact you later today. I'd like to come down to your house after business hours. Is that possible?"

Mark said something about having dinner arrangements at the Decatur Country Club with one of ADM's distributors from Venezuela until at least 9 PM, looking over at the Enforcer while he said it. The Enforcer shrugged his shoulders as if to say, just go along you pawn.

Turning back to the agent, he said, "Anytime after about 9:30 PM should be no problem."

"OK, I'll be at your house at 10 pm."

Mark agreed and quickly left the room. Driving back to his office, a host of fears surfaced. He had a strong desire to please The Chairman and get ahead, and that is what compromised his moral compass. From a strictly business point of view it had paid off, because Mark had just become the youngest corporate vice president in ADM's history and knew he was being groomed. However, he knew he had Ginger to deal with.

Ginger had seen the dark side of her husband's supervisors much sooner than he himself had. Call it a woman's intuition; call it having some distance from events. Call it what you will.

What Ginger *didn't* understand, however, was the lengths the imperious Chairman was willing to go to keep his minions in line. Back in those days, if Mark had said to the FBI guy in the presence of the Enforcer that he thought executives inside the firm might be breaking the law, he would have been terminated.

That night, on the way home from dinner at the Country Club, Mark told Ginger the whole story about lysine price-fixing. She was appalled and said, *make sure you tell the FBI everything.* She could not have been more serious. Moments after arriving home from a dinner meeting with one of ADM's Venezuelan distributors, they met FBI agent Shepard at the door.

Mark looked over Shepard's shoulder. "I thought you'd be sending someone else, someone like a phone technician or something."

Shepard looked at him, opened his arms, and said, "I'm the only game in this town, Dr. Whitacre."

"Call me Mark."

They both smiled. Then Mark escorted Shepard upstairs to the family exercise room, just off the master bedroom, where the OPX phone line was. Shepard got behind the desk, attached some sort of recording device to the phone, and tested it. Mark made no mention of the meeting from earlier in the day. Ginger had deliberately stayed within earshot and realized her husband was waffling. She didn't like it.

The recording apparatus seemed to work fine, so he and the agent went downstairs and were just saying their goodbyes when Ginger turned Mark toward her and gave him one of her piercing looks. She repeated what she had said in the car on the way home from dinner, "Corky, if you don't tell him—RIGHT NOW—I will."

He gazed painfully into his wife's determined eyes. He was frozen. She walked to the front door, eyes still on him. She was getting ready to call Shepard back herself, when Mark quickly stepped forward.

"Mr. Shepard, got another minute?"

The agent looked back at him quizzically. He glanced down at his watch and said, "What is it?"

This was it, the moment of truth, Mark's fork in the road. Either fear The Chairman and stay silent, or align with Ginger and speak out. He was stuck in the middle of forces he couldn't control. Shepard stood just outside the front door; Ginger stood just inside it. Both were waiting. Shepard was waiting for anything. Ginger was waiting for her husband to do the right thing. Mark looked first at Shepard, then turned and looked at Ginger . . . then back to Shepard . . . . then back again to Ginger. From the uncompromising look in her eyes, he knew there was no getting off the hook.

With a deep exhale, he uttered the two words that would change his life forever.

"There's more," he said and then looked down at his shoes like a shy little boy.

"What do you mean?" the bewildered agent asked.

He looked back up. "I mean there's more going on at ADM than Mick Andreas, me, or anyone else has told you."

"Like what?"

"Like stealing technology from other companies. Like engaging in an international price-fixing cartel. That sort of thing."

Shepard took a step backwards, as if he were absorbing the sudden impact of a blunt-force object hitting him in the chest.

As Shepard recoiled away from Mark, Ginger, almost in lock-step, stepped forward toward him. She gently took his hand and squeezed it, as if to say, *tell him the whole truth. I'm with you all the way.*

"Wait a minute, wait a minute here," Shepard said. He paused, swallowed, and then continued, "Mark, you're taking this thing into a whole new realm. What exactly do you mean?"

By now, Mark was ready to go into as much detail as this guy wanted but, in the first of what would later become many displays of paranoia, he suggested they move into Shepard's car—in case ADM had bugged the Whitacres' home.

Once inside Shepard's standard-issue government vehicle, Mark unleashed the whole tale in rapid but measured tones.

"To be exact," he said, "my bosses at the company are systematically and deliberately impeding free trade and open discovery of market prices in certain commodities. ADM arranges with other companies throughout the world to agree to volume allocations and prices on certain raw materials and commodities that they are involved with. That means ADM participates in a cartel. As a cartel, ADM and these other companies do not compete with each other. Instead, they talk on the phone and go to 'trade meetings,' as they're called, where they all agree on production, pricing, and marketing in a number of products. As a cartel, we divvy up the global market and maintain an artificially high price in restraint of free trade. Ultimately, the consumer, the end user, overpays because he is paying an artificially high price for whatever product a consumer buys that has any of our ingredients in it. Direct buyers from us have no place else to go for lower prices because we are all in collusion. The price is pre-arranged, as are the volumes."

"That's a real mouthful Mark," Shepard said, as he wrote furiously on a notepad while the two of them sat freezing in Shepard's car in the long circular Whitacre driveway.

For the next two hours, Mark talked non-stop. Even though Shepard did not understand a lot of what Mark was saying, he understood that the FBI very likely had a company in serious violation of the Sherman Antitrust laws. Shepard's hand must have been ready to fall off, he was writing so furiously.

Just after midnight, he was finally talked out. Shepard, not wanting to waste any time, said he would arrange to have Mark meet with an FBI supervisor from the Springfield office named Dean Paisley just as soon as Shepard could get Paisley over to Decatur as soon as possible. Paisley was a highly experienced and very senior FBI Special Agent.

When Mark met Paisley in less than 48 hours, Paisley made it clear that the FBI would need hard evidence of price fixing, not just Mark's disjointed explanation of two nights before. He then asked Mark if he would volunteer to become a Cooperating Witness. It would involve signing a release, wearing a wire, and recording an indeterminate number of price-fixing meetings. Paisley said it would be for only a short time, just until the FBI had enough evidence.

Mark hesitated, knowing that, once he started down that path there could be no turning back. His major worry was retaliation from The Chairman. Paisley assured Mark he would be doing the right thing.

"You mean I'll be one of the good guys, one of the guys wearing the white hat?"

"That's right Mark."

More importantly, Mark knew that Ginger believed very strongly that he was doing the right thing, and Ginger had world's best moral compass bar none. After discussing the matter with Ginger, he agreed.

Years later, Mark and Ginger discussed with their children, despite what ultimately happened to Mark, how, once you establish that one choice is good and another choice is bad, there is no justification—no matter what the consequences—in choosing what you know to be the bad choice. In this case, the principle they wanted to establish with their children was that free societies must have free trade as a condition of their freedom, and any company in any country should be free to compete in any product or service on the basis of price, quality, and ability to deliver, totally free from any controlling influence beside fair and open market forces.

What a few senior executives at the firm were doing was the opposite. They rigged the game. They were already controlling the price and production levels of several commodities by colluding with their competitors. Sadly, it was entirely unnecessary in lysine. Mark knew that, eventually, he would solve the contamination problem, and, once he was going full steam ahead, he could compete aggressively but *fairly* by selling ADM's lysine on the basis of quality, efficiency, vast economies of scale, and an abundant marketing budget.

Mark and Ginger, being basic and uncomplicated people, didn't like the country-club mentality of a few of the company's senior managers and their wives. Despite the perks, title, private jet, and money, Ginger didn't like the vibe she picked up from certain co-workers of her husband's, such as the blatant displays of wealth by certain of the managers. She encouraged Mark to keep his eyes and ears open and take calls from headhunters about employment opportunities elsewhere. By his third year as President of the BioProducts Division at ADM, he realized that the mantra adopted by several senior executives was, "the competition is your friend; the customer is your enemy," and he knew that that mantra, the mantra of price-fixing, would be coming his way sooner rather than later.

Hearing footsteps like that, and knowing that one man alone would never be able to persuade his bosses to compete strictly "on the merits," he and Ginger now say they should have quit immediately, before "it" got to his division. The company simply had too many managers who had been there too many years and had made themselves and the shareholders too much money to see things his way. Mark's bosses had long since been desensitized to the possibility that the very premise on which their divisions made money was not only unnecessary in lysine, but flagrantly violated established antitrust law.

Given ADM's vast global reach and entrenched management, it was one thing to be dissatisfied with your company's policies and actions—but quite another to tape a wire to your chest and start recording criminal conduct of those who trust you most.

Were it not for Ginger, Mark never would have done it. He had no plans to blow the whistle. He'd been around The Chairman enough to believe that he had, by far, more power than the FBI. He believed that The Chairman could use the FBI for his own purposes. Ginger believed the opposite. The FBI is our nation's top watchdog, she reasoned, and they'll protect my husband.

It turned out he was right, and she was wrong, but it places the location of purity of motive. Mark was not the one with purity of motive. Forget any "I'm-going-to-bring-down-the-bad-guys" reason that motivates most whistleblowers to initiate contact with federal authorities about misconduct inside their companies. Purity of motive had absolutely nothing to do with his becoming "the most productive whistleblower in the history of American business," as the media said *ad nauseum* once the case broke. He had just been named a corporate officer. He was too high up in the organization and had too much to lose.

Ginger came at it from a different angle. She strongly believed in the fundamental goodness of our nation's institutions and held fast to a few basic truths, one of which was that if any federal institution was above corruption and influence, it was the Department of Justice of the United States of America. Any thought that the DOJ might have a few political magnets attached to its moral compass that could be moved and redirected at the discretion of those in power, like The Chairman, was beyond her.

It was she, not Mark, who possessed purity of motive. She admits now how naïve she was at the time. Ginger was relying on nothing more than an entirely understandable trust that all Americans ought to be able to place in our nation's top law enforcement agency. That's how this whole thing was pure serendipity. That's how, thanks to Ginger's trust in them, the FBI stumbled on to the largest price-fixing scandal since the very creation of the Sherman Antitrust Act in 1890, made into law more than one hundred years earlier.

As far as how he ended up going undercover, that's the reality. No heroics. No grand ethical battle, at least in Mark's mind, of good versus evil. It was Ginger. The FBI stumbled onto this massive price-fixing case thanks to Ginger. Mark did it under pressure from his wife. He never voluntarily would have gone to the FBI. In fact, he did not go to the FBI. They found him; he didn't find them. He told a little lie, and now he was forced to expose the big truth.

Once on board as an informant, however, and with Ginger's help, Mark thought through what would have happened had he not drawn the line then and there. Had he gone along with Mick and hid the schemes, they would have been able to blackmail Mark the rest of his life. When he first signed on as an informant, he never imagined that anyone would go to prison for what his undercover work would bring to light, least of all him. He thought ADM would pay a hefty civil fine but figure out a way to blame most of it on the Japanese. He also thought that, because he was dealing with the big guys, the FBI itself, that they would protect him and that nobody would find out he was the mole. They could protect him from everybody but himself.

Had the Whitacres known back then what they know now, Ginger never would have compelled her husband to talk to the FBI, and Mark never would have agreed to go undercover. He would have simply followed both his and Ginger's initial instincts: quit the firm, find another job, and move on. In the words of the writer, O. Henry:

> **My advice to you, if you should ever be in a hold-up, is to line up with the cowards and save your bravery for an occasion when it may be of some benefit to you.**

Mark was in a hold-up; he did not line up with the cowards; and what he did was of almost no personal benefit.

PART TWO—THE ADM YEARS
CHAPTER SIX

LEADING TWO LIVES: WIRED & DANGEROUS

"Without you, Mark, we had nothing.
The whole case against ADM rests on the tapes, and you
made the tapes."

ROBERT HERNDON
FBI Special Agent, *Operation Harvest King*
Letter to Mark Whitacre

Except for the lysine contamination problem, Mark ran his business to his bosses' entire satisfaction for the first years he was there, from 1989 to early 1992. He made numerous acquisitions and joint ventures. During that time, there was no interference in how he ran his division. This was in part due to the fact that he was a relative newcomer to the firm, and in part due to the fact that he had started a new and very high-tech division from scratch.

But just as night follows day, the suggestion that he try learning some "tricks of the trade" came from higher up the day that Mick dropped by to say that Terry would be getting back from vacation the following week and Mick would be assigning him to work with Mark, on a "strictly temporary" basis.

Mark wondered if this new development had to do with the contamination problem or was it the other, bigger, thing. Because, sooner or later, Mark's people *would* solve the contamination problem.

Mick and The Chairman and Randall all knew that Mark would eventually bring the contamination problem under control. They were thinking beyond such short-term production hiccups. Terry wasn't coming over to BioProducts to help Mark run his business. Terry would not be getting involved in Mark's high-tech side of the business. He just needed to show Mark how ADM does business.

Mark knew it was now or never: Mount a defense or get on board with price fixing. He mounted his defense.

He demonstrated to Mick as graphically as possible the company's competitive advantages: (1) *Low raw materials cost* from the corn division (dextrose); (2) Vast *economies of scale* due to the huge new fermentation plant; (3) Improved *granular grade* product versus powder grade of competitors; and (4) sophisticated, *well-trained salesmen* hand-picked by Mark who knew the business.

Mark went to the white board and drew a flow chart, hoping that the visual approach would help Mick see what Mark saw.

Mark continued, "So corn (the corn division) sells my division their dextrose at intercompany rates, meaning *cheap*. Since what I'm buying from corn is mostly reject dextrose, Accounting could actually argue a *zero* inter-company transfer cost for raw materials. Either way, I've got low-to-no raw material costs. Ajinomoto doesn't have that. They have to buy their dextrose from outside vendors, and I know what they are paying. It's high enough that they can come down in price only so far without making this their loss-leader, and Ajinomoto does not have significant cross-selling opportunities for MSG because the buyers of lysine are not necessarily the buyers of MSG.

Mick was only half listening.

"Our fermentation plants are literally connected by pipe to our dextrose source at corn, so transportation costs are nil. And we have the largest single fermentation plant in the world right there."

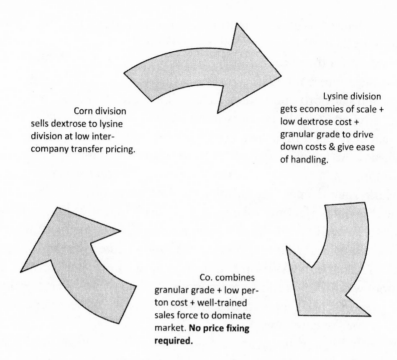

Corn division sells dextrose to lysine division at low inter-company transfer pricing.

Lysine division gets economies of scale + low dextrose cost + granular grade to drive down costs & give ease of handling.

Co. combines granular grade + low per-ton cost + well-trained sales force to dominate market. **No price fixing required.**

Mick remained unmoved.

Mark kept trying. "We feed our dextrose into our fermentation plants, and, bingo! Out comes pure lysine at a fraction of their cost. And in granular form, not powder. Ajinomoto only has the powder stuff. It's like flour, a cloud of dust everywhere. Handlers have to wear face masks. We've solved the handling problem with our granular lysine, bud." Mark threw in that he had assembled a polished and experienced sales force, and then sat down.

But Mick had ten years on Mark and a perspective that had been handed down over many years from The Chairman himself. He told Mark they couldn't trust Ajinomoto or the Japanese government because of how they subsidized their agricultural commodities. Subsidies were already in place for Japanese lysine producers, whereas the product was so new that Archer Daniels had not yet lined up support from the U.S. Department of Agriculture. That could take years.

Mark had translated a broad competitive strategy into the specific action steps he outlined, but it fell on deaf ears. He knew his division had created value for the buyer through cost leadership, product differentiation, and focused selling. Yet Mick was correct that a price war could materialize that would eat both companies alive. Ajinomoto would incur losses to match Archer Daniel's lower pricing for as long as they needed until they had developed their own economies of scale and granular grade of lysine, and the Japanese system of subsidies would support them. Then Ajinomoto could run ADM into the ground. Not vice versa.

Mark paused and then admitted, "The **only** thing we lack at the moment is the perfect microbe, and that's evolving." But he stuck to his guns, "After that, this half-billion dollar market is low-hanging fruit for us."

But Mick was adamant, and ADM didn't like to leave things to chance. He and Terry Wilson had been around a long time, and, besides, the proof was in the pudding. Years ago, Terry had gotten everyone on the same page in citric acid, and that product went on to become a money machine for the company.

Price-fixing was being shoved down Mark's throat, so he did what he had to do. He went along with it. Call it a coping mechanism, call it rationalization, call it poor judgment, call it what you will, but at that moment, in his mind, Mark shifted gears. *Let it be,* he told himself. *I'm the up-and-comer. The Chairman's in his seventies. The president is in his sixties. Once they're gone, and once Mick starts spending more time in the sun in Boca, I'll be running day-to-day operations. When I do, I'll turn this ship around and run an ethical company.*

Mark actually believed that he could turn such a deeply entrenched corporate culture around. Believing in a clean ADM in the future was the only way he could justify doing things Mick's way. *Be patient, bide your time. Wait until you're in position. Then clean up our act.*

Anyone could see that Mark's division had no reason to reach out to its competitors and start slicing up, via secret agreements, the world pie in lysine. Mark could fill the pie, bake the pie, take it off the countertop and eat it whole. They could slice it any way they chose—all by using above-board, straight-up legitimate business practices. Were Mick and Terry simply to do it this way, Mark was sure that, within three years, the world lysine market would be ADM's and ADM's alone.

A week after that conversation, a tanned Terry Wilson, fresh from a golf vacation, strolled into his office. Mark and Terry were polar opposites in almost every respect. Terry had been at ADM for years; Mark was a relative newcomer. Terry was Mick's and The Chairman's most senior crony; Mark was (at least he thought) still very independent. Terry was almost sixty; Mark was just 34 in early 1992. Terry drank and smoked heavily; Mark almost never drank and had never smoked in his life. Terry had little formal education; Mark was an Ivy League PhD. Terry barked orders rudely at subordinates in his gravelly smoker's baritone; Mark consulted them collaboratively in a low-key, respectful tenor voice. Terry projected a Bogart-like tough-guy image, cigarette dangling from his lips; Mark projected the image of a modern young manager with both business and scientific backgrounds.

Terry plopped down behind Mark's desk as if he owned it. He lit a cigarette, propped his feet up, spat a little piece of tobacco out of his mouth straight onto Mark's neat clean desk, and spoke.

"OK, kid, here's what I need. First, who are your competitors? Second, where are they located? Third, how big is the overall market for this—ah—product? Fourth, who has what share of it currently? Fifth, who are the decision-makers at each company? And finally, how many of these so-called decision-makers do you know personally?"

He asked absolutely nothing about the product or the process.

Mark, whose knowledge of the lysine business was encyclopedic, rattled off precise and detailed answers to every one of Terry's questions without reference to notes or files.

"Our biggest competitor," he began, "is Ajinomoto, the Japanese firm. 'Ajin-O-Moto' stands for 'Essence of Taste,' and MSG is their signature product. Right now, they control over fifty percent of the world lysine market, 52.5 percent to be exact. Number two is Kyowa Hakko, also Japanese, but smaller in lysine, less than 10 percent. Then come two small Korean producers, one of which is just as new to the lysine production business as we are, but without our resources."

He continued, "In addition, Ajinomoto also has a fifty/fifty joint venture with a French company called Orsan. That joint venture is known as 'Eurolysine.'

"Good, kid, real good," Terry replied. "Got any kind of personal relationship with anyone at Ajin-O . . . . whatever-you-call-them?"

"There's a guy named Mimoto I know pretty well. He's in charge of their entire lysine production, including their facility here in the U.S. called Heartland Lysine, which is headquartered in Chicago. I've run into Mimoto at conferences, and his English is decent. I would say that I know him well enough to pick up the phone and call him."

"What about the other, smaller Japanese outfit?"

"Kyowa Hakko? They're a bit player in the global lysine market. We recently hired a guy away from their St. Louis office named Marty Alison, so I can talk to him and look for a back-door intro that way."

"Just do whatever it takes, kid. We need to get a meeting set up with all these guys as soon as possible. Our cover is that we wanna form a lysine trade association to improve quality and efficiency and help the overall market, that sorta thing. Got it?"

"Sure thing, Terry," he grimaced.

Mark did not like this guy. Not his assumptions, his style, or his sleazy vibe. But he looked at the old-timer, smiled through it all, and did what he was told.

It took Mark at least fifteen phone calls over the next month to get the heads of the various global producers of lysine to reach terms on when and where to meet. Neither Japanese firm could figure out why in the world ADM wanted to meet with them. Their mistrust was palpable.

After much jawboning on Mark's part, Ajinomoto finally agreed to meet, but only once, and only on their turf, in Japan. The other Japanese firm, Kyowa Hakko, fell in line behind Ajinomoto, also stipulating in Japan only.

Terry hated to fly, so when Mark said the only way a meeting was going to happen was if they flew to Japan, Terry initially rejected the offer. At his age, he had no desire to make such a long trip. But Mark made it clear that neither Japanese outfit trusted Terry's intentions, and the only way a meeting was going to happen at all was if Terry and he flew to Japan. Reluctantly, Terry agreed, so after some more back-and-forth with Japan on the phone late at night, Mark scheduled April 14th, 1992, to meet Ajinomoto at their headquarters and April 15th to meet with Kyowa Hakko at theirs. Both were in the business section of Tokyo.

The morning of April 12th, Terry and Mark were settling into soft leather seats in the inviting cabin of a lavish *Falcon 50*, one of ADM's many well-appointed private jets. With its triple jet-engine layout and high cruising speeds, the Falcon would have them at LAX Los Angeles in less than two hours. From there, they would fly first-class commercial to Tokyo. The trans-pacific Gulfstreams IV and V did not exist in 1992. If they had, Archer Daniels would have owned several.

Shortly after the Falcon took off for Los Angeles, Terry gave Mark his first mini-lesson on how to enforce volume-allocation agreements among competitors. You get the other four competitors together and show how much more money there is to make if there is a cartel than if there is no cartel. "We're gonna cut this market up like a good-tasting pie," Terry said. He was still completely clueless as to what lysine was, how it was produced, or what it was used for. It didn't matter to him. He was the Fixer. All he wanted or needed to know was who, where, and how much. This Japan trip would be Terry's show, his opening salvo in what would become dozens of meetings about lysine price-fixing. As far as Terry was concerned, Mark was just along to make the introductions.

During the long trans-Pacific flight on JAL, Mark saw first-hand why Terry had not wanted to make the trip. Wilson had emphysema and could not deal well with the recirculated air in the plane cabin. In fact, his breathing and overall health was so bad on that trip that Mark was worried Terry would arrive in Tokyo too sick to function. It didn't help that Terry drank one glass of scotch after another the whole flight.

Mark told himself that it was only because Terry was in poor health and The Chairman in his seventies that he put up with this old-school way of doing business. Mark adopted the mantra of, "think long-term," rationalizing that both of those business anachronisms will be gone from the ADM scene in a few years. After that it won't be hard to change the corporate culture at Archer Daniels to a more ethical one and stress legal competition on merits, not on fixes.

JAL's first-class service was superb, right up there with Singapore Airlines. But Terry was his usual rude self to the flight attendants. Mark had anticipated that Terry's drinking and gruff manner would be a problem, but he didn't think it would start this soon. What happened on the airplane would be a harbinger of things to come in Japan.

ADM's Japanese competitors were suspicious and wary of this meeting, but they had no real alternative. They had seen the price of lysine fall from $1.50 per pound to $0.60 per pound in just the few months since ADM had entered the market. They knew there was a problem, and they knew something had to be done about it. They did not know, however, that ADM had raw-material costs of low-to-none, and they refused to believe that Archer Daniels had capacity as great as Mark said.

Terry's brashness and provincial views worked against him. Mark had been to Japan many times before, both for ADM since joining the firm and for his predecessor employer, Evonik. Terry had scoffed when Mark said you must always bring gifts when traveling to Japan. He had scoffed when Mark said you must bow this deep or this much deeper, depending on the seniority of the manager you were greeting. And he had scoffed when Mark tried to explain that businessmen ceremoniously exchange business cards in a certain, precise way. Terry could have cared less, but Mark saved the day because, as usual, he brought lots of Mont Blanc ink pens with the logo "ADM BioProducts Division" on them. He brought ADM silk ties. He even packed some ADM golf putters. The Japanese love golf. Mark wanted to make sure these guys stared down at an ADM logo every single putt. Mark also brought large coffee-table books about the State of Illinois. Since the Japanese reciprocated with their own gifts, imagine if Terry and Mark had shown up empty-handed.

Terry didn't realize the importance of these gifts and acts of ceremonial etiquette until he saw the faces on the Japanese businessmen at the first meeting at Ajinomoto on the fourteenth. ADM's foreign hosts lit up like Christmas trees as Mark passed out the gifts. Terry later told Mark he almost puked watching those guys genuflect like puppets on a string and smile their phony smiles. "It made me sick to see those boys grovel like that over trinkets, but you did make your point."

Much to Terry's chagrin, that first day's meeting in Tokyo turned out to be nothing more than an ice-breaker. With urgency in his voice, he had told Ajinomoto he wanted to form a lysine producers' secret association immediately. He echoed that urgency the next day at the Kyowa Hakko meeting. But an impatient Terry Wilson was finding out just how cautiously and slowly the Japanese move on certain delicate business matters.

On their last day in Japan, when he least expected it, Terry got his Big Moment. It happened in the middle of a round of golf. If you're a scratch or one-handicap golfer, you have a skill that your average inscrutable Japanese businessman does not. That generated respect. Seeing how in awe they were of his game, Terry loosened them up with suggestive remarks like, "the winner of this hole gets more volumes." He managed to get the promise of a future meeting out of executives from both companies.

Mark and Terry left Japan the next day. Terry thought the trip was an abysmal failure, because a promise to get back to "Dr. Mark" concerning a meeting sometime, somewhere, felt too vague to him. But Mark explained the trip was in fact a huge success. The Japanese seldom promise anything, particularly after just one meeting. Whether it was his golf skills or the declining price of lysine that got their attention, they understood Terry's remark about sharing—not hiding—information on lysine. Accordingly, Mark soon got commitments from all the lysine players worldwide to meet in eight weeks in Mexico City.

Back in Moweaqua, Mark's long absences were not going down well with his family. Over the past two years, he had been away on business more than fifty percent of the time. Ginger had to work hard at explaining Mark's long absences to their children. Much of Alex's childhood was passing by without him, yet the family could not know at the time how much worse it was going to get.

Ginger's growing intuition about certain senior managers led her to tell Mark bluntly one evening after the children had gone to bed that, sooner or later, Mick would cross some lines and do things Mark would never dream of doing. Her insight into human nature would later help tip the scale in favor of Mark's cooperating with the FBI and against his staying loyal to Mick while he knowingly violated the law.

Long before the FBI ever showed up and got to Mark, Terry was agitating him for yet another price-fixing meeting. After dozens of calls, Mark got everyone to agree on Paris, France, as the next location. The date would be sometime in October of 1992. Like all prior "trade association" meetings, this one was also being held offshore. ADM's foreign competitors, well aware of how strong the anti-trust laws were in the United States, were terrified of having any meetings on U.S. soil.

Whenever in Paris, Mark always stayed at the Ritz on the Place Vendôme, one of Europe's finest hotels. Terry stayed there for the October trip as well, but it could have been a Red Roof Inn for all he cared. What Terry cared about was making the competitors his friends. Their Japanese counterparts stayed at the more modest Pullman Windsor, since the yen was weak against the French franc in late 1992 and the Euro had not yet come into existence. The "trade association" meetings took place at the Windsor, which pleased Terry because it was a low-profile hotel off the beaten path and perfectly acceptable in terms of facilities and conference-room logistics.

This time all the lysine players from around the world were there. Ajinomoto had three representatives, including Mr. Mimoto. Kyowa Hakko had two. Eurolysine sent a delegation, and the two Korean competitors sent delegates. This would be the last important price-fixing meeting before Mark started working undercover for the FBI.

From Terry's point of view, the Paris meeting accomplished two important objectives: one, all lysine producers agreed on market-share for every location around the world; and two, they all agreed to meet once a quarter to maintain the cartel and make any necessary adjustments.

In the beginning, neither Shepard nor Paisley nor Mark imagined, in their wildest dreams that Mark would have to wear a wire for almost three years. Yet, to allege price fixing is one thing; to prove it in a court of law, quite another. The FBI grossly underestimated how difficult it would be to obtain irrefutably incriminating evidence against ADM. It is impossible to imagine that Mark would have agreed to wear a wire if he had known going in that it would have to be for years.

Once Mark did sign on as a cooperating witness, his FBI handlers quickly discovered they had stumbled onto a super-mole. As Mark succinctly put it years later on a radio talk show on National Public Radio, "my government needed me, so I got intense." He was excellent at compartmentalizing, keeping the business of business separate from the business of snitching. And, psychologically, he was rhinoceros-skin tough.

Or so he thought.

By the end of month one, he stopped taping. Serious inner conflict seeped into his consciousness. He had lied to his FBI handlers, who were still knee-deep in a useless investigation of his phony sabotage story.

The sabotage story didn't check out, so his handlers poly-ed Mark (gave him a polygraph test). He blew the polygraph ink off the charts! Only in the face of this evidence did Mark finally admit to his handlers that he made up the sabotage story to buy time to get the lysine plant up and running.

Mark also failed a second polygraph test after the FBI took the unusual step of polygraphing him again when he tried to convince his handlers that the company was no longer engaged in price fixing because he wanted out of being an undercover informant. Again, he blew ink off the charts. Considering that lying to the FBI is a crime and Mark did it twice, it is safe to say that they stood by him through thick and thin. They could have instead prosecuted him for lying twice to the Federal Bureau of Investigation. Mark had started thinking twice about what The Chairman could do to him, and his FBI handlers understood how this created fear and confusion in their mole.

So for one month, he was adroit at leading two lives. In hindsight, he may have done so for no other reason than that he didn't want his own embezzlement to get exposed. Whatever his reasons, it is undeniable that he was able to insulate his executive self from his mole self: by day, playing the hard-charging, up-and-coming divisional president; by night, playing the stealth operator, meeting FBI handlers at all hours in out-of-the-way motels on the outskirts of Decatur.

Mark was leading a life of profound duplicity. The fact that he stayed undercover for so long was entirely his own decision. Whether he did so from purity of motive is not entirely clear, but the fact remains that he received no training in how to do so and stay sane. His composure would sometimes just crumble, and his handlers would write it off as fatigue—"get some sleep Mark"—when in fact the crumbling was screaming proof of severe inner conflict.

Perhaps there should have been a better system of checks and balances as part of Bureau policy. The FBI has vast resources, including psychiatrists trained to identify and help combat the common tendency among informants to demonstrate short-term symptoms of bipolar disorder (manic-depression) and acute situational stress disorder. Bipolarity's classic symptoms are grandiose thoughts, lying, and erosion of judgment, especially in financial matters. Mark exhibited all of these negative qualities simultaneously within months of going undercover.

For what then seemed like valid reasons, namely to save the case, the field agents in Illinois did the opposite. Logically, they realized that Mark could not attend sessions with a local psychologist or psychiatrist. Decatur is a company town. Had Mark spilled his guts about being an informant to any shrink within a hundred miles of Decatur, word would have gotten back to the company in a matter of hours. Given that "leaky" aspect of Decatur, the government probably should have, in hindsight, flown in the specially-trained mental-health professionals from the FBI

Academy's Behavioral Sciences Unit at Quantico to Springfield and let them work with Mark. But it did not happen that way and as a result Mark lost his mental balance so that by his third year undercover, Mark was completely out of control.

———————

There is substantial empirical data to support the conclusion that one year is about the maximum that an undercover witness can function. Keeping a mole undercover for longer than that has, according to numerous case studies, almost always led to erratic behavior, in particular to a mole's "flipping," that is, crossing over to the other side and becoming, in effect, a double agent, where he is now working against the original mission.

Mark led two lives for almost *three* years. By mid-1993, he was mentally adrift and profoundly conflicted. He lived in constant fear of being discovered by The Chairman or Mick as a hard-wired whistleblower. Mark's biggest emotional conflict related to The Chairman. On one level, he lived in sheer terror that The Chairman would find out. He was a ferocious competitor and used hardball tactics when things didn't go his way. In business matters, The Chairman took no prisoners.

On another, more personal level, Mark was like a surrogate son to The Chairman. He and Mark had had many father-son type conversations, both before and after Mark began wearing the wire. Mark despised any thought of collusion with competitors in restraint of free trade. Yet Mark still felt tremendous loyalty toward The Chairman. *The Chairman trusted him, and he was betraying that trust.* That betrayal was eating Mark alive, day by day and hour by hour.

While wearing the wire, Mark was facing another huge problem that should have been clarified before he ever agreed to work with the FBI: that he had no financial safety net whatsoever were he to be found out and summarily dismissed.

———————

Mark was the centerpiece of the biggest international cartel bust in the history of American business, but he was getting nothing in return. When it hit him that his career could be ruined if it came to light that he was the whistleblower, he did what anyone else in his position would have done. He asked the feds for compensation in return for risking his life and career for them. By his conservative calculation, what he was doing was worth at least ten years' salary, bonus, and stock options. His aggregate annual compensation package, after he became an officer of the corporation, was worth at least a million dollars per year, higher if the stock continued to perform well. That made the stock options worth more than Mark's base salary of $350,000 per year (worth $490,000 in 2009 dollars). He asked the FBI for 10 years of salary (or $10 million) minimum.

This was not an unreasonable request. He was the highest-level executive ever to turn whistleblower in U.S. history. He was a human evidence-gathering machine, a "vessel" for the government to gather immense quantities of information so they could indict one of the largest corporations in the world for bilking unsuspecting consumers out of many hundreds of millions of dollars. Why should he get nothing from his government as an offset? Mark's FBI handlers agreed, at least in principle, to look into some way to compensate him for the career-risk he was taking. However, the handlers had to get authority from "higher-ups." The higher-ups procrastinated for months, never committing to an explicit agreement on compensation, yet continued to use him as an intelligent robot to record meetings and gather evidence.

During this time, his handlers were making trips to Washington, D.C. in an effort to obtain for him some sort of monthly stipend, specifically the payment of $17,500 per month, should Archer Daniels fire him, until he found a new job. One of his handlers, FBI Agent Robert Herndon, even carried with him at all times a Christmas photograph of Mark and his family to remind himself and others that Mark was a human being with needs. Agents Shepard and Herndon never abandoned Mark, even though by all rights they could have done so at many intervals during the investigation.

But Mark did not know what his handlers were doing behind the scenes, so he knew nothing of their efforts to obtain the $17,500 safety net. In his mind, he had received nothing but hollow reassurances. Thus, from that moment, Mark knew he would have to take things into his own hands. And he did just that.

PART TWO—THE ADM YEARS

CHAPTER SEVEN

WHISTLEBLOWER EXPOSED

"A man cannot be too careful in the choice of his enemies."

OSCAR WILDE

A whistleblower's greatest fear is getting caught and punished. They crack or slip up because of the inner conflict created by snitching out those who trusted them, because of the fear of getting caught, and because of the fear of retaliation if they do get caught. In Mark Whitacre's case, the fear was justified. From the moment he was given up by his attorney as the mole, until now, some fifteen years later, Mark's life and the lives of his wife and three children have gone from the normal to the tragic to the totally catastrophic—and, now, back again to something approaching normal. In between, however, life for the Whitacres went completely and totally haywire.

The biggest question on most people's minds is how the whistleblower ended up getting a sentence many times longer than the sentences meted out on the people he exposed.

Due to the bizarre twists and turns of this massive, complex, multi-year antitrust case—a case that he alone brought to light—his immunity agreement with the federal government got revoked. He had embezzled $9.5 million to protect his family in the event of discovery. However, he avoided telling his FBI handlers, since they would have repatriated the funds back to ADM when the case went overt.

Once he lost that protection, the company's public-relations machinery adroitly managed to paint Mark as a thief and mentally unstable, both of which were arguably true at the time.

Without that immunity agreement, Mark was fresh meat for the powerful Fortune 100 Company he had snitched out. It was only a matter of time before attorneys for the company maneuvered the government into gang-tackling him on the fraud charges. A few more stumbles after that, stumbles of his own making, and Mark had managed to go from heroic whistleblower to disgraced convicted felon. When the dust finally settled, he received a 108-month (9-year) sentence for the embezzlement and a 30-month sentence for the very price-fixing case he exposed. Ten of the thirty were to be served concurrently, the remaining twenty consecutively, so the whistleblower received a 128-month sentence, or 10+ years before any good-conduct credit.

By the spring of 1995, after nearly three years of undercover work for the FBI, Mark had accumulated so much damaging evidence against ADM and several of its top executives that the Justice Department was ready to convene a secret grand jury in Chicago and lay out their charges.

Mark was the government's main—make that *only*—witness. He was summoned to Chicago, where he would be asked under oath to deliver the *coup de grâce* against the very company of which he was not merely a division head, but also a corporate officer and heir apparent. This would expose the largest price-fixing scheme in modern business history.

To avoid detection within the company and remain beyond suspicion, Mark had to concoct a plausible business cover as to why he would be in Chicago for two days in late May. Such duplicity was no longer difficult for Mark. The FBI had turned him into a master dissembler, an expert at the art of subterfuge. As far as his wife Ginger was concerned, they had also turned him into a basket case. She saw first-hand how the psychological pressure of leading two lives was making him increasingly emotionally fragile when he was out blowing leaves off the driveway at 2 AM in a thunder and rainstorm. The FBI had simply pushed Mark too far. He had reached the point of such inner conflict that he no longer knew whose side he was on.

What Ginger could not have possibly known, however, was that the situation was actually much more acute for Mark. The stress of being an informant was overlaid on top of the stress of running a major division of a major public company, which itself was overlaid on top of the tremendous guilt Mark felt at betraying those who trusted him. He was in an impossible situation.

From a strictly business point of view, Mark was a young man with a big responsibility, that of running a company-within-a-company, one that itself was larger than many stand-alone companies trading on the New York Stock Exchange. He had to keep the business wheels rolling, undercover agent or not, which meant coping with all the problems indigenous to any fast-growing business. This meant fielding long calls from Asia and Europe at all hours in connection with joint ventures in progress, and heavy travel, both foreign and domestic.

His primary FBI handlers, Agents Brian Shepard and Robert Herndon, showed great concern, but Mark was an exceedingly difficult Cooperating Witness. As such, both Shepard and Herndon focused more on the goal and less on the vehicle that was helping them reach that goal. That vehicle, Mark Whitacre, was difficult and unpredictable.

Shepard called Mark as soon as he got word from the Chicago U. S. Attorney's Office, the entity that would bring criminal charges against ADM and its executives, that they were ready to convene a grand jury.

"Mark, we now need you to formally affirm under oath before a grand jury that you made these hundreds of hours of surveillance tapes and that they are true and accurate. Do you understand the significance of this, Mark?"

"Tell me," he replied listlessly.

"It means we are taking *Operation Harvest King* from covert to overt status.

"That's what you call this beast that I've unleashed? *Operation Harvest King?*"

It was the first time he'd ever heard the label the FBI put on Mark's sting operation.

"Yep," Shepard replied.

Mark was bemused by the cloak-and-dagger, spy-novel sting operation nomenclature, and knew that the case he had so diligently built for the

FBI over the past three years put any James Bond movie or John Grisham thriller to shame.

The massive antitrust case brought against the Archer Daniels Midland Company began with a grand jury indictment in Chicago. Some legal scholars have come to question the use of grand juries in the way they are used today. Many countries have outlawed grand juries. In fact, grand juries are today virtually never used outside the United States.

In practice, grand juries rarely act contrary to the wishes of prosecutors. Too often they acquiesce to a prosecutor's desires with little or no careful consideration of all the evidence. That is what led Chief Judge of New York State Sol Wachtler to observe that a prosecutor could persuade a grand jury to "indict a ham sandwich."

Given that Mark was the prosecution's sole source of evidence in the grand jury indictment against the company, and given the secret nature of the indictment, when Mark's FBI handlers met him in Chicago in late May of 1995, they had to slip him surreptitiously into the DOJ building, whose main entrance is on LaSalle Street. On the way up in the elevator, Mark noticed how much space was devoted to the DOJ's antitrust division. *Must be a growing business,* he thought to himself.

Once inside and on the proper floor and in the proper conference room, Mark met for the first time the three lead government prosecutors on the case. They were there to prep Mark for his testimony. The most experienced in antitrust cases was a sharp woman named Robin Mann (who, sadly, died in 2007). She walked Mark through exhibits that the government was going to present to the grand jury. She was well-prepared with a compelling Power Point presentation that provided a logical build-up to the obvious charges of price-fixing.

During the proceedings, Ms. Mann would turn to the grand jury and say, "what you will now hear, ladies and gentlemen, is a voice recording of Mr. Michael Andreas, Vice Chairman of the Archer Daniels Midland Company, at a secret meeting with world lysine producers, telling other members what their volume allocations would be in lysine for the coming year."

Then everyone would listen to a tape of Mick's voice that Mark had gathered with the recording device that was taped to his body during a meeting in Irvine, California. After the tape played, she prompted Mark, making sure to call him "Doctor" in the belief that his status as doctor would give him greater authority in the eyes of the grand jury.

"Can you confirm, Dr. Whitacre, that the voice which the grand jury just heard is that of your boss, Mr. Mick Andreas?"

"Yes ma'am."

"And can you further confirm that he was in collusion with those present at that meeting to fix quantities and prices in lysine?"

"Yes ma'am, that is correct."

The doctor tactic worked, as did the prosecution's emphasis that Mark was a very senior manager, a corporate officer, and president of an entire division. Mann noted for the grand jury that Mark's name, salary, and stockholdings had to be disclosed in the company's proxy material. The combination gave Mark high credibility with the jurors.

By the standards of credibility of most Cooperating Witnesses brought forward at a grand jury, on a scale of one to ten, with ten being the highest, Mark was somewhere around fifteen. The Feds' usual CWs were small-time drug dealers trying to get their sentences reduced by implicating others or low-level disgruntled former employees out to get back at the company that fired them. Mark was neither low-level nor former, as he still worked at ADM as of May 1995. And disgruntled? Not really. Mark derived great satisfaction from his work as head of BioProducts.

Mark managed during the review session to keep Jim Randall, president of ADM and the man just below The Chairman in rank, from being included in the indictment. Mark told the prosecutors that Randall was not the man calling the shots. Mick and Terry Wilson were the ones calling the shots. Randall was an engineer, mainly in charge of overseeing ADM's massive construction projects. Mark found Randall to be a fundamentally decent and honest man, someone Mark could work with once the other two had been swept from the stage.

Much later, legal observers would remark at how rare it was to have so many indictments come down on so many senior executives at a company, yet leave the named president of the company, James Randall in this case, unindicted.

What was clear from Mark's thought process was that he was in denial about what would happen once the indictment came in on ADM. Mark still thought that he would be put in charge of a new, more ethical ADM in a year or two. Only much later would Mark realize how delusional he was.

As a result of Mark's expert testimony and a well-organized presentation by the government, the grand jury had no problem indicting the company and its executives. Presenting the evidence to the grand jury for the first time laid the necessary groundwork for the FBI to raid simultaneously all ADM's offices, managers' homes, and related sites so that crucial evidence would not be destroyed. Once everything was coordinated at the Bureau, Shepard and Herndon informed Mark that the raid had to be planned for June 27, 1995, about one month after the grand jury convened.

Mark then had to make sure that all the ADMers who were going to get served would be in Decatur when the FBI came swooping down. This took Mark weeks of planning. ADM was a busy, multi-national corporation with a fleet of private jets, and it was difficult to get all of the senior management team in Decatur at the same time. Mark anchored the key players to headquarters by inviting the head of ADM Asia to come to Decatur on the 27th of June, along with top executives from Asia's version of ADM, known as CP (Charoen Pokphand) to discuss joint venture opportunities in Southeast Asia.

The date of the raid was not cast in stone, however. The plan was to confront Mick Andreas first with a surprise visit. The FBI wanted to see if he would cooperate or lie, but most importantly they did not want him to have a heads up that they were going to visit him unannounced and ask him point-blank about the price-fixing. After the Mick interview, during which he tried to cover up the price fixing, Herndon called all units standing by and told them to execute the search warrants.

It was a multi-city hit. They hit simultaneously ADM's Decatur headquarters, the Chicago headquarters of Heartland Lysine, the New Jersey office of Sewon (a Korean competitor), and the St. Louis subsidiary of Kyowa Hakko (the smaller Japanese competitor). In addition, they would at exactly the same time appear at the doors of the homes of The Chairman, Mick, Randall, and others. In all, the FBI hit over a dozen places at once on June 27th.

At six pm on the day of the raid, Mark was sitting down to dinner with Terry and ADM's president of ADM Asia, Stephen Yu, in the main dining room at the Country Club of Decatur. The dining room was empty, and they were at a distant table for additional privacy.

Two strange, out-of-place looking men strode purposefully across the dining room. They were headed directly toward them. Mark tried to act as nonchalant as possible and pretended to barely notice the strangers heading their way.

The men pulled up abruptly in front of Mark's table. One of them asked sternly, "which one of you is Terry Wilson?" Terry gave a nod, not sure what was going on. Then the stranger asked "which one of you is Mark Whitacre?" to which Mark raised a bewildered hand.

"We are federal agents of the FBI," they said as they pulled out and flashed their badges. "We are here to discuss very serious matters of a criminal nature with you both."

Terry nearly had a heart attack on the spot. Mark play-acted to appear equally mortified. The agents immediately separated Terry from Mark. One agent took Terry over to a private corner of the club, while the other marched Mark out of the club and into a government vehicle. They pretended to interrogate him just as they were interrogating Terry. Sitting in that car, Mark gave the appearance of being quizzed intensely. In reality, he and the agent talked a little baseball and a little weather until a decent interval had elapsed.

After half an hour, the agents released both Terry and Mark. They resumed dinner, which for Terry would be Dewar's only for the rest of the night. Stephen Yu was dumbfounded and speechless. Terry was shaken almost beyond recognition. Mark gave an Oscar performance of anger and incredulity, sputtering that someone had set them up.

Terry put calls immediately into The Chairman, Mick, and Jim Randall. Mick and The Chairman confirmed that they, too, had been visited by the FBI. They also told Terry that they had been given the opportunity on the spot to turn government witnesses, but had declined as defiantly as Terry had. Mark said the same thing, only he was lying through his teeth.

Following the raid, Mark assessed that no one at the company suspected that he was the mole. Within hours of the raid, The Chairman had mobilized a SWAT-team of defense lawyers to fly in to Decatur as soon as possible. Most of the legal team came from Washington DC, The Chairman's power center and hub of influence. A Williams & Connelly, DC, lawyer was lead corporate counsel. He was the *de facto* field general. His firm had represented President Bill Clinton in the Monica Lewinsky case.

One of King & Spaulding's top criminal defense lawyers would represent Mick. Steptoe & Johnson's best would represent Terry. And

Akin Gump's finest would represent Mark. These were all high-powered, expensive lawyers, paid for by the company.

The day after the raid, lead corporate counsel for Archer Daniels, a high-powered senior partner from Williams & Connelly, separately debriefed each company executive who had been subpoenaed. Mark's corporate-assigned attorney would be one of the best criminal defense lawyers from the renowned firm of Akin Gump. Mark was told to meet him the next day in downtown Decatur at the Decatur lawyer's office in the Citizen's Bank building.

What happened next was one of those seminal events that alter the course of one human being's life forever. Or in this case three, four, or many more human beings' lives—forever.

Mark first met his new company-appointed, company-paid lawyer in a private office where the two could pow-wow alone and plot strategy going forward. Understandably his new counselor wanted to know as much as Mark could recall about what he said to the Bureau agent the night before when the agent pulled Mark outside into a government car and asked questions while another agent had debriefed Terry separately. Mark made up a story for "his" lawyer that meshed well with Mick's and Terry's and led the attorney to believe that Mark had stone-walled the FBI agent in the car the night before.

The attorney was pleased to hear that Mark had stonewalled the feds and told Mark not to talk to the government again under any circumstances. Because Mark now had company-paid legal representation, the FBI had to run everything through counsel. He warned Mark that they would try not to, and that they would threaten him with fines and penalties if he didn't talk, but not to worry, the lawyers would make sure that the company indemnified all executives against monetary penalties. In other words, public shareholders were going to get stuck with paying the hefty fees due to the malfeasance of certain executives that should have come out of those executives' own pockets. While it may have been reassuring on one level that no individual would have to pay personally any fines, penalties, or legal fees, it smelled too much like the company wasn't being run for the ultimate owners, the shareholders, but rather for a few managers who may have committed crimes detrimental to the creation of long term shareholder value. There are no shortcuts in business, just as there are none in life.

At that meeting, the attorney emphasized, upon repeated questioning by Mark, that he was Mark's personal attorney. The lawyer had close ties to a company board member, but that was a connection Mark did not make at the time. If he had, the attorney's conflict of interest would have been clear. The two men spent several hours getting what Mark thought were the ground rules straight. Mark asked for and received repeated assurances that everything said between them was attorney-client privileged. Mark recalls that the company-hired attorney specifically told Mark he represented him and not the company. This gave Mark comfort that, if he revealed that his position was truly adverse to the company's, if there had to be a "bifurcation," the lawyer would bifurcate in Mark's direction, not the company's. Mark says he even made the lawyer repeat that principle under various scenarios, such as "even if I get sued by the Chairman, you represent me and not ADM?"

Agents Shepard and Herndon spent hour after hour explaining to Mark the very real likelihood that his company hired attorney would attempt to elicit a confession from him. They repeatedly told him that the lawyer would represent the company and not Mark, no matter what the guy told Mark. Even the prosecutors told Mark this. They had drilled into him the importance of rejecting company appointed counsel by just saying, "no thank you, I already have an attorney in this matter and he will represent me."

Yet Mark blew that part as well. After long thought and several more pullbacks from the edge of trust, Mark took the plunge and foolishly confided in the company hired attorney, saying, "OK, here's the deal . . . . I'm the whistleblower. I'll tell you flat out, I'm the mole. I'm the informant. I was a Cooperating Witness for the FBI and wore a wire for almost three years. It was me who taped all the meetings. Any evidence the government has about illegal price-fixing, they got from me. Nobody else inside the company was involved. Just me. I'm the beginning and the end of why the FBI conducted those raids yesterday."

Mark went on, "I knew the raid was coming. Plus, I was the sole witness at a secret grand jury session last month in Chicago that was the impetus to give the FBI raid the go-ahead."

The attorney grew completely silent, then turned and stared out the window for what seemed an eternity. Mark knew at once that he had grossly miscalculated where this man's loyalties stood. Finally, after turning back from the window, the lawyer shook his head back and forth slowly and gravely and told Mark that he had just taken down the last of the great cowboys of the Wild West and that there would never be another risk-taking visionary like The Chairman, a man who built the company into what it had become. It had, after all, generated an average annual return to shareholders of twenty-one percent per annum for the prior decade from 1985 to 1995.

The cat was now out of the bag, and a young, confused, ambitious executive had just put his trust in the wrong man. Mark knew this lawyer would take Mark's revelation straight to the top. *I'm a dead man,* he thought. The meeting wrapped up quickly.

It's as if Mark had looked at a cactus, saw its sharp thorns, but sat on it anyway. Mark would be screaming ouch from those thorns for a long time to come. His problems weren't ending. They were just beginning.

At home later that night, Mark's OPX line rang. He looked at the clock. It was midnight. He picked up the phone to hear the voice of lead counsel for Archer Daniels tell him that it would not be in either his or the firm's best interest for Mark to show up at work the next day.

Disturbed by what he clearly considered a threatening phone call, Mark woke Ginger. They needed to talk, so they did long into the night. At this point, Ginger had the more level head of the two, but even under the best of circumstances Mark's behavior had become unpredictable. He proved how clouded his judgment had become by foolishly ignoring the entreaties of his Bureau handlers and blowing his cover to a company-paid lawyer. With Ginger helping him sort things out in his mind, and not knowing what to do after such a telephone call, they finally agreed that Mark should first consult his FBI handler, Shepard, before buckling to the demand that he not show his face at company headquarters.

At 7 AM sharp, after just three hours of sleep, Mark placed an anxious call to the FBI's Regional Springfield Office. He left a message to please call him back as soon as possible. It was urgent.

Five minutes later, the home phone rang. It was Shepard.

Mark told Shepard the whole story about confessing to the attorney that he had been the informant, and Shepard almost dropped the phone out of his hand. He could not believe Mark had been so dumb.

He told Mark to report for work anyhow, as if nothing had happened.

"They can't do this to you," he said. "You could 'own' that company based on what you know and all the evidence you've collected over these years. They know that. They're bluffing."

That was good enough for Mark, so he drove to work like it was any other day, except that he had a sense of dread and foreboding unlike anything he had ever experienced, the day before being the only exception.

He quickly realized this was not going to be just another wonderful day at work. As he tried pulling into his usual reserved parking space, an ADM security guard was standing there. The guard immediately got on his walkie-talkie.

Despite his extreme paranoia—and outright fear of being shot point blank through his windshield—Mark calmly backed up his company car and parked somewhere else. The security guard was nowhere to be found, so he tried to stay calm as he ascended the back stairwell to his office on the second floor. He made it to his office, put down his briefcase, and took off his jacket. He paused for one brief moment to enjoy the sad irony that this was the first time in nearly three years that he was not wearing a recording device and could thus take off his jacket.

Mark had begun returning his backlog of phone calls when a house lawyer, whose usual habitat was the sixth floor, abruptly appeared in his office, closing the door behind him. At first, Mark wondered if the man was lost. Then he realized that the lawyer had been sent down from six to advise him to vacate the premises. He told Mark that he was outed. Based on the extreme gravity of the man's expression, Mark snapped out of the reverie that led him to believe that anything about this day was going to be normal. He took the man's advice and made a beeline for the back stairwell.

He was flat out terrified. *I'm only just beginning to learn what it means when you mess with The Chairman,* he thought as he hustled down the stairs and broke into a trot to get to his car. *I may not make it through the day alive.* While that thought was potentially over the top, Mark strongly felt that he needed protection from physical harm at this point. He needed to get his wits about him. There was only one safe place to go: Brian Shepard's office in the federal building in downtown Decatur.

Once Shepard and Herndon learned that Mark had voluntarily outed himself, they pushed aside their dismay and concluded that the first thing

Mark needed was a replacement lawyer. He needed someone immediately and someone who would be exclusively loyal to Mark, with absolutely no conflict of interest.

Uncertain as to how to proceed, the agents called the U.S. Attorneys in the Chicago antitrust section, the same ones who had convened the grand jury. As Mark sat in Shepard's office and listened to the back and forth, he realized the prosecutors were clearly more concerned that their informant's self-induced exposure could compromise the antitrust case than they were for Mark's safety. Mark felt the other way around. *Just keep me alive,* he thought.

Shepard asked the prosecutors to select a top-flight, criminal defense attorney from their large network of contacts in and around Chicago. The prosecutors said "no way." No way were they going to assist a witness by hiring his defense counsel for him. Shepard reminded them, however, that the entire case now hung in the balance, and if Mark did not get someone good, fast, everything could be ruined.

Mark was flapping in the breeze, and the U.S. Attorneys were unable to assist him. Mark thought *I helped them build their whole case; how can they even think of not helping me now?* Mark did not know at the time that there are specific DOJ rules based on legal practices that specifically prohibit DOJ personnel from recommending outside attorneys. After much pleading on Mark's behalf by Shepard and Herndon, the prosecutors agreed to fax over a list of leading, reputable criminal-defense attorneys.

DOJ stressed, however, that the final selection would have to be Mark's, with absolutely no coaching from the U.S. Attorney's Office. Mark believed that, in the event the government's interests somehow became adverse to his, he would need a tough lawyer in his corner, someone who would in no way be beholden to the Justice Department. From the list the prosecutors faxed over, Mark and Ginger did some checking around. They ended up choosing a highly regarded criminal-defense attorney named Jim Epstein, whose office was in Chicago.

James R. Epstein was a Chicago lawyer with the criminal trial firm of Epstein, Zaideman & Esrig when Mark and Ginger hired him in 1995. Prior to starting his own firm, he gained excellent experience as a trial lawyer and negotiator—while also doing something pro-social (helping indigents obtain competent legal advice)—as a Public Defender in Cook County. Today in 2009 he is a distinguished Cook County, Illinois judge. The Whitacres picked him from a short list of three lawyers.

Mark and Ginger called Epstein from Decatur and interviewed him by phone. Whatever he said reassured them. They quickly decided he was the right man for the job, and without hesitation the next morning—June 30, 1995—drove from Decatur to Chicago to meet Epstein in person.

During the three-hour drive, Ginger and Mark talked and worried—and worried and talked. Mark's future with the company had come to an abrupt and callous halt. Any illusions to the contrary—and Mark was full of illusions—had gone out the window with that ominous late-night call.

Ginger was fully grounded. She understood that the past is beyond even the power and mercy of God. She had to bring Mark into present reality, and Mark is not an easy man to jolt out of the script he plays in his head. Usually that script is reality-based and flexible. No longer. Mark needed to replace past error with new truth. The new truth was that they were flinging themselves into the blank future.

The gathering storm and the nearly three years of being undercover continued to take a heavy toll on Mark's mental condition. Ginger had one thing. She had prayer. As they were driving and talking, she was also praying that a merciful God would protect her husband and family from harm. *Dear God, in your perfect kingdom no sword is drawn but the sword of righteousness, no strength but the strength of love. Spread your mighty spirit that we may all, even Mark's enemies, be gathered under the banner of your Son Jesus Christ, who is the Prince of Peace. Amen.*

Word that Mark Whitacre was the mole traveled fast. Within forty-eight hours of telling "his" lawyer that he was the informant, Ginger started receiving threatening phone calls at the house, including an anonymous call from someone who said to "expect a bullet in your head, Whitacre." This greatly alarmed Ginger, and she made sure Mark saved that recording and gave it to FBI Decatur for follow-up. Such a recording would also confirm that Mark wasn't delusional about the force with which the company would strike back if left unchecked.

At the Chicago meeting with Epstein, Mark signed a retainer agreement and paid Epstein from his and Ginger's own funds. When it comes to lawyers, it's important to keep in mind the German proverb, "Whose bread I eat, his song I sing." That's the best way to ensure that your attorney works for you.

Once the check cleared, Epstein moved quickly: he placed a call to the company's lead attorney and told him point blank he could no more fire his client than he could fire The Chairman. He went on to say that the call did, however, succeed in creating a climate of intimidation for his client Mr. Whitacre. As such, he would never be able in good conscience to work at the company, so why don't the two of them, lawyer to lawyer, just work out the little matter of Mr. Whitacre's severance agreement and let bygones be bygones. For emphasis, Epstein added, "It will save you guys a lot of headaches."

The Williams & Connelly lawyer saw the wisdom of Epstein's suggestion. Over the next two to three days, they negotiated. After some back-and forth, Epstein faxed them his draft of a reasonable severance agreement that provided for $7.5 million in cash severance pay, immediate vesting of all stock options, transfer of the title of Mark's company car to Mark personally and several other smaller perquisites such as health insurance that Epstein shrewdly leveraged out of the company.

The company's lawyer agreed to those terms. In return for such a severance package, however, he wanted Whitacre to come in and tell them everything he had done while he was undercover for the FBI. Epstein insisted that both sides would have to wait for that to come out in the legal process that lawyers call discovery.

ADM's lawyers wanted the information before discovery. Obviously, their goal was to build an iron-clad defense before the case made it to the discovery phase. Epstein knew that any such preliminary disclosures by his client would tip the government's hand and jeopardize the entire price-fixing case.

The two sides *almost* came to terms on a severance deal. It was so close. However, one of Mark's accounting friends called him and said that the company was going after Whitacre for embezzlement. This occurred only after the company found out Mark was the mole? Why now? Why not earlier? The company lawyers leveraged this "new" revelation with Epstein to cause the severance deal to fall apart.

When those negotiations fell apart, so did one Mark Edward Whitacre. Upon learning that he would not get a pay package that would provide a financial safety net for his family, he went into the twilight zone. In his paranoid and manic condition, he wrongly saw the occurrence as proof that Epstein wanted to protect the government and its antitrust case more than he wanted to protect Mark. This was a variation on what he had just been through with the company-hired "personal" attorney who outed him, so for a second time Mark asked himself, *who does my lawyer really work for?*

Unable at this point to help himself, Mark made another serious mistake. Without telling Epstein, he placed his own call to the company's attorney—the Williams & Connelly honcho—in an attempt to obtain a severance package on his own. *Epstein isn't the one going down. I am. And I have to protect my family.* However, the call proved to be a foolish move because the Archer Daniels lawyer immediately called Epstein. Within minutes, Epstein was on the phone to Mark, furious. He said that if Mark ever tried to make an end-run around him like that again, Epstein would cut him off at the knees, quit on the spot, and sit back and watch him get eaten alive by The Chairman's lawyers.

Mark felt like a fool, but he was so strung-out, hung-out, and chewed-up from the remnants of the years of being undercover and from watching the sting operation unfold against one of America's most powerful companies that he had nothing but inner turmoil and outer numbness. Peace can only rule the day if reason rules the mind, and Mark's mind had lost all reason. He was frightened, as much for Ginger and the kids as for himself. *What if they try to kidnap my little boy? What if they drain the brake fluid out of Ginger's SUV?*

One week after Mark's exposure as the mole, he received a call from Howard Buffett, who said he had resigned his board seat and position as an officer of the company. He had severed all ties. Because Howard was the son of legendary investor Warren Buffett, the resignation triggered considerable national media attention. Howard volunteered that he had spoken on the record to a *Wall Street Journal* reporter whom Howie trusted. The reporter's name was Scott Kilman, and Kilman was thorough in his research and balanced in his reporting. Mark thought, *that's the same Scott Kilman who has been standing in front of our Moweaqua house for days trying to get an exclusive interview.* Howard said he thought it would be best if Mark talked to Kilman because the *Journal* was going to break the big ugly ADM story the next day anyhow. Mark might as well give the reporter his side.

Epstein, however, was adamant that neither Mark nor Ginger speak with the press about any matter, under any circumstances. In an attempt to follow—for a change—his lawyer's advice, Mark did everything he could to avoid the newshounds. It got comical: He hid out in the horse stables and peaked around corners of horse stalls to see if the coast might be clear.

Meanwhile, the family in the house kept the curtains closed day and night and became prisoners of the media. Epstein had himself been swamped with hundreds of media calls. Epstein maintained the discipline of "no comment" and repeatedly admonished his client to do the same. Absolutely no comment.

Alas, Mark Whitacre is Mark Whitacre. He was being constantly barraged, and he felt he was being railroaded. He had a strong personal need to tell his side of the story. He failed to understand that nothing gives one person so much an advantage over another as to remain cool and unruffled under such extreme circumstances. Based on Howard's recommendation that Kilman could be trusted, Mark invited the *Wall Street Journal* reporter in. Not just "in" to his house, but into his life and head. That was another huge mistake on Mark's part.

The *Journal* article ran on the front page on July 10, 1995. It was favorable to Mark but set off a chain reaction that was not. Well-researched and well-written, Kilman's article made it clear that the resourceful reporter had figured out a number of things about the case on his own. He had definitely done his homework. Unfortunately, the piece triggered a media battle between the embattled company and the informant, and the informant didn't stand a chance. He was David, without the slingshot, to their Goliath.

Mark once again did not listen to his lawyer. He was out of control and melting down fast. He had taken the battle to the streets. Whether that was the right thing to do against such a formidable opponent is clear today, in hindsight, but it was not so clear at the time. When you are in the middle of a battle for your life, when you are melting down but don't know you are melting down, when you believe in yourself, you take your enemy on. You take the battle to the streets.

If you make a decision to take your battle to the streets, you need allies. Mark had one—not one but two—very good allies: David and Carol Hoech (pronounced "Hague"). The Hoechs took it straight up and in your face right beside Mark. They fought shoulder-to-shoulder with him against a common enemy for at least four years.

———————

With or without allies, Mark Whitacre got bloodied. He had both the company and the government turning against him. The street fight got messy.

PART TWO—THE ADM YEARS
CHAPTER EIGHT

THE MELTDOWN

"When I make a mistake, it's a beaut."

FIORELLO LA GUARDIA
Mayor of New York City, 1934-1945

Mark Whitacre had now outed himself as the mole, gone repeatedly against the advice of both his FBI handlers as well as the lawyer hired to protect him, and spoken to the press. When combined with his inability to see that his embezzlement had damaged his credibility, taking the battle to the streets against an opponent with almost unlimited resources, Archer Daniels Midland, was a colossal mistake. Street brawls are never won by the weak and wounded. Even the strongest of private individuals is not strong when his opponent is the Archer Daniels Midland of 1995.

In other words, Mark didn't stand a chance. But he had not come to that realization. To himself, he was behaving logically. Ginger, the only one who had been along for the full ride with him, understood why he thought he was behaving logically. There was plausibility to every single issue he raised. However, there are times when logical behavior often comes dangerously close to toppling over into the absurd, and Mark's had toppled over into the absurd and then gone even further—into the zone of the delusional. But it made sense from his point of view. As

Benjamin Franklin said, "so convenient a thing it is to be a reasonable creature, since it enables one to find or make a reason for everything one has a mind to do."

Mark had a mind to fight back. When Mark believes he has been wronged, his reflexive response is to fight back. Isn't it also common among all of us? When we feel wronged, we want to fight back. Natural instinct. The problem here, however, was that he was fighting against friend and foe alike, and the foe was no mere mortal. Mark was either going against the advice of his lawyer, Epstein, or he was combating an enemy so powerful he couldn't possibly win. This enemy was among the most influential Fortune 100 companies in America and its law firm, one of the toughest in the land. Who in his right mind would get in a street brawl with such an opponent? And who in his right mind would then turn against his own legal counselor?

Mark Whitacre would. But he was a bird with a broken wing, maybe even two broken wings. Normally he stayed rational, optimistic, and confident, no matter how dire the situation. But this was no normal "dire situation." The length of his undercover work and the peculiar turns the case had taken—whether of his own making or not—led to hesitation, clouded judgment, and a fragile mental condition that, by Christmas of 1995, even Ginger was unable to set him straight. Mark grew more distracted by the day. Worse, by thinking that the FBI would soon come to his rescue, he was playing a fool's game.

By January of 1996, Mark seemed like a man riding a runaway horse that he could not bring under control. He exhibited an attitude of brash defiance toward Archer Daniels and its powerful attorneys. Worse, he ended up turning against his own criminal-defense attorney.

To most objective observers, two events in particular stand out as proof of the fragility of Mark's mental condition. One was lying to his wife, something he never did; specifically, he lied to her about being abducted. The second was Mark's firing of Attorney James Epstein after he had worked out a plea deal that could only be described as the "deal of the century." Without the behind-the-scenes fighting for Mark that Shepard and Herndon were doing, there would have been no "deal of the century" because many of the arguments proposed by Epstein either originated with his FBI handlers or reinforced Epstein's arguments.

While both occurrences were strange, the firing of Epstein was, without question, the biggest blunder of this saga and had the longest-lasting and most far-reaching negative effects on the Whitacre family. Looked at from a writer's perspective, both demonstrate conclusively that Mark needed immediate mental-health counseling, which should have been provided by the Federal Bureau of Investigation.

THE ABDUCTION STORY

Mark came running into the house one Sunday in March. His shirt was ripped half off and his face smeared with dirt; his glasses were bent. He told Ginger he had been abducted by two men who were hired by the company to scare him into shutting up. She had no reason to doubt him. A few days later Mark and Ginger were being interviewed together on live television on Decatur's local TV station, WAND-TV. Mark told the reporter about the abduction and went into great detail, saying he had been forced into a brown sedan in a parking lot by two thugs. He said the thugs threw him into the back of an unmarked car and drove around for half an hour with sawed-off door locks, telling him to keep his mouth shut or he would suffer severe consequences. Once they put the scare on Mark, they pushed him out of the car, and he rolled onto the street, later finding his way back home.

As the reporter pressed Mark for details, Ginger noticed that Mark stumbled. What did the men look like? Did he file a police report? Were there any witnesses? Was any of this caught on security cameras anywhere? She sensed doubt in the reporter's manner and, at first, was indignant that he might question the veracity of her husband's story. As the interviewer pressed on, however, Ginger realized that he was on to Mark long before she was. Mark was spinning a widening web of lies—on live television and to a local Decatur public that would never give him the benefit of the doubt.

Mark later confessed that the abduction story was a complete fabrication. He did indeed pay a Chicago thug to kidnap him. He gave the man five thousand dollars cash in an unmarked manila envelope and expected him to appear the next day as agreed. However, the man took the money and was a no-show. Therefore, Mark had ripped his own shirt, smudged dirt on himself, and bent his own glasses. He staged his whole disheveled appearance. Ginger hit the roof: Mark's lying to anyone at any level was unthinkable, but lying to *her*, his wife of almost twenty years at the time and closest confidant since the age of fourteen, was so far removed from the moral essence of the man she had known for more than twenty-five years that she was furious beyond words. And worse, that pathetic, unnecessary lie rolled off his tongue as effortlessly as the words "I love you Ginger" did. Once she realized that he had completely duped her, the last person on earth he should want to dupe about anything, she sat him down for a major talking to. Why, she asked, would you tell such a lie? But like all liars who are unmasked for their deception, Mark had no valid explanation.

Ginger went through a range of feelings. At first she saw the lie as an unforgivable violation of one of God's Ten Commandments, that of bearing false witness. Then she moderated her view and realized that Mark's fabricated story was in fact a desperate cry for help. Ultimately, she saw it is as irrefutable proof that her husband's mental state had become seriously compromised.

As it would turn out, however, the abduction fabrication was merely a prelude to Mark's more damaging act, firing Epstein, who had taken a sour lemon and made good lemonade out of it.

THE FIRING OF ATTORNEY JAMES EPSTEIN

Sound judgment and wise counsel are a lawyer's stock-in-trade. James Epstein had acquired a good deal of both over the years. The most difficult aspect for Mark to resolve in his own mind was how the government he had so faithfully served for nearly three years could ignore the whistleblower side of the equation and see only the fraud. The closer I looked at the fraud charges, the more I concluded that charging Mark alone with fraud was selective prosecution.

Certainly, the magnitude of Mark's contribution to the federal government as a whistleblower in the price-fixing case should have "mitigated away" some of the fraud charges. Both Lieber and Eichenwald in their books agree with me on this point. To anyone who looked beneath the surface of the fraud allegations, including Mark's FBI handlers, the emphasis on the fraud charges gave every appearance of being a tactic to divert attention away from the much larger price-fixing case.

The federal prosecutors in Chicago understood implicitly that the fraud case was minor in comparison to the antitrust case. When asked by the FBI to give Mark the names of lawyers to represent him, they did so assuming that FBI Springfield would be handling the case. They did not assume that a team out of Washington would be running both the fraud and the antitrust cases on the government's side. After all, this historic case had occurred at ADM, which comes under the jurisdiction of the Central District of Illinois Office of the FBI.

Mark—a man in desperate and immediate need of independent counsel after foolishly believing that his company-paid lawyer worked for him and not the company—thus received a gift from the Chicago U.S. attorney's office. When they gave Mark a list of names of potential attorneys to represent him, that list had, most likely, been carefully vetted.

The fraud case was miniscule compared to the price fixing case. The huge imbalance between the two could only be made clear if both were run out of Chicago and preferably in the order in which they occurred: price-fixing case goes first, fraud case second. Based on the information I have reviewed some fourteen years later, including recent pardon letters to the president, I would say Chicago's primary goal at the time was not to be altruistic to Mark, but to save the potential collapse of the price fixing case by making sure that Mark appeared at trial as witness for the prosecution, not as a price-fixing defendant alongside Mick and Terry.

But The Chairman had so much influence in Washington, D.C., that he was able to (1) move the fraud case there, (2) get Mark's immunity agreement revoked, and (3) cut off all communication between Mark and anyone inside the government who could help him, including his FBI handlers from *Operation Harvest King*.

That's power.

The Chicago prosecutors cautioned Epstein to be wary of the fraud prosecutors out of Washington, so Epstein arranged a meeting in Washington with the Deputy Assistant Attorney General of the Criminal Division. This effectively allowed Epstein to go over the heads of the Washington fraud division. To anyone who looked beneath the surface, the DC fraud division appeared to be nothing but a puppet of the powerful D.C. law firms hired by the company.

By going higher up the Justice Department food chain in Washington, Epstein was able to end-run the Washington fraud division and plead Mark's case directly to the Deputy Assistant Attorney General. Thus, he was able to interject into the fraud case the mitigating circumstance of Mark's extraordinary undercover work. At that meeting, Epstein gave a brilliant performance and negotiated the best possible plea deal anyone in Mark's situation could have hoped for, the "deal of the century."

Epstein did so through good instincts no doubt developed during his eight years as a Public Defender. Mark brought him a complicated and bizarre case, then behaved erratically the entire time he was Epstein's client. Yet Epstein turned many big mountains into manageable molehills. For one thing, when Mark first hired him, Epstein correctly anticipated the company's probable aggressive moves to discredit Mark once they fired him. Epstein got out in front of that by going public in advance with a statement that he expected the company to "invent some pretext to fire Mark." That is exactly what happened, and Epstein's anticipation and public pronouncement in advance that such a predictable and transparent tactic on the part of the company's lawyers would be coming soon helped blunt its potentially damaging effects.

For another, Epstein had negotiated a favorable severance package for Mark, but it was later revoked by Archer Daniel's attorneys once they were able to document Mark's embezzlement activity and use it as a pretext.

Not long after the Whitacres hired Epstein, someone on the other side persuaded the Justice Department to run the fraud investigation out of Washington, D.C. instead of Springfield. Their argument, tenuous at best, was that the FBI agents in Central Illinois had condoned Mark's phony invoice scheme and were dirty as a result. The FBI did *not* condone Mark's embezzlement and most certainly were not "dirty." Mark hid the embezzlement from them, yet another act of total stupidity on his part.

Notwithstanding how it was accomplished, getting the nexus of the government's fraud investigation against Mark shifted from Chicago to Washington was a major strategic victory against Mark. The Chairman had power and influence in Washington—not just with legislators, federal agencies, and paid lobbyists, but also with the Oval Office itself—versus virtually no influence over the Chicago U.S. Attorney's Office. Somehow, the various Justice Department attorneys working on Mark's embezzlement investigation got shuffled around, and soon the prosecution took its marching orders from DOJ Washington only, even though Mark's alleged transgressions occurred in Decatur. If it had been any other case but one involving ADM, the Justice Department's Chicago office would have in all likelihood retained jurisdiction.

Epstein understood what an advantage this was for the opponent, so he went on the offensive. Prior to his meeting in Washington with the Deputy Assistant Attorney General of the Criminal Division, he called the chief of the fraud section in Washington and invited her and her deputies to a meeting in Chicago. She came with enough other lawyers at her side to field a football team, while on the Whitacre side of the table it was just Epstein, his partner, and Mark.

Epstein had prepared Mark for this meeting. He made sure Mark unloaded the whole sordid tale with both barrels blasting and with as much solid proof as possible. At that meeting, Mark came totally clean on his own fraud scheme, providing detailed documentation as to how the phony invoices occurred, exactly how much money was transferred, to whom, when, and where. Then he specified a vast array of crimes that had nothing to do with him. He took no prisoners as he laid bare the full extent of his bosses' misconduct. With as much backup as possible, including taped conversations, he alleged (1) theft of other companies' proprietary technology; (2) bribing competitors' employees; (3) hiring prostitutes for managers at other companies in order to elicit information; (4) circumventing federal campaign finance rules; (5) using company aircraft for personal vacations; and (6) dumping lysine biomass into corn gluten feed.

Epstein's goal was to have Mark establish a pattern of such egregious wrongdoing by his supervisors that Justice would—based on *all* the evidence and not just the evidence against Mark—turn its focus away from Mark's transgressions and toward the multiple and much bigger crimes his bosses were committing.

Once Mark's enemies knew they had the focus limited to Mark's fraud, the company's public relations machinery pumped out press releases to the media portraying Mark as the sole ringleader in a bogus-invoicing scandal involving just him and those under his direction.

When the Justice Department failed to act on any of Mark's allegations and instead revoked his immunity agreement, the Whitacres knew their problems were going to get worse. Mark was David against Goliath, and Ginger's David had just lost his slingshot, the immunity agreement. This turn in events was huge and made Mark's prior manifestations of mental disturbance look tame in comparison with what followed. The speed and force with which the company was able to influence public sentiment drop-kicked Mark into a red zone of self-destruction. Even his deep faith in God seemed to be inadequate as a spiritual antidote to the onslaught that followed.

The big shift in the company's favor shook Ginger's faith as well. Especially since she had admonished Mark so many times to "just give the

Good Lord time" and "don't worry, honey. God knows what to do with this." By the winter of 1995, in the middle of their sea of fear and doubt, those words were sounding hollow, and their faith was being tested to the max. It was looking increasingly like vengeance was not the Lord's, but the exclusive domain of the company and their lawyers and publicists.

Mark was drowning under the pressure, and Ginger was barely treading water herself. Epstein was the only lifeboat in sight, and when he threw Mark a lifeline in the form of a favorable plea deal, Mark was too mentally disturbed to take it. The plea proffer that *almost* came about resulted from Epstein's moving and persuasive performance at a meeting he had in Washington with the Deputy Assistant Attorney General. He had gone over the heads of the DC fraud division in an attempt to show that the only reason Mark had perpetrated any crime of embezzlement or fraud was because he cracked under the pressure of having to be an informant for so long.

Epstein explained how FBI agents get trained in advance for the stresses of living a double life when they go undercover by an elite Behavioral Sciences Unit in Quantico that trains and debriefs professional agents put in such undercover situations. He went on to say how Mark received no such training. The FBI sucked him in, shaved and wired his chest, and told him to just go out there and capture it all on tape for the good of the country. It has been well-reported that even well-trained agents can run a high risk of cracking under the pressure, of flipping, and of losing their true sense of self if left undercover too long.

Epstein continued eloquently, "So I ask you, did Mark Whitacre dupe the US government, or did the government dupe him? Did it draw him in and then fail to safeguard him against the inevitable retaliation and meltdown? Who breached whose trust? You have ample proof that the government failed him. There's the length of time he was undercover—three times what FBI protocol says a professional agent should be hung out on undercover assignments. There's the Chinese wall that went up between him and his handlers after he was outed as the mole. There are the many indicators along the way that he was buckling under the stress that the FBI ignored."

"Yes, Mark committed a crime. He stole nine million dollars. That's indefensible. But the company he worked for stole at least one hundred times that from innocent consumers all over the world. And not only did Mark alert you to what was going on, he and he alone got you the hard evidence you needed to prove it. He broke new ground in your understanding of how price-fixing cartels work and has improved your ability to prosecute future violations of the antitrust statutes. He should be given a medal, not a prison sentence."

Epstein didn't stop there. He threw down the gauntlet.

"If I don't get a deal, we go to trial. And if we go to trial, I will lay out every single detail—the good, the bad, the ugly. And the media will report it all. And then the public will decide who duped whom. If you let my client take the fall, then somewhere inside some other big corporation that's doing bad things, some potential future whistleblower will stop and think twice because he or she saw what happened to Mark Whitacre once he got exposed as the mole. Instead all future whistleblowers will just shut up and refuse to step forward. Is that the message you really want to send?"

Epstein gave a brilliant performance. The DOJ listened and was moved. Given such an eloquent defense of Mark's behavior and the long-term consequences of an obvious failure to protect the whistleblower, Epstein got a deal. Or more precisely, he broke through the company stranglehold and got the Deputy Assistant AG to agree to at least think about a deal.

Epstein got the go-ahead to work up a draft of a deal whose terms would have Mark plead out to wire fraud. He would get three to five for that, but the prosecutors would not object to a downward departure by the judge to only six months, due to the mitigating circumstances of Mark's substantial assistance in the antitrust case and his mental condition. He would also have to pay $9.5 million (the amount he embezzled) in immediate restitution.

Unfortunately, as this negotiation was going on in the autumn of 1996, Mark was at his most psychologically confused. When Epstein brought the deal to him, he not only balked, he flew off the handle. He wasn't about to plead out to any jail time! End of debate. To him, it was inconceivable that, after all he had done for his government, he would have to serve *any* time, let alone anything close to that of his bosses, Mick and Terry. Mark simply could not comprehend how much trouble he was in. Ginger's perspective was clear: take the deal. Plead out and put the whole matter behind him, her, and their children—as quickly as possible. She and Mark strongly disagreed on whether or not to take the plea deal. In words that still haunt both of them to this day, she told him, "This will be our biggest mistake of the whole ordeal."

Epstein was vexed and exhausted by his client's total disconnect from reality. He had a deal that would have given Mark the least possible time. He tried to persuade Mark of the merits of the deal, of how the justice system works in situations like this, but the meeting ended with Mark saying only that he would consider it. Epstein got him the deal of the century, and all Mark could say was that he would consider it.

A few days later Mark fired Epstein. By fax.

He faxed Epstein a letter saying he could not accept the recommendation of signing a plea agreement and wanted to "go in a new direction." Mark was so delusional that he soon thereafter told his psychiatrist, Dr. Derek Miller, that he believed Epstein worked for the Russians.

Firing Epstein was the most disastrous decision in a daisy-chain of bad decisions that proved beyond a reasonable doubt that Mark was suffering from an acute mental breakdown. There is no stronger indication that his judgment was severely impaired than that decision to fire Epstein.

It was a watershed event that cost him and his family dearly.

The Epstein deal was now off the table. Chicago prosecutors had no influence on the fraud case because it was being handled out of DC. A new deal was created between the DC prosecutors and Mark's new attorney, Bill Walker, in which Mark agreed to plead to thirty-seven counts of tax fraud, money laundering, and related charges. Instead of six months, Mark Whitacre was now facing the very real possibility that he would be serving over ten years behind bars.

He was scheduled to be sentenced for tax fraud and money laundering in Urbana, Illinois, on February 26, 1998. He had been awaiting sentencing since the previous October 10th. The bizarre turns in the case and Mark's even more bizarre behavior had brought the situation to this different—far less attractive—plea bargain. The D.C. prosecutors were asking the judge to impose a sentence of at least nine years in prison.

Unfortunately for Mark, the main event—the ADM antitrust trial—had not even started by the time he had pled out to fraud. Thus, neither the Urbana-based federal judge presiding over the fraud case, Judge Harold Baker, nor the press nor a broader public, was focused on what was far more important, namely Mark's outstanding service to his country as a whistleblower. He had single-handedly exposed one of the largest price-fixing conspiracies in the history of American capitalism, a fact that should have been sufficiently mitigating to make the fraud case simply go away. Yet his opponents manipulated the flow of information to make sure that the whistleblowing side of the equation was not only barely mentioned, but *not mentioned at all*, during Mark's fraud-sentencing hearing.

It is not unreasonable to assume that, had the antitrust trial occurred first, and had Mark's FBI handlers not been muzzled by their higher-ups in D.C., Judge Baker would have recognized Mark's service to the FBI as an overwhelmingly positive offset to the fraud case.

But the case sequence was fraud before antitrust, so neither the judge nor the public had any real understanding of just how heroically Mark had served his country. Was it The Chairman who had orchestrated the delay in the antitrust case? He was, after all, a man of vast influence in the corridors of power in Washington DC. For years, ADM had been making large campaign contributions to both parties and using highly paid lobbyists in Washington to get legislation favorable to ADM enacted. Someone once joked to me that an honest politician is one who, once bought, stayed bought. My first thought was, that describes The Chairman's view of politicians exactly.

Why did Mark's fraud case open and close months before the price-fixing case even got put on the docket? Mark was to be sentenced in February of 1998, whereas the price-fixing trial did not even start until July of 1998. This meant that Mark and the family had to live in suspended animation for more than a third of a year. While he was to some extent able to focus on family during that period, it was a time of profound confusion and uncertainty for both him and Ginger. Ginger, ever Mark's equalizer and ballast, willed the family into enjoying these months together.

After his firing from ADM three years earlier, Mark had easily secured a new job as the CEO of a biotech start-up in Chapel Hill, North Carolina. His strong suit was that tripartite mix of decisive management capability, broad scientific background and outstanding salesmanship and congeniality. He led the company from August of 1995 until February of 1998.

Chapel Hill was a long way from Decatur, and the Whitacres couldn't have been happier about it. It was here that Mark found a stimulus that helped restore his Christian roots. In the Research Triangle area, there is a fraternity of biotechnology executives, and Mark had the good fortune to meet an Englishman named Ian Howes in the spring of 1997. Howes is a strong Christian who started a small bible study group specifically with Mark in mind. Thanks to Ian, Mark started building one of the first layers of trust that not only restored his faith, but helped it reach a new level in the months and years to come, long after Mark was forced to leave Chapel Hill. This little band of Christian brothers met two to three times a week to draw on the wisdom of the Bible.

They felt as if they were finally putting the nightmare behind them and enjoying a period of relative normalcy and family closeness. They also held out hope that the FBI would step in on Mark's behalf. It never happened. As sentencing day got closer, despite the best efforts of Herndon and Shepard, nobody was coming to the rescue. This sent Mark into a tailspin. The thought of going to prison terrified him.

He decided, as many do when they are facing jail time, that prison simply was not an option and just wasn't going to happen. The day before Mark was supposed to fly out from North Carolina to Urbana and get sentenced, he had gone to a local hardware store in Chapel Hill and bought tubes, a garden hose, and some duct tape. He had decided he was going to "do it right this time." Early the next morning, at approximately 3 AM, he went out to the driveway where his Lincoln Continental was parked and, instead of driving off to the airport, hooked up the hose and pipes and ran them into the passenger compartment of the car. Ginger and the three children were all upstairs sleeping. Mark turned on the engine, sat down in the driver's seat, and waited for sweet death to embrace him.

What he failed to realize was that this particular model of Lincoln had a triggering device that automatically blew out carbon monoxide and blew in fresh air through special vents once the carbon monoxide levels got too high. Mark passed out, but this, his second, suicide attempt failed again. When he awoke, he was in an ambulance with Ginger, en route to the UNC Medical Center.

"What happened Ging? How long have I been unconscious?"

"About twenty minutes Sweetheart," she said lovingly, as she stroked his hand. "Everything's going to be all right. You just lie back and try to breathe."

The irony of this, Mark's second suicide attempt, was that, following his first attempt on August 9, 1995, and after months of therapy, he had been given a clean bill of mental health just weeks earlier. His Chapel Hill psychiatrist, Dr. Eric Jensen, a Professor of Psychiatry at the University of North Carolina at Chapel Hill was widely considered to be one of the foremost authorities in the four-state area on suicidal tendencies. Mark had been seeing Dr. Jensen two or three times per week for a full year and a half.

Because of that first attempt, Mark was put on lithium and ended up taking the drug on a long-term maintenance basis for two and a half years, from mid-1995 to early 1998. He said the lithium helped considerably; it drastically reduced the severity of his mood swings. He found that the drug helped particularly to keep him from getting depressed or panicked at the prospect of going to prison.

What none of the doctors knew was that he surreptitiously went off the drug. When I asked him why, he said his "manic highs" lasted longer and were more pronounced, whereas his lows were no longer unbearably low. Thus, he far preferred the extended manic highs without the lithium, believing he could handle the more modest lows.

In Urbana, Mark's lawyers, Bill Walker and Rick Kurth, were expecting him, and the media was set up at the steps of the courthouse. But the convicted felon was a no-show. Ginger called Mark's attorney, Bill Walker, just as soon as she could.

With a sad and tearful tone, she said, "Bill, you won't be seeing Mark at his sentencing hearing today."

"What!?!" replied Walker, stunned. "What happened?"

"He tried to commit suicide at about 3 am this morning. Fortunately, it was unsuccessful, but I'm calling you from the hospital, and he's in bad shape."

Walker was silent for several seconds while he absorbed this news and said, "this will not be well-received by the judge." Later that morning in court, Walker asked the judge to let him fly to Chapel Hill and personally escort Mark back to Urbana for a re-scheduled sentencing hearing. Walker assured the judge that, if he would permit this extraordinary, special dispensation, Walker would be able to keep Mark calm and get him to his sentencing hearing without further incident.

The other side—the DC Attorneys who were prosecuting Mark's case—hit back hard. They expressed outrage that the judge would even consider Walker's petition. They requested that U.S. Marshalls be dispatched to Chapel Hill, sent to Mark's bedside to arrest him and take him into custody. The DC Attorneys argued cogently that Mark's next attempt could well prove fatal.

Once the U.S. marshals arrived in Chapel Hill the next day, things changed dramatically. They denied visitation rights to Ginger and the children and shackled Mark into wrist-ankle-waist chains and focused on one thing: getting their "cargo" to the Urbana, Illinois, courtroom without incident.

With a still-fragile Mark sequestered in his hospital room after being admitted under the name Mack Lard by his psychiatrist, Dr. Eric Jensen, who specializes in suicide cases and knew the case was high profile and put him in under an assumed name, Ginger and the children made it a point to show strong support for their husband and father. They knew he had been on the brink for some time because they were right there living it with him. The only way they could show their support was to stand vigil outside the hospital, in the parking lot, waving huge signs readable from his ninth-floor window that said, "HANG IN THERE DADDY!" and "WE'RE WITH YOU FOREVER!" and "WE'RE BEHIND YOU ONE HUNDRED PERCENT!"

Mark shuffled over to the window, looked down, and felt a rush of many different emotions: Encouragement by his family's visible support. Joy at the depth of their love. But also shame at attempting to take the coward's way out, and a deeper sense of shame that he might not be living his life in a way that was a credit to his children. His overriding concern, however, was the one immediately in front of him: His sentencing hearing was yet to happen in that Urbana courtroom in Illinois, and he knew that, whether he got the minimum (108 months) or the maximum (156 months), he would be taken directly from the courtroom to jail to begin serving time. This was a dreadful thought.

Although the man on the outside was still alive, the question remained: Was the man on the inside already dead? The late Norman Cousins said, "The tragedy of life is in what dies inside a man while he lives—the death of genuine feeling, the death of inspired response, the death of the awareness that makes it possible to feel the pain or the glory of others in yourself."

When it came time to leave the hospital the next day, the marshals had arranged for an unmarked dark-blue transport van to be stationed at the hospital's obscurely-located rear service doors. The marshals remained laconically all business. When Ginger asked when they might be transporting him, they told her nothing. Their refusal to provide even the detainee's spouse, Ginger, with basic information was, in her view, over the top, so she simply redoubled her effort to show her support by holding an all-night vigil in the parking lot.

Lucky she did, because in the wee hours of the morning, the transport van appeared out of nowhere and drove quietly to the double-door exit in the back. She roused the kids, and they all hustled to the back where he would be brought out and loaded into the van. It wasn't until approximately 10 AM, after Ginger and the kids had waited several more hours, that the marshals moved their wheel-chaired, ankle-shackled "cargo" as quickly as his short-stepped, shuffling gait would make possible, out the hospital doors and into the back of the van. He was loaded in swiftly and given the "don't hit-your-head" control push that all law enforcement agents seem to feel a need to do, as if they really care whether you hit your head or not. This prohibited Mark from looking left or right. He was confused and dazed anyhow, so at first he didn't see them, his entire family standing 100 feet away. But once he was in the van and able to stretch over and look out the van's small side window, he saw them—wife and all three children—standing tall, waving their support, and yelling out that they loved him. They had been keeping vigil for hours. Mark, in restraining cuffs, smiled at them through bittersweet tears. He could not make hand gestures or give two thumbs up. He was shackled. He was in reality in a prison cell; it just happened to be a rolling prison cell.

The scene overwhelmed Ginger. She felt completely helpless. As the van pulled away, she stood and waved, then, like a deflated balloon, collapsed into Tanya's arms, taking them both to the ground. With the tragic visual experience of seeing his family collapse on the lot in a rag heap of despair, Mark managed to mouth to Ginger, "I love you." He couldn't quite tell, *did she see it?* Could she make out what he was trying to say? Before the van got too far away, he saw her mouth move. Yes, she had seen it! She responded, only not in silence, but shouting at the top of her lungs: "I love you too!" while running after the van.

Two hours later, the van pulled up, not to the airport as Mark expected, but to the Winston-Salem County Jail, eighty miles west of Chapel Hill.

They off-loaded their cargo and processed him in for a night's stay at the jail. At 4 am the next morning, the marshals pulled Mark out of his cell and gave him his old blue jeans and shirt. The clothes still smelled of carbon monoxide.

After a lengthy out-processing from the Winston-Salem County Jail, they shackled Mark and loaded him back into the van and headed for the Winston-Salem airport. They removed his handcuffs for the flight so that he would look more or less like any other passenger.

The trip was a series of indirect commercial flights that took all day and ended in Chicago. There they loaded Mark into a mid-size airport rental car and drove three hours due south. Instead of stopping in Urbana, however, the car turned southwest and headed for, of all places, Decatur. As he was ushered out of the van, Mark looked up and saw a sign on the building that said Macon County Jail, Decatur, Illinois. Why Decatur? Why not Urbana, where the courtroom was located and which had its own county jail? *What are they doing, setting me up for a shank?* He thought, referring to a prison stabbing, often fatal, by a make-shift knife.

This unusual resting spot for Mark could have occurred only as a result of the behind-the-scenes machination of one man, The Chairman. In that jail, in that city, Mark feared for his life. It was one thing for Mark to attempt suicide and take his own life; it was quite another to think of getting murdered by a local enemy.

Everyone in Decatur knew about Mark, but they knew only one side of the story: that Mark Whitacre was a "snitch" who cost many people their jobs and the stock price to plummet. The antitrust trial against ADM had not yet started, and none of the other executives had been charged with anything. This meant that the whole story had not yet come out, only the stories damaging to Mark.

Even the head jailor at the Decatur Macon County Jail knew Mark. His sister worked for Mark in the BioProducts plant (and still works in the BioProducts plant). Mark remembered her well and tried to explain to her brother, the jailor, how bad he felt that all of this had happened. The jailer actually showed some sympathy, indicating that he saw through to the truth of the matter. But there is one entity that controls the way things are seen in Decatur.

Mark and Ginger were greatly concerned that his Decatur enemies were orchestrating behind the scenes a possible hit, shank, skirmish—something that would bring harm or "accidental" death to the despised whistleblower that had somehow ended up in the Decatur jail general inmate population. In my view, The Chairman was Machiavellian enough to enlist one of his minions to see that Mark got taken out, all the while keeping his hands clean.

As a result of Mark's suddenly life-threatening exposure in the Macon County jail, the relief he had felt after the hearing was replaced with terror and hyper-vigilance. Ginger knew there was no logical reason for Mark to be driven 45 minutes further south and detained in Decatur rather than Urbana. Urbana's Champaign County jail was right next to the courthouse and had plenty of empty cell beds. When Mark called her from the wall phone in his cell pod and told her he'd been put in the general population rather than protective custody, she made a beeline for Mark's lawyers with one mission: to keep her husband alive until he got designated. She warned them that her husband's life was at risk; she called the news media, anyone who would listen, and complained loud and hard. Meanwhile Mark was having nightmares of the shower scene in *Psycho* or the pillow-smothering scene in *The Godfather.*

PART THREE

THE PRISON YEARS

Whitacre Family First Prison Christmas at Yazoo Low (December 25, 1998)

A Prayer for Prisons & Correctional Institutions:

Lord Jesus, for our sake you were condemned as a criminal: Visit our jails and prisons with your pity and judgment. Remember all prisoners, and bring the guilty to repentance and amendment for life according to your will, and give them hope for their future. When any are held unjustly, bring them release; forgive us, and teach us to improve our justice.

Remember those who work in these institutions; keep them humane and compassionate; and save them from becoming brutal or callous. And since what we do for those in prison, O Lord, we do for you, constrain us to improve their lot. All this we ask for your mercy's sake. AMEN.

The Book of Common Prayer

PART THREE—THE PRISON YEARS
CHAPTER NINE

INMATE NUMBER 07543-424

**"His first night in the joint, Andy Dufresne cost me two
packs of cigarettes. He never made a sound . . ."**

"Red"
Played by actor Morgan Freeman
The Shawshank Redemption (1994 Movie)

It was Wednesday, March 4th, 1998. Sentencing day. Mark had
finally reached the end of the line. All the docket shuffling, delays, suicide
attempts, and appeals were over. He was now on the threshold of the
abyss, and it did not feel good.

The media grapevine was humming. Reporters were trying to
handicap not just how much time the once high-flying executive would
get, but also whether something bizarre, another mini-circus, might pop
up at the last minute. One thing they agreed on was that our protagonist's
behavior was in those days totally unpredictable.

One day earlier, Ginger had delivered a nice jacket, tie, and a crisp white
shirt to the Macon County Jail for Mark to wear to the sentencing hearing.
She didn't want him standing before Judge Baker in prison orange.

As the courtroom began filling up, Ginger came in quickly and alone,
taking a seat one row behind Mark on the gallery bench reserved for

family. She managed against all odds to maintain a reassuring exterior because today, of all days, she had to be ballast for her husband. She willed herself to remain calm, a process aided by her belief that Christians live by love above all else. Love was something she had in abundance for her husband.

She gathered her thoughts while sitting there, calling to mind Scriptures and the peace of Christ, who said, "*My peace I give unto you*" (John 14:27). She knew that the peace of Jesus must fill her heart now more than ever and that—for her husband's sake as well as her own—she had to call on the divine serenity that Jesus himself demonstrated throughout His life.

> My peace I give unto you.
> John 14:27

Yet beneath that calm exterior was a woman living in a man-made world that made her furious, not toward the beautiful planet that God made for all mankind, but toward a legal system that was so badly broken and callous that it had brought her husband to this degrading moment.

In minutes, the Honorable Judge Harold Baker would listen to Mark's acceptance of responsibility speech, say a few words himself, then deliver his sentence, bang his gavel down and signal the bailiff to escort Mark away. Mark understood full well that, once that gavel came down, he would have to start serving his sentence immediately. No cozy white-collar self-surrender after three months at home to "put his affairs in order." This wasn't Monopoly™, but he would be going directly to jail without passing through Go.

The press hounds were clearly disappointed that the courtroom proceedings that afternoon were entirely devoid of the theatrics they had come to associate with Mark at the time. Since they got no last-minute surprises, the media the next day described the hearing as anti-climactic, even boring.

Boring is relative. The proceedings may have been boring when held up against such rich cannon fodder as Mark's suicide attempt the week before. And maybe they are boring if you aren't the one being sentenced. But for Mark and Ginger, this was a major inflection point in their lives, a moment of indescribable sorrow. Whatever their shared life experiences had been up to that point—whatever it all meant—life as they knew it was over. For Mark it meant removal from society for at least eight and as many as thirteen years. For Ginger, it meant the start of more than three thousand days of forced separation from her husband and loss of the primary breadwinner in the family.

In the months leading up to Mark's sentencing, Ginger had gone from reading her Bible weekly to reading it several hours each day. Writer Ernest Hemingway called the Bible "the Sea of Wisdom." Ginger's well-worn "Sea of Wisdom" got some extra workouts during those trying days. She maintained then, and does to this day, a daily routine of rising early, 4:30 AM, and reading some passages from Scriptures. Only then does she go forth into the world.

Her bedrock Christian faith gave her the courage to make it through that day. When asked later how she managed to get through it, she said what she would come to say many times over the ensuing years, "I put my trust in a loving, caring heavenly Father. I believe God has a purpose in making us suffer and experience the problems we are facing, and I know God will see us through it." *Put your faith in Jesus, who has experienced every kind of problem we can have* (Hebrews 4:15).

The burden, Ginger said, was simply too great for her alone. She placed that burden on God's shoulders. Between God's shoulders and Mark's following a few years of pumping iron in prison, she was using the strongest shoulders in the world.

At 2:15 PM that afternoon, Judge Baker was about to emerge from his chambers and preside. The Clerk of the Court handed him a stack of the afternoon's hearings. Mark's folder was on top. Baker quickly reviewed the day's most unusual folder, stood up, and walked briskly into the courtroom to mete out sentences to a motley crew of convicted felons, among them Mark Whitacre.

As the judge entered from the side, a bailiff called out sonorously. "All rise!" Then, "be seated."

The Clerk then looked at the court stenographer but spoke to the entire courtroom, "Case number Nine-Seven-Two-Oh-Oh-Oh-One, Unites States of America versus Mark Edward Whitacre!"

The background buzz bouncing off the marble courtroom walls came to a halt. You could hear a pin drop. Mark's case had a high public profile. Throngs of media hung from the rafters. Those who couldn't get in waited out front in media vans with towers sticking up, ready for live transmission to TV audiences around the state and the nation.

As Mark and his attorneys rose from their seats at the defendant's table, all eyes were on the whistleblower. As he huddled with Bill Walker, his lead lawyer, he glanced back at Ginger. The two can give and receive mutual assurances with the slightest facial flicker, and this time she gave him her biggest, best, heart-swelling transfer of love and support. He caught it and saw that she was calm and confident. That steadied him.

Judge Baker, annoyed at Mark for delaying the hearing by a week with that attempted suicide back in Chapel Hill, shot Mark an exasperated look that was not confidence-inspiring, then resumed studying Mark's PSR.

A PSR—Pre-Sentencing Report—is supposed to be an impartial report prepared by a probation department to assess an offender's reasons for the offence and the relevant conduct and proposed actions that will assist a judge in determining appropriate sentencing. PSRs typically start with damaging recitals of the charges, a brief family and work history, and an explanation of any prior convictions or arrests, of which there were none in Mark's case. PSRs also indicate whether the person has a history of drug or alcohol abuse, needs anger management counseling, has community service requirements. The PSR will also state in detail any dollar amounts of restitution.

PSRs are something the average person on the street has never heard of. But when you brush up against the criminal justice system, you soon realize it is the single-most important document in the judge's hands when he metes out a convicted felon's sentence. PSRs often recommend curfew orders, drug treatment and testing, and victim impact assessments. U.S. Probation Officers will argue that all PSRs are impartial and objective. However, I have yet to see or hear of any PSR being impartial.

Instead, because U.S. Probation Officers work hand-in-glove with federal prosecutors to generate PSRs, they are invariably damaging to the defendant and favorable to the prosecution. Such a biased collaboration gives rise to selective recall. Your PSR may contain three long paragraphs about the candy bar you stole as a kid but omit any mention of how you saved someone's life in a fire, became a Rhodes Scholar, or volunteered to read to the blind. It is a charade of objectivity. PSRs that don't tilt the narrative toward the strongly negative are rare.

A sticky point in most defendants' PSRs is the portrayal of the defendant as not being serious about accepting responsibility. In Mark's case, nothing could have been further from the truth. Like all defendants, he had been extensively questioned about his upbringing and business activities by the probation officer preparing his PSR. Then the officer writes it up, starting with a verbatim repetition of the prosecution's highly-charged wording of the crimes as found in the transcripts.

With Mark's PSR, for once our protagonist caught a lucky break. When you're as down and out as he was, you take any break that comes your way. He was assigned a sympathetic probation officer who strove for greater objectivity, which helped offset the damaging opening recital in the PSR in which the DC prosecutors tried to cast the fraud conviction—for Mark's $9.5 million embezzlement—in the most negative terms possible and clearly had gone way too far in ascribing unflattering motives to all of Mark's activities, including Mark's suicide attempt a week earlier. By casting Mark's behavior as erratic and dangerous, they hoped to convince the judge that he deserved no offense-level reduction for acceptance of responsibility.

Fortunately Mark's assigned probation officer had been following his case in the press and made it clear he thought Mark was being treated unfairly. He offset the negative language in Mark's PSR with a well-worded argument supporting leniency. This helped blunt the DC prosecutors' attempt to steamroll over their defendant.

Mark had been forced to accept four months earlier the plea agreement that led to this sentencing hearing. Now he was ready, even eager, to state on record that he accepted full responsibility for his crimes and wasn't falsely denying any conduct that might be inconsistent with that acceptance of responsibility.

Ginger knew the system was out-of-whack, so she was not surprised when the DC prosecutors used the lure of an offense-level reduction as a carrot for pleading out rather than going to trial but backed out once they had his signed plea-agreement in their hands. Clearly, these prosecutors would do anything to make themselves look like major winners and brilliant prosecutors.

Judge Baker was limited by the mandatory sentencing guidelines in effect at the time to a range of months of incarceration for Mark. Disastrous consequences have followed the enactment of legislation creating mandatory guidelines which had been made into law some thirty years earlier. Under the guidelines, Mark was eligible for a two-level reduction based on Judge Baker's assessment of the sincerity of Mark's acceptance of responsibility.

However, Baker appeared to have issues with that sincerity. Mark was not one of Judge Baker's typical offenders, but an educated man full of complexity and contradiction. For another, Baker was annoyed that the hearing got postponed a week due to Mark's attempted suicide, suggesting it had been nothing but a ruse and delaying tactic, not a sincere effort to end his life. The question that pops into mind when you hear that is, how can a judge out in Urbana, Illinois, make such a call about an incident that had occurred in North Carolina?

If Baker decided that Mark was sincere, and if there was no contradictory relevant conduct, he could reduce Mark's offense by two levels and thereby impose a less severe sentence. As Ginger listened to the judge deliver his soliloquy, it was hard for her to tell which way the judge was leaning.

––––––––––––

Before changes in the law under the *Booker* decision, prosecutors had more clout than judges when the offense level was sixteen or above. Since Mark was well above offense level sixteen—he was at offense level 33—his DC prosecutors had sole authority to grant him an additional one-level decrease but they had to file a formal motion at time of sentencing in favor of that third offense-level reduction.

The reasoning behind ceding such power to prosecutors is that they, not judges, are best positioned to determine whether a defendant has assisted authorities sufficiently to warrant a further reduction in the offense level. Critics of mandatory sentencing laws claim such power vested in prosecutors is too strong a bargaining chip in their favor and discourages defendants from exercising their legal right to take their case to trial.

The *Booker* decision let prosecutors know that the U.S. Supreme Court agreed with the critics. Yet the fact remains, even after *Booker*, that you may get an extra brownie point if you plead out and save the government the expense and time of having to prepare for trial and the risk of embarrassment should it lose at trial, but there are no guarantees. Federal prosecutors can still extract a plea bargain out of a frightened defendant, receive all the benefits of not having to prepare for trial, and then, for capricious reasons, decline to file a motion recommending the additional one-level reduction in the offense calculation.

Bill Walker, Mark's new attorney, was not about to let that happen. Thanks to his good preparation and deceptively down-home oratorical skills in the courtroom, he kept the DC prosecutors under control. He gave his speech and sat down, confident Baker would give Mark the lowest possible sentence.

Mark and Ginger weren't so sure. After Walker sat down, Judge Baker turned directly to Mark and told him to rise. He stood up like a marine recruit whose drill sergeant had just entered the barracks. Baker then asked him if he had anything to say.

Mark's speech was short and to the point. He apologized to all the people in the courtroom and also to those not in the courtroom. He spoke in a strong, clear voice. He was there to accept his punishment. His tone was sincere and contrite, but its degrading nature was too much for Ginger. She sobbed.

Everyone in the courtroom believed Mark's short speech came from the heart. After delivering his statement, Mark stood ramrod straight. He held the judge's gaze. He knew the end was near.

Baker responded to Mark's short soliloquy by remarking that Mark was quite different from the petty thieves, drug dealers, and racially disadvantaged defendants from broken families who usually stood before him. He cited Mark's intact family situation. He itemized one-by-one Mark's seven advanced degrees. He noted with respect Mark's meteoric rise at ADM. He said these were all contra-indicators to criminal conduct. Then the judge went silent for what seemed like an eternity.

Mark remained standing and at attention. He was ram-rod straight. Walker believed the judge's disparaging remarks were just a smokescreen to divert attention away from the fact that he was about to give Mark the lowest sentence possible, which, based on a fraud amount of $9.5 million, and given the absence of any criminal history, ranged from 108 months to 156 months. That forty-eight month spread between high and low equaled four years, so the stakes were high.

Judge Baker sentenced Mark to 108 months, the minimum under the guidelines, exactly nine years. Prison sentences are stated in months I think to make them sound less severe than they are when stated in years.

As good as that was, Mark's sentence was a catastrophe compared to the deal his prior attorney, Epstein, had worked out two-and-a-half years earlier. Back then, the deal on the table was for three to five years, with mitigating circumstances bringing it down to six months of jail time for Mark. Nine years is a different matter entirely, a staggeringly long sentence.

Baker also ordered Mark to disgorge $11.4 million as restitution, which consisted of the $9.5 million of embezzled funds, plus $1.9 million in interest, calculated at a compound average annual rate of five percent. Mark would also be required to do three years of post-incarceration supervised release, referred to by ex-offenders as "three years of paper."

As for designation, federal judges can recommend a facility but have no power to make it a required part of the judgment. It's the Prison Bureau that has the final say, and it is under no obligation to heed the judge's recommendation. In most cases, however, if a judge recommends an inmate be designated to a facility near his family, the Bureau tries to honor the judge's recommendation, absent over-crowding or other issues.

Baker recommended that Mark be remanded to Federal Correction Institute (FCI) Butner Low, a new satellite facility built that year to house low-security male inmates. Butner Low is about forty minutes northeast of Chapel Hill just off I-85 in the Research Triangle area (Raleigh-Durham-Chapel Hill) in the eastern part of North Carolina. It's part of a multi-building, multi-security-level prison complex located in the midst of a whole cluster of other federal buildings in and around Butner, North Carolina.

———————————

The judge ordered Mark to undergo psychiatric evaluation because of his two documented suicide attempts, so he would first be sent to a medical administrative facility to check for mental soundness before going on to Butner Low. This was not a good development for our protagonist. Medical administrative facilities in the federal prison system hold inmates of all security categories and have special missions: they house inmates who are extremely sick (often with terminal cancer), exceptionally violent, escape-prone, or severely mentally ill. That meant low-risk white-collar offenders like Mark get mixed in with extremely dangerous criminals.

———————————

Judge Baker's hearing ended quickly. When the hammer went down, Mark's freedom was gone. The judge nodded to a court bailiff and said sternly, "Take him away."

With that, Mark was unceremoniously escorted out of the courtroom. His back was to the main courtroom gallery, so, although he tried to turn toward Ginger, he was being ushered out, so he caught only the briefest of glances. Ginger was sobbing openly.

Thus began the long, great tragedy of Mark's incarceration. He was escorted to a cold-soldered steel holding cell behind the courtrooms and left to himself there.

A sense of relief engulfed him. One would expect a sense of dread, but his was relief because, for the first time in years, he actually felt safe. Safe from the retaliation of the machine, safe from the immense burden that led to his mental breakdown and two suicide attempts. Whatever nightmares lay ahead, whatever prison facilities he would pass through, and whatever was about to come of his long prison stint, he felt nothing could be worse than the nightmare he was leaving behind.

As it would turn out, he could not have been more mistaken. He was at that moment living in ignorant bliss of the ordeal that lay ahead. This newly-minted prisoner, Inmate #07543-424, had no clue that things were going to get so much worse before they ever got better.

PART THREE—THE PRISON YEARS
CHAPTER TEN

SPRINGFIELD MEDICAL

"I don't suffer from insanity: I enjoy every minute of it."

BUMPER STICKER

Ninety minutes into his nine-year sentence, with an eternity in front of him and barely a heartbeat behind him, Mark was handcuffed again, this time tighter around the wrists, and whisked out the rear exit. The media frenzy was intense. The press wanted blood, and, if it couldn't have blood, it wanted at least a quotable zinger from Mark.

They got nothing.

Cuffed to the side rails in the non-descript plain-vanilla prisoner transport van, Mark bounced around in the back. *Why do all the other convicts who were in that courtroom holding tank get taken to the Urbana county jail while I'm alone in this van and the only one being hauled down to the Decatur jail?*, where he would await transport to the medical compound in Springfield, Missouri.

Prison time is slow time. It would take another three weeks for this to occur. All the while, Mark was thrust into the general population. This was not the place for him to be in a Decatur jail. He would have preferred protective custody, given that the Chairman could have easily planted someone in the general population to shank him at an opportune moment. The Chairman owned that town, and he badly needed Mark out of the way before the price-fixing trial started.

Knowing this, Mark—and Ginger by telephone—first tried explaining why his life was in danger in such an environment. When their pleas feel on deaf ears, he spent those three weeks on high alert. He was a sitting duck in the general inmate population and knew that a shank contract had to be out on him. On behalf of the company. Despite a three-year absence from Decatur, everyone in town knew only one side of Mark's story, the side promulgated by the company's public relations machinery, which had all-too-deftly painted Mark as nothing more than a large-dollar embezzler and a snitch who cost many people in Decatur their jobs.

Mark felt certain there was a contract out on him in the Macon-County jail. This was, after all, a one-company town with a powerful man running the show. After spending three weeks sleeping with one eye open, he finally got the call-out and two US marshals drove him non-stop from the Macon County Jail in Decatur, Illinois, to Springfield Medical, a distance of some 350 miles. By car, it's a six-hour drive. The van took seven.

Springfield Medical is a paradox. Built during the Great Depression, its grounds and physical structure are among the most beautiful in the entire federal prison system. It has an elegant architectural half moon design for the various buildings, with the main building in the middle. It also has an underground tunnel system connecting the main building with the other buildings that form an arc of brick buildings.

This is what the Lord says: Yours is an incurable bruise, a terrible wound. There is no one to help you or bind up your injury. You are beyond the help of any medicine.

JEREMIAH 30:12

All inmates move from building to building via this interconnected web of tunnels. The only inmates seen at ground level are the ones doing the landscaping. The grounds are exceptionally well maintained.

For Mark and Ginger, Springfield Medical offered a gigantic yard for visits. Ginger flew from Chapel Hill to Kansas City, Missouri, every other weekend to visit Mark and brought their three children most of the time.

Yet Springfield Medical is a serious penitentiary with turrets and concertina wire and guards pointing rifles from multiple towers surrounding the complex at inmates at all times. Rifles were never at ground level because a guard could be overtaken at ground level and disarmed. When he got to Springfield Medical, Mark told Ginger he felt like he was in a scene from *The Birdman of Alcatraz*. Little did he know that the real birdman of Alcatraz spent his final days at Springfield Medical. In fact, within Springfield Medical's walls, the two prime requirements for coping with a prison sentence—youth and good health—are almost nonexistent among the inmate population. A huge percentage of the inmates there are being treated for cancer.

Many famous people have done time in Springfield Medical: John Gotti died there of throat cancer in 2002. Robert Stroud, the Birdman of Alcatraz, died there in 1963 after 54 years of incarceration. Larry Flynt, the paraplegic who started *Hustler* Magazine, spent time at Springfield Medical. And Don Vito Genovese, leader of the Genovese crime family, died there in 1969 of a heart attack. Even the fictional "Johnny Sack" from the hit TV series *The Sopranos,* died of cancer at Springfield Medical in the season six episode, "Stage 5."

Despite the difficult environment of severe mental instability that Mark encountered in the mental health ward at Springfield Medical, he says his healing first started at Springfield Medical. This was due to several factors. Most important was that he finally felt out of reach from his enemies and thus safe for the first time in five years. In addition, he was permitted unlimited phone minutes, so he talked to Ginger and the kids for long stretches. This kept Mark and Ginger emotionally connected despite the fact that prison had sequestered him in dreadful places designed specifically to separate him from his family.

What's more, Mark decided to get fit physically. He arrived at Springfield Medical forty pounds overweight. The stress of the past years had caused him to overeat, and he had grown flabby and lethargic. By walking the track every day, or the indoor treadmill on rainy days, and by beginning a weight training program at Springfield Medical's weight pile, which was underground and way to the back of the compound, he shed twenty pounds during the two months he was there.

When talking with Ginger, Mark was able to make calls three ways: direct debit from his commissary account, collect, or pre-paid. One of the infuriating aspects of prison life is that the prison-industrial complex is a huge profit centers for subcontractor like telephone companies. For collect calls, the rates are dramatically higher than the equivalent rate for a collect call made from outside prison. Thus, crime does pay—if you are a long-distance provider with a prison contract.

Mark knew he needed help in reclaiming his mental stability, and Springfield Medical had a battery of mental health specialists meeting with him on a rotating basis. Most of the psychiatrists he talked to at Springfield Medical had considerable experience in diagnosing men who engaged in abnormal behavior and whose crimes were due to mental illness. One could argue that almost everyone has some form of neurosis or another. Most of us on the outside, however, manage some degree of impulse control, keeping our neurotic behavior to a controllable minimum. By contrast, the inmates in the psychiatric ward at Springfield Medical can be dangerous, including to themselves. In prison, they call the mental health ward the "ding wing."

Self-mutilation and suicide are not uncommon in prison ding wings, and Springfield Medical when Mark was there was no exception. He described it like a scene from the Ken Kesey novel, *One Flew Over the Cuckoo's Nest*. Kesey's premise was that most patients in mental wards are not insane, just individuals who get pushed away by society because they don't fit into conventional stereotypes of how to act and behave. It would be difficult to document how many crimes are committed because of mental illness.

Mark's initial diagnosis prior to his incarceration was bipolar disorder, and the mainstay treatment for bipolar is lithium. Mark's father, Farmer Whitacre, had a sister who had been diagnosed as bipolar—called manic-depression in those days—so perhaps a case could have been made that manic-depression ran in the Whitacre gene pool. Mark definitely displayed various forms of anxiety disorder, ranging from feelings of fear (some real, some imagined) to the two suicide attempts. However, the psychiatrists at Springfield Medical were, in fact, impressed by Mark's relative sanity, given what he had been through. In their view, having been undercover for nearly three years and not showing more signs of post-traumatic stress disorder or acute situational anxiety indicated to them that he was emotionally resilient, not emotionally disturbed.

After hundreds of hours analyzing and talking to Mark, the Springfield Medical doctors reached the unanimous clinical conclusion that he did not in fact suffer from bipolar disorder. Rather, he suffered from the short-term mental condition called *acute situational stress*, which often gets misdiagnosed as bipolar disorder because the symptoms are the same except that the former is only acute, i.e., short-lived, while bipolar disorder is chronic, i.e., long term. Although Mark's team of prison doctors—based on their new and more informed diagnosis—took him off lithium, he and Ginger both knew that, for the rest of his life, they would need to monitor his mental stability.

His unit team immediately cleared him to go to Butner Low located in Butner, North Carolina not far from Chapel Hill and his family. Getting cleared to go to Butner Low, however, was not the same as getting to Butner Low.

Mark got his first taste of diesel therapy on this transit from Springfield Medical to Butner Low. Nothing moves fast and linear in the federal prison system—except of course the disciplining of an inmate who has the bad luck to get caught fighting or snitched out for holding contraband like a cell phone. In those situations, the warden moves very fast and very linear: the offender is forcibly removed from the prison population immediately, in tight handcuffs and gets "shipped out" in the language of prison—usually to a holding tank on the premises first, then to the local county jail, then to a much worse facility somewhere in Timbuktu. In addition, the offender gets his sentence lengthened by virtue of add-on charges for the offense.

Mark got slammed with his first dose of diesel therapy transiting from Springfield Medical to Butner Low. He went through USP Atlanta, otherwise known as the Atlanta holdover facility. Atlanta holdover is a despicable, inhumane place that defies description. It is so overcrowded that, when Mark ended up as the third man in a two-man cell, he considered himself lucky because many two-man cells have four and five prisoners in them. As the third and last man in, his spot was on the concrete floor next to the toilet.

Mark's two cellies were in transit too, but one was doing a twenty-year jolt and the other thirty, so for them to spend ten or twenty months in the Atlanta holdover was but an instant in time.

Although these three men were in lockdown together twenty-three of every twenty-four hours, Mark has no recollection of ever talking to them. He couldn't tell you their names or even what they looked like. They slept the entire time except for rec hour.

Recreation in the Atlanta holdover consisted of one hour in an enclosed area. Showers were permitted twice a week and lasted exactly five minutes each. The other two slept most of those twenty-three hours. Mark read the Bible. With nearly the full nine years in front of him, he felt at that moment in that cell as if the darkness of his dark hours was at its deepest. The same three questions screamed from inside his breast: *Will I even have a family when I get out? How can Ginger possibly get by and feed and clothe the kids with so little money? And how can I possibly get a job when I get out, nine years down the road?*

At that moment, Mark's was the voice of true desperation. His need for spiritual light was far greater than his need for physical daylight during that one hour of recreation time. That one hour, when his two cellies were gone, was the only time he could be alone.

Then it came. On a day just like any other, it came. His two cellies had stirred from their sleep, gotten up, and shuffled out to the line that would take them outside for their allotted hour of outdoor recreation. God is often most active in an invisible way when the darkness seems deepest.

Right then and there in that Atlanta holdover cell, as Mark was hitting bottom, something took him down on his knees. It was the words of David in Psalms 139 that brought him to his knees. With no one else in that tiny cell, Mark fell down and prayed more fervently than he ever had in his life:

Dear God, I can never escape from your spirit! I can never get away from your presence!

PSALMS 139: 7

Even in darkness I cannot hide from you. To you the night shines as bright as day.

PSALMS 139:12

Then Mark realized that the Holy Spirit was with him and inside him at that very moment in that cell. God in that instant forgave and redeemed Mark simultaneously. He is always with us through every situation, in every trial, he reminded himself.

Calm and contentment began to overcome Mark when he realized this and felt it deeply within his heart. Still on his knees he became infused with a deepening peace. God is always protecting, loving, and guiding us. God knows and loves us completely.

God may move more slowly than we like, but even the first verses of Genesis tell us something: Not only is God always working, but in Genesis He spoke: "Let there be light." And there was light.

This was the beginning of Mark's true conversion. *Genesis* means "beginning," and this was Mark's own beginning, his true epiphany, his true revelation that God has a purpose, that God believes in the value and dignity of man and the value and dignity of Mark himself. Mark read Genesis over and over again and realized, yes there is hope! No matter how dark his situation, God has a plan. No matter how insignificant and useless Mark may have felt a moment earlier, now he felt that God loved him and wanted to use Mark in His plan. God's salvation is always available.

David, the great writer of Psalms had many troubles. He had been a young shepard and faced both bears and lions. He had protected his sheep from them. After killing Goliath, David was taken into King Saul's house but then was nearly killed by Saul, who became jealous with rage. After David became king, he suffered the terrible blow of losing a child. When he grew older, he was betrayed by his own sons who wanted to take the throne from him.

But God took David through all those dark valleys in safety, and He would take Mark through all his dark valleys in safety. "The righteous face many troubles, but the Lord rescues them from each and every one" (Psalm 34:19).

And so, in that manner, in that cell and on his knees, Mark moved from fear to serenity, from desperation to affirmation, from darkness to light, from the negative to the positive. *From hoping to knowing. From the general to the specific.*

The Bible is very specific about the presence of God. David sang this song to the Lord on the day the Lord rescued him from his enemies and from Saul: "In my distress I cried out to the Lord; yes, I prayed to my God for help. He heard me from His sanctuary; my cry reached his ears" (Psalm 18:6).

Mark cried out no less than David. He felt the wondrous power at that moment in the touch of the Master's hand. At that moment, there were no longer any cell walls. There was only God's loving smile. He felt God's hand touch his and thrilled to that miraculous touch.

Then Mark got up off his knees. *God lifted him off his knees and back to wholeness and joy.* It was at that moment that Mark finally and truly felt God. He knew that nothing could keep him down if he would just let the Lord lift him up. There is always a way through or around every problem.

A few minutes later Mark's cellies returned, unaware of what had happened. Mark thought, *didn't they just leave?* Whereas to him, only an instant had passed, in fact it had been a full hour. He had been praying on his knees for almost a full hour, but it felt like an instant.

Mark Whitacre had been saved. Ginger's prayers were finally answered.

His worries about his family, the money, a job when he gets out—gone. The "key of David" in Revelations 3:7, which represents Christ's authority to open the door into God's Kingdom, had been opened to Mark. Once the door is opened, no one can close it. Mark had just had the door of salvation opened to him, and from that moment on, none of the squalor and noise and stench and chaos of the Atlanta holdover bothered him anymore.

Soon he was in transit and finally on his way again to Butner Low.

———————

No sooner did Mark get to Butner Low than he had to "pack out" and head for Chicago, where the price-fixing trial was to commence on July 9, 1998. With two marshals, he flew by private jet from North Carolina. Mark scratched his head and wondered how our taxpayer dollars were being spent. The aircraft had been confiscated in a drug deal. *"How many of these do the feds have?"* he thought, *"Why not just sell them at auction and lower our taxes? I could have flown commercial . . ."*

En route, Mark was fully focused on the upcoming price-fixing case. On arrival, the marshals released him into custody at the Metropolitan Correction Center in downtown Chicago. This would be his home when not in court for the antitrust trial, approximately sixteen out of every twenty-four hours.

Mark's focus took an unexpected turn away from the case. He was about to bump into unexpected trouble at his temporary overnight accommodations, MCC Chicago.

PART THREE—THE PRISON YEARS
CHAPTER ELEVEN

MCC CHICAGO: URBAN WARFARE

**"It was no individual's fault that his difficulties were
suddenly compounded by the unexpected series of events
that followed . . ."**

Erwin James
"Reason and Rehabilitation"
A Life Inside

O nce Mark Whitacre arrived in Chicago in the sweltering July
heat of 1998, he was better prepared for his defense arguments in the
price-fixing case than he was for his stay at the Chicago city jail, otherwise
known as the Chicago Metropolitan Correctional Center—or MCC
Chicago in prison lingo.

MCC Chicago is an urban high-rise located at the intersection of
Clark and Van Buren Streets. The building has a triangular footprint.
On its roof is a poor excuse for an exercise yard for prisoners. MCC
Chicago is an administrative facility designed to house prisoners of all
security levels who are appearing in federal courts facing felony charges
in the Northern District of Illinois. Both male and female prisoners are
housed at the facility, and the twelfth floor is restricted for females only
and can hold approximately forty-five women on that floor. Access to the

rooftop exercise area is limited to twice a week for two hours each. Men and women are never allowed to be on the elevator at the same time, and since there are twenty times as many men as women at MCC Chicago, the female inmates end up waiting as much as forty-five minutes for transport to other areas of the building.

Realizing he was going to be mixed in with prisoners of every security level, Mark felt an onrush of panic. MCC Chicago is twenty-six floors of nastiness and as rough-and-tumble as it gets in the Bureau's system. It is also a place of high stress, because everyone there is facing uncertainty as to his permanent disposition involving a court case. It is little more than a poorly run human warehouse. Michael Santos, a former inmate who was confined in a variety of different federal detention centers numerous times during his twenty-one year journey through imprisonment says of MCC Chicago, "Despite the name, no one in the building gives much energy to 'correcting' anyone."

MCC Chicago is particularly notorious as a thriving gang center. Gangs can thrive no less efficiently on the inside of a prison as they can on the outside. Many gang members are serving thirty-years-to-life, so they have nothing to lose. For that reason alone, it is widely held that first-time non-violent offenders like Mark should not be held in such dangerous prison facilities as MCC Chicago. Soft newbies or affluent white-collar criminals are easy prey for extortion and harassment by hardened gang members. Mark was thrown in their midst, something he had not counted on, and he quickly became one of their prey.

When you become the object of a gang squeeze in prison, there's nowhere to hide. Mark was no exception. Within two hours of his arrival at MCC Chicago, while he was making up his bed and putting the single, thin prison-issue sheet (MCC Chicago had stopped issuing two sheets to each inmate coming through Receiving, presumably due to scarcity caused by overcrowding) and lone threadbare wool blanket on his steel bunk bed, he saw standing suddenly in front of him a young, compact, well-muscled man of five-feet-five with jet black hair. He had a menacing grin on his face and dark, wild eyes. Standing just a few feet behind were three others, equally menacing. They had their arms folded across their chests.

"*Amigo*," began the leader, "on behalf of my associates," gesturing with one arm to the posse of three behind him, "I woud lie to wakum you to byoo-ee-full dow'town Zhicago."

"Thank you," replied an exhausted, pre-occupied Mark, who continued making his bunk bed. The group of four edged a little closer, the leader glaring at Mark with those dark, wild eyes, saying nothing for at least fifteen seconds. Then, pointing to Mark's attire, he said, "I lie your outfit *Amigo*."

Lie? Mark wondered to himself. Then he looked down. *Oh, he "likes" my . . . . what, orange jumpsuit?* Not sure what there was to like about a prison-issue orange jumpsuit, Mark looked quizzically at this thug, then continued about his business. Lead thug and his three associate thugs just stood there.

Realizing they weren't going to go away anytime soon, Mark tried small talk. "So where you from, Bud?" he asked the leader.

"'Bud?' Whooosss name isss 'Bud'?" My name, *Amigo,* isss none of your biss-ness." Then raising one arm and making a circle in the air with his index finger, lead thug said, "I fro' here *Amigo*. We all fro' here." Pause. "An' aass' I joss said, I lie your new outfit."

Mark stopped what he was doing and stood up to face the group. *This is no time to show you're not afraid of them,* he thought. *Let them have whatever they want.*

He kept his eyes on the leader. "You mean you want my jumpsuit? No problem, Bud . . . ah, I mean Sir. I leave here in a week or so, and you can have it then."

"No than' you, *Amigo,* bekoss you see, I lie your outfit right NOOOWWWW." He let the "nooww" extend a bit too long for Mark's comfort. Mark looked at each of them one by one, then without question or comment undid his orange jumpsuit, pulled it over his canvas prison slippers, stepped out one foot at a time, rolled it up, and handed it to the man whose name was "none of his biss-ness."

Standing alone now in only the threadbare jockey undershorts with torn elastic given to him at Receiving, Mark thought *man, it's cold.*

However, he was so stunned by what had just happened that he wasn't sure which made him shiver more: the cold jail temperature or the fear that what just happened could be repeated tomorrow, and the next day, and the day after that.

Most jails and prisons keep their facilities cold, in part to reduce the spread of airborne diseases such as tuberculosis, in part to keep the natives from getting restless. MCC Chicago was no different. It may have been ninety-five and humid on the streets of Chicago that July day, but it was probably fifty degrees inside the Chicago Metropolitan Correctional Center. The warden keeps it cold so inmates will spend most of their time under their covers trying to stay warm rather than being up and about making mischief.

Lead thug passed the rolled-up jumpsuit over his shoulder to an associate without looking back. With a growing smirk on his face, he continued to glare at Mark. He wasn't done with Mark yet, and Mark knew it.

"You know what, *Amigo*? I lie your mattress an' I be needing tha' too."

Mark deemed it prudent, under the circumstances, to climb up to his bunk, the upper one in his new cell, roll up his thin mattress, bring it down, dust it off, and hand it over with a smile. As Mark held it out, lead thug gave a small flick of his head. One of his posse stepped forward to receive Mark's "gift."

"Oh, an' the blanget *Amigo*." Silently Mark handed yet a different "associate" his wool blanket, hoping now that lead thug wouldn't also ask for his shoes or the only sheet he had left.

Lead thug took another half minute to gaze around Mark's area, trying to decide if there was anything else he wanted. Not spotting any more items "of value," he turned and walked away with a leering sneer, posse in tow.

Mark stood motionless except for the shivering. He had on nothing but the threadbare, loose-fitting jockey undershorts. He felt humiliated, helpless, and scared. He grabbed the thin towel he had been issued at intake, spread it out on what was left of his bed, a flat cold length of metal, climbed up, lay down, and pulled the sheet over his head, trying to block out the nightmare just beyond its thin veneer.

He froze that night and knew pneumonia wouldn't be far off if he didn't do something. After two days of shuttling between the purgatory of the courtroom and the quadruple purgatory of MCC Chicago, word about Mark started leaking back to the metro jail. It turned out that Mark had a much bigger problem at the Chicago correctional facility. Any leak of his status as a government witness—a snitch—in the Archer Daniels price-fixing case would mean bodily harm, if not death, by shank. Any subtle distinction between a street snitch and being undercover against a Fortune 500 company—one that inmates by definition would love to hate—would have been lost on the gang members. Each cell pod had one TV that hung down from the ceiling on a swivel base. It was turned on and off by the guards, but it was always on during the evening news. If a local news broadcast blew his cover and let it be known that he was a government mole, he was a dead man.

It would only be a matter of time before the Latin Kings or the Crips or the Aryan Brotherhood, all active prison gangs, learned about it. The contract to take out Mark would have come from somewhere higher-up in the gang hierarchy, and order-fulfillment at the Chicago Metropolitan facility was no problem. Prison gangs constitute an efficient enforcement network. Furthermore, in Chicago, thanks to budget cuts at the time, the gangs had the added advantage of being able to operate under a low guard-to-inmate ratio—about one guard for every one hundred inmates.

The only type of inmate hated worse in prison than a snitch is a child molester. Gangs accomplish the elimination of snitches and molesters by forcing a cellblock member to either kill the target or be killed himself for failure to carry out a direct order. Someone who needs to get "made" as a member of the gang is usually the one told to fulfill the contract. The Chicago facility was a world of shank-or-be-shanked.

Mark's fear of having his cover blown while in the Chicago high-rise prison and getting shanked as a snitch far outweighed any trial-room benefit to his being physically present in the Chicago courtroom of Judge Manning, the presiding judge in the price-fixing case. The other inmates were catching wind of something and already asking questions. Someone had stolen his legal papers. Mark had to get out of there. After much talking and persuading, the Chicago facility warden relocated Mark to the sixth floor of MCC Chicago. This was considered the PC floor, the protective custody floor. It housed many dirty cops or gang informants.

The next day he told his attorney, Walker, that he wanted to be tried *in absentia* and be returned to his low-security setting at Butner in North Carolina. The two disagreed on the matter, but Walker wasn't the one sitting in the MCC every night fearing for his life. Mark told Walker he would in fact be more effective, not less, from Butner via telephone hookup to the courtroom. Walker disagreed.

Over his lawyer's objections, a frightened and worried Mark Whitacre stood before Judge Manning and stated directly to her that he wanted to waive his right to be present at trial and be returned to his assigned facility in Butner. The judge told him that she did not think that was a good idea, but she recognized a defendant's right to be tried *in absentia* so she permitted him to return to Butner. Walker warmed to the idea that removing Mark as a physical presence at the trial would allow the jury to focus on Mick and Terry, not his client.

After the judge granted his return to Butner, it took the government two weeks to move him from MCC Chicago to Butner. For safety reasons, two pleasant U.S. marshals flew with him on a private cargo plane with no one else on board. It would be the last time he traveled in such comfort for a long time because another dose of diesel therapy was in his future.

PART THREE—THE PRISON YEARS
CHAPTER TWELVE

DIESEL THERAPY TO YAZOO

**"No hour is to be considered a waste which
teaches one what not to do."**

CHARLES B. ROGERS

No sooner did Mark get back to Butner than he was dealt another heavy blow. By now he felt like a punching bag.

He got profiled on nationwide TV while he had been in Chicago for the price-fixing case as "troubled former FBI informant, Mark Whitacre."

Only one word in that profile filtered back to the inmates at Butner Low. *Informant.* Informant equals Snitch. Snitch equals Bad. Snitch equals Dead, as in shanked real fast. The only con in the general population who gets shanked faster than a Snitch is a Diaper Sniper (see *Glossary of Prison Slang* under child molester).

Until the media attention in Chicago, none of Mark's fellow inmates knew he had worked undercover for the FBI. They thought he'd been a businessman on the outside who got caught with his hand in the cookie jar. Now his cover was blown.

No sooner did he get back to Butner from his horrific Chicago ordeal than the warden ordered him into protective custody (solitary confinement). The risk that he would get shanked was too high. While cooling his heels in the hole, Mark got word that the warden was conferring with his higher-ups in Atlanta about where to designate The Informant.

It didn't take more than a day for the order to come down to ship him out as soon as possible and diesel him until they could relocate him somewhere where the other inmates were not likely to have heard about his case. Mark found out before he got shipped out. It would be Yazoo Low in Yazoo City, Mississippi, birthplace of writer-editor Willie Morris and Mississippi Governor Haley Barbour.

Going to Yazoo was not a good development. All inmates at almost all federal facilities can get the word—good, bad, or ugly—on any other facility through the efficient grapevine that develops inside prison.

The word on Yazoo was it was a nasty place. Mark knew life there would be much harsher than it had been at Butner. Ginger tried to undo it. She made a flurry of calls to see if she could get him sent somewhere else, but the decision in Atlanta had been cast in stone, so within twenty-four hours of his return to Butner, Mark was packing out for Yazoo. He was not aware at the time that there would be four months of diesel therapy in between.

By car, the trip from Butner, North Carolina, to Yazoo City, Mississippi, takes less than thirteen hours. For Mark, the transit took four months.

Diesel therapy is the cruelest aspect of being a federal inmate. Diesel therapy is a nightmare involving shackles, deprivation, and weeks or months of getting bused and flown through a zigzag maze of interim moves and holdover jails. Diesel therapy has no directional logic. It is pure punishment, and the guards make sure you get demeaned at every step in the process.

On Day One of his diesel therapy, Mark packed out at Butner and awaited further instructions. On Day Two, he got called out at 3 AM to be taken to R&D where he got strip searched, processed, and placed in a holding cell with other prisoners who would be boarding the same bus, themselves headed for destinations unknown. He got handed a baloney sandwich and carton of milk for lunch, then continued to wither in the crowded holding tank until 3 PM. With no explanation, at 3 PM the assistant warden sent the inmates back to the Butner Low protective custody area. So far he had gone nowhere. He overheard one inmate say that the bus crew never showed up due to a flat tire. Back at his hole in protective custody, he spent the night on a cold steel bed with no sheets or blankets. He was given no towel, toothbrush, or any of his personal property because all of that had been boxed up and taken away the day before, presumably forwarded by parcel post to Yazoo.

On Day Three the process started all over again. He got posted up at 3 AM, strip searched, processed, and placed in the bullpen. This time, at 11 AM, an old white noisy diesel bus showed up. Hence the name diesel therapy. Neither Mark nor the other men being dieseled got food because it was too late for breakfast and too early for lunch when they boarded the bus—in ankle bracelets.

At least a third of the inmates loaded on the bus had the black-box handcuff covers and belly chains. This combination restraint system is used to ensure officer safety when transporting dangerous criminals. Every black box is made of high-strength, high-impact plastic with a security clip and a dead lock, designed to protect the keyhole. This eliminates any possibility that an inmate will pick or tamper with any part of the lock. The box has an adjustable feature that allows the officer to restrict the movement of the prisoners' hands to any degree he deems necessary, loose or tight.

Mark got shackled into a lumpy bus seat, and, once everyone else from the bullpen got loaded and shackled in too, off they went. Exhausted, he was lulled to sleep by the motion. He dozed for what seemed like three minutes but could have been three hours. When he awoke and looked out the window, he noticed that, instead of heading west on I-40 to get to I-59 where you would normally turn southwest in the general direction of Mississippi, the bus was heading north on I-77, toward Cleveland, Ohio. He had no clue what was going on. That night, Mark vaguely recalls that they might have been held over at FCI Gilmer in West Virginia. He didn't know and he didn't care. All he remembers is that he was going in the opposite direction from his ultimate destination, Yazoo Low.

The next day, Day Four, the process started all over again: up at 3 AM, strip searched, and held in the bullpen to be loaded onto a different bus. As far as Mark could tell, only one face had changed. The other twenty-two were the same forlorn faces of the men who had shuffled off the bus with him the night before.

———————————

After repeating this process many times in many holdovers at a blur of other facilities, Mark weeks later looked out the window and saw that the bus was finally headed in a southerly direction. But it wasn't I-55 toward Yazoo City; it was I-75 toward Atlanta. He didn't care any longer. He just wanted one night of real sleep. Exhausted and sick after several weeks of diesel therapy involving already well over a thousand miles, he prayed, *Dear Father, is there no rest for the weary?*

Finally, the bus pulled up in the middle of the night to a combination penitentiary and transfer facility complex in Atlanta known as the Atlanta Federal Transfer Facility, known by inmates as the Atlanta Holdover. The place was huge. He and a gaggle of fellow prisoners got herded off the bus like cattle. Mark estimated this was the nineteenth time he had been loaded off and on one of the system's buses. The gaggle was once again thrown into a processing bullpen. This time they were held there for three days with no explanation. Eventually the hacks at the Atlanta Holdover issued Mark a clean orange jumpsuit. They also stood him in line to go off somewhere into the bowels of Atlanta Holdover. This was different from the holdover procedures he had gotten used to since he left Butner Low. *What does this mean, a longer stay in Atlanta? When am I ever going to get to Yazoo?*

———————————

Mark spent three full months as a holdover inmate at the Atlanta Federal Transfer Facility. He had gotten a brief taste of the Atlanta holdover back in March of 1998 while en route from Springfield Medical to Butner Low, but that had lasted only a few days.

The Atlanta holdover facility is such a mammoth movement of human cattle that it took many hours before they had Mark processed through intake. When he got to his cell, it was so crowded he had to—yet again—sleep on the cement floor. The cell intended for two inmates was now holding three.

Since Mark was the newcomer, his mattress was next to the soldered-down stainless steel toilet. He lay down and watched an army of cockroaches go by before finally falling asleep. Sometime in the middle of the night, one of his cellies had to go potty. Mark had nowhere to move to, so all he could do was turn his head the other way, cover himself with a sheet, and hold his nose. Both of his cellies were somewhere in the middle of twenty- and thirty-year sentences, respectively. Mark had little information other than that. He didn't want any; the three of them seldom spoke.

Since he was officially only in holdover in Atlanta, no visitors were permitted. This interrupted any comforting appearances from Ginger and the kids. Telephone calls were permitted, but only twice a week. During those, Ginger could readily detect from Mark's voice that the only two things holding her husband together were the voices of the family on the phone, and that of the Good Lord above in his head and heart.

As inhumane as Atlanta Holdover sounds, it is commonplace throughout this nation's vast prison network. Lockdown lasts twenty-three out of twenty-four hours per day. Showers are allowed only three times a week and then only under a row of scalding shower nozzles in the open where guards, including female guards, watch "for security measures."

On the cock-roach infested concrete floor of his cramped cell, Mark slept on a razor-thin mattress and used a thin, threadbare towel as his pillow. At first, he spent the one free hour per day getting some fresh air and exercise, walking around the facility's big outdoor "dog cage," walking lap after lap. However, with fifty men out there at a time, most of whom stood around smoking and strutting, trouble was but one wrong glance away.

For Mark, that one hour of fresh air and so-called freedom was so fraught with potential pitfalls that he soon chose not to go out at all. Instead, he holed up in his cramped, smelly, over-crowded cell for days and weeks on end. Time of day became a big blur, and he was unable to sustain any quotidian pattern. He approximated time of day by when a nasty tray of food arrived. Otherwise, he used the time in the Atlanta Holdover as best he could by reading an old rag-tag Bible that he had retrieved from the library cart. He read it from cover to cover, from Genesis to Revelations and back again.

Ginger helped him through his extended Atlanta Holdover stay by phone. She painted for him an image of the good-bad difference. *Mark, the good things are the non-visible things, the images in your mind of the family that loves you and the concepts of faith found in your ragtag Bible. The bad are the visible things, the physical environment in front of your eyes and the bad-intentioned inmates around you.*

Mark clung to Ginger's image prompts with all his might. He made no friends. He spoke hardly at all. And he remembers little about his cellies other than that their sentences were so long and their unwashed bodies were malodorous.

Three months later, sometime in the middle of the night a prison guard rapped on his cell and said loudly, "Which one of you is Whitacre?" Mark raised his hand from the concrete floor. "Get up and pack out! You're leavin' this place, mister!"

Mark stood up and departed silently. His cellies didn't stir; there were no goodbyes.

At Discharge Processing, Mark was handed khaki pants and a white t-shirt. Then he was shackled and taken outside to a waiting bus, full of other inmates. He was shocked by how cold the weather had gotten. The seasons had changed. He had been in his Atlanta cell for so long that it went from sweltering summer weather to a chilly autumn cold. It was late November of 1998. The bus transported them to Robins Air Force Base to be put on a prisoner aircraft—a "Conair" plane.

Ginger got scant information from the Bureau as to where her husband was at any point in the long diesel therapy transit from Butner Low to Yazoo. She always had to wait for Mark's calls. On this round, he was put on a prison airplane but not told where he was going. Mark was not cuffed this time and got assigned to pass out meal bags on the flight. He noticed how many of his fellow passengers had their cuffed hands in black boxes again.

Mark had gone from a six-year stint as the head of a large division of a Fortune 100 company to a three-year stint as the CEO of a Research Triangle biotechnology company to this, the early stages of a nine-year stint sitting beside men deemed so dangerous they had to have their hands cuffed and black-boxed, with marshals holding shotguns aimed at them at all times.

This for tax fraud and money laundering? he thought, more than a little bewildered.

He eventually found out he was being flown to the Oklahoma Federal Transfer Facility, Oklahoma Transfer. It was a straight air shot to Oklahoma Transfer. The plane landed and taxied over to a tunnel. As he hobbled down off the plane in leg irons like all the other inmates, he realized he was part of an ant colony, part of a massive operation of moving human cargo. Aircraft were landing and taking off about every fifteen minutes, and throngs of inmates, all in leg irons and belly chains, were being shuffled into or out of a concourse inside an enormous brightly lit tunnel. Such activity goes on every night of the year at the Oklahoma facility and goes unseen and unheard-about by the average citizen on the outside.

———————

Inside, he was surprised to see that Oklahoma Transfer was cleaner, newer, and more comfortable—relatively speaking—than Atlanta Holdover. Oklahoma permitted freedom of movement inside the compound from 6 AM to 10 PM. Showers were abundant and not rationed, and the water was temperate and adjustable. The outdoor area, while still fenced in with concertina wire and overhead fencing, was available for inmate use all day. Best of all, Mark was permitted unlimited calls, albeit only collect. Throwing cost and caution to the wind, Mark spent hours and hours on the telephone with Ginger.

After several weeks at Oklahoma Transfer, Mark suddenly found himself on a bus headed due south for Yazoo City, Mississippi, home of Yazoo Low. He arrived at Yazoo Low in mid-November of 1998. *If Yazoo is going to be my home for a while, this place is heaven compared to Atlanta Holdover.*

Once he settled into his daily routine at Yazoo, Mark enjoyed visits from Ginger every other weekend. His job assignment at Yazoo was in education. Mornings he taught other inmates English as a Second Language (ESL). Afternoons, he taught preparation for the General Education Development (GED) tests, which are a group of five rigorous subject tests that, when passed, certify that the taker has high-school level academic skills. The GED can only be taken by individuals who never received a high-school diploma. More than fifteen million people have received their GED credential since the program began—some of them taught by prison professor Mark Edward Whitacre. Evenings he taught corporate law.

Mark, who can't really hold a tune, joined the Yazoo chapel choir. Out of several dozen very good singers, Mark was the only Caucasian. He sang off-key and loved every minute of it.

Whitacre Family at Yazoo Low between Thanksgiving & Christmas (December 1998)

Within two weeks of his arrival at Yazoo, Thanksgiving came. Ginger and the children made the trip from Chapel Hill by first driving to the

Winston-Salem Airport, then flying to Atlanta, changing planes, and connecting to Jackson, Mississippi. In Jackson, Ginger rented a car and drove the family one hour north on I-55 to Yazoo City. It was tough on the kids and a marathon session for Ginger. They returned to Chapel Hill after a wonderful Thanksgiving visit with Mark, but Christmas came a few weeks later, so they repeated the same grueling trip for Christmas.

So for Thanksgiving and Christmas of 1998, Ginger and the children had to hole up in a cookie-cutter motel in the small town of Yazoo City in central Mississippi. Ginger kept everybody in line. If the kids started doing what kids do, like complaining about the quality of their accommodations or the holiday itself, Ginger reminded them that, unlike many families, particularly those in the military, at least the Whitacre Family was together, and they should give thanks for that.

The Yazoo hacks actually went out of their way to decorate the prison visitors' center nicely. In a testament to their eternal optimism, alluded to by Paul A. Willis in the Foreword, Mark and Ginger tell me that their Thanksgiving and Christmas at Yazoo were wonderful times together for the family.

In general, Mark and Ginger recall their eight Christmas celebrations in prison with as much kindness as possible. The kids have a bit of a different recollection. Christmas can be emotional under the best of circumstances; it can bring out the inner child in all of us. Alex recalls those Christmases as sad times with a lot of waiting around. The family had to arrive even earlier than normal and wait an extra two hours in the car queue. The visitors' centers never opened before 8:30 am. This meant Ginger woke the kids at 3 am in order to leave by 4:30 am and get there by 5 am. Any later and they would not be at the head of the car waiting line.

They did this for eight Christmases in three different states at three different prisons. Prison visitors' centers can get decked out with boughs of holly only so far. Typically, there would be a small plastic Christmas tree in a corner, then the same old nothing-to-do. They still were limited to playing cards, eating lousy vending-machine food, and shouting over the din to be heard. Christmas in prison visitors' centers consisted of wall-to-wall people in a cramped space.

The kids would look at their father and want to cry and hug him as hard as they could. However, hugging and other displays of affection are frowned upon by the BOP. For eight long Christmases, Ginger maintained a wonderfully positive attitude. She was remarkable like that, not the norm because the statistics regarding the breakdown of families caused by incarceration are horrendous. Most wives leave their husbands by the third year, often much sooner if they find a reliable "Jody" (see Glossary of Prison Slang).

For Ginger, it wasn't in the realm of the possible. The longer she was separated from Mark, the stronger the bond. She was determined that the Whitacre Family, would beat the system; it would not beat them.

———————

Young Alex always did what his mother told him to do before going in: put on a happy face for his father. But it took its toll: back home or back in the motel room, he would close his door, lie on his bed, and cry for hours. The pain of separation at such a young age was unbearable for Alex. He prayed deep into the lonely night. *Dear God, please protect my father in prison and bring him home safely to me as soon as possible. Help me to become wise and learn from my own father just as King Solomon learned from his father David.* (1 Kings 2:1-9 and 1 Chronicles 28-29).

> "DEAR GOD, PLEASE PROTECT MY FATHER IN PRISON AND BRING HIM HOME SAFELY TO ME AS SOON AS POSSIBLE, AND HELP ME TO BECOME WISE AND LEARN FROM MY FATHER JUST AS KING SOLOMON LEARNED FROM HIS FATHER DAVID."
>
> 1 Kings 2:1-9
> 1 Chronicles 28-29

In January of 1999, shortly after Ginger and the children spent their first Christmas with Mark in the Yazoo visitors' center, and thinking Yazoo would be her husband's prison home for some time, she began making plans to move the family to Jackson, Mississippi, one hour south of Yazoo City on Highway 49. But she got a call from an elated Mark.

"Honey, it looks like we caught a lucky break."

"That doesn't happen often when comes to the Bureau of Prisons," said Ginger, who then asked with heightened curiosity, "What could it be?"

"The BOP just changed its 'time-remaining' requirement for eligibility to go from a low to a minimum from 84 months to 120 months. I'm at a little over a hundred."

Suddenly Mark had become eligible to transfer out of Yazoo and down from a low to a minimum. Under the old rules, he would not have been camp-eligible for another two years.

He quickly made an appointment with his unit team counselors at Yazoo. They were sympathetic and told him he could select any minimum in the system—subject to space availability and clearance with the designation bureaucrats in the Atlanta Regional Office.

Ginger did her research online while Mark used the scuttlebutt approach of letting other inmates tell him which minimums throughout the system were the best. He and Ginger discussed their range of options and narrowed their choice to either Eglin Air Force Base in the Florida Panhandle or a new camp that had just opened in Edgefield, South Carolina. Since Ginger's sister and her family lived in Greenville, South Carolina, they chose Edgefield Camp, which was just up the road from Aiken, South Carolina. Greenville and her sister were only three hours north of Edgefield. The extended Whitacre and Gilbert families were painfully aware of the importance of proximity to aunts and uncles for the kids, given the rupture in Mark and Ginger's nuclear family. The move to Edgefield Camp afforded them exactly that.

PART THREE—THE PRISON YEARS

CHAPTER THIRTEEN

EDGEFIELD CAMP

"The wise man does not expose himself needlessly to danger; but he is willing, in great crises, to give even his life—knowing that under certain conditions life is not as honorable as death."

Aristotle

Ginger Whitacre went house-hunting in Aiken, South Carolina, excited that Mark would finally be settling into his own long-term home—and some sort of prisoner's routine—just twenty miles up the road at the Federal Prison Camp in Edgefield, South Carolina. Although Aiken is the second largest metropolitan statistical area in the state, in 1999 there were still fewer than five hundred thousand people in the four-county area.

This meant lower human density than she had in either Decatur or Chapel Hill. After so many years in the limelight, Ginger was looking forward to being tucked away in a quiet setting and leading a life of relative calm and anonymity. She found a good school for young Alex and moved into a house with several acres of abundant woods. The Aiken home afforded the Whitacres, without father, a degree of privacy they had not had in years.

The calm verdant setting also afforded Ginger some long overdue time to reflect and pray in peace. Her husband was finally in a new, stable minimum-security facility very close to her. Alex, their youngest, took well to his new school. With their two eldest grown and gone, Ginger's thoughts turned to full-time school teaching. She had been a teacher's assistant in Chapel Hill in North Carolina for several semesters and enjoyed it. Every one of her academic credentials transferred from Ohio State even though they dated back some twenty years earlier, so she needed just one more year of course work to get her bachelor's in education. She accomplished that while still in Chapel Hill, shortly after Mark had been remanded to prison in Urbana. By the time she moved the family to Aiken, while her husband had been bouncing around the federal prison system, she was fully certified to teach. She started teaching kindergarten at Saluda Elementary School in Saluda, South Carolina. She loved teaching then, and she loves it now, in 2009.

———

Once he and Ginger made the decision to put in for a transfer, Mark quickly completed the necessary paperwork. He got designated to the Edgefield Camp in January of 1999, but, like I said, prison time is slow time, so he would not depart for Edgefield for another two more months. When, in March of 1999, his Yazoo case manager said the coast was clear and the Yazoo hacks finally ordered him to pack out, he found out that, since he was being re-designated from a low to a minimum and had no shots in his jacket, he could furlough transfer from Mississippi to South Carolina. His Yazoo case manager gave him a bus ticket and eighteen hours to get from Yazoo Low to Edgefield Minimum. He was thrilled.

———

The Edgefield Camp, is a mere twenty six miles north of one of the most exclusive golf clubs in the world, the Augusta National Golf Club, host to the U.S. Masters golf tournament each April since 1933. The proximity of "Club Fed" to "Club Augusta" has a certain irony to it. Both are exclusive. Both are members-only. I am sure that neither is even aware of the other's existence.

Meanwhile, the bus terminal in downtown Augusta, Georgia, was Mark's drop-off. His transfer furlough had taken most of the allotted eighteen hours. If you were to travel by car from Yazoo, Mississippi, to Edgefield, South Carolina, you would need no more than nine hours. Mark was happy he got double that to go by Greyhound. As he sat back and cruised easterly along I-20, he was euphoric: The bus made restaurant stops, meaning real—non-prison—food, and he wore civvies, so he blended in, just like "normal" folk.

Shortly after Mark's arrival at the Greyhound bus terminal in Augusta, a prison van—driven by an inmate—pulled up. Something gave Mark a sense of new beginnings. Certainly, he would be living in better conditions. Going from a low to a minimum is hugely positive when you are incarcerated. Minimum-security camps are far less harsh than low-security correctional institutes and have many amenities absent from even the best lows. Furthermore, as minimums go, Edgefield was better than most, not least because it was newly built and only twenty percent filled to capacity—one hundred inmates on the count versus a capacity for five hundred inmates. Mark welcomed this respite from the norm. The norm is, sadly, over-crowded prisons.

Mark spent the next four years and two months at the Federal Prison Camp in Edgefield, South Carolina. His first job detail at Edgefield, starting in March of 1999, was in landscaping. He worked the grounds of the prison compound and was allowed to drive a John Deere Gator™ utility vehicle. On the inside, piloting such a machine is considered, at least by those who enjoy the privilege, to be a status symbol.

After two years in landscaping, Mark was allowed to work off the compound, so he spent the next year and a half on loan to Habitat for Humanity, building houses for the needy.

Becoming a carpenter-builder was a learning experience for a man who had the soft hands of a manager. Mark's Habitat work detail taught him how to hammer a nail, mix concrete, install electrical wiring, and even use an electric saw without cutting off his thumb. It was especially gratifying to stand before the finished Habitat house and watch a young single mother with her three children move into that house.

Mark also got serious about his personal fitness at the Edgefield Camp. He began a regular routine of calisthenics and running. He had never done much, if any, running before. Beginning in May of that year, at age forty-two, he shed pounds, getting down to 188 lbs, and toned up his body. The running track was a new blacktop-paved quarter-mile track. The smooth surface made it great for push-ups; in the hot summer heat, he had to wear gloves to do those pushups because the blacktop was so intense. Edgefield had a great cardio-room.

There were several benefits to working off the compound for Habitat. Chief among these for Mark was a sense of purpose. Mark was helping others by building new homes for qualified recipients under the Habitat for Humanity program. Another was being able to order take-out lunches from a different restaurant every day. And a third involved small perks such as taking a ride in the van with a community volunteer to go to the local hardware store for parts.

Because Edgefield was new and dramatically under-populated at the beginning, Mark enjoyed relatively loose regulation enforcement. He still had to make the 4 PM count. You do not miss the 4 PM count in prison. Overall, however, Edgefield offered a lower-stress environment than any institution he had been at since the beginning of his incarceration. The chow-hall food was not, however, particularly good even by modest prison standards. This forced inmates to get creative back in the units. They purchased food items at the commissary based upon recipe needs and made heavy use of the microwave ovens provided in the living units. Mark's favorite concoction at Edgefield was Prison Nachos. Prison Nachos, if properly branded and marketed on the outside, would sell like hotcakes. They are made using a few bags of chips, cheese-in-a-jar purchased at commissary, and inmate ingenuity.

MR. T. WHITE

Even the best-equipped prison is not a happy place. It's still prison. A poignant reminder of that is Mark's recollection of one Mr. T. White.

Mark ran out on the blacktop track every day, sometimes in the morning, sometimes later in the day. No matter what the hour, he ran into an elderly, quiet, stooped-over inmate, who was either shuffling slowly toward the picnic bench that abutted the track or already sitting on it. In total silence, the old man smoked one cigarette after another. A hollow expression seemed permanently etched in his face. Mark does not recall ever seeing the man speak to another person on the compound.

From his prison nametag, Mark noticed the name "T. White."

Mr. T. White waved meekly to Mark every day, and Mark returned the gesture. The two traded those gestures for many months. In prison, you learn to respect another inmate's privacy, so they never spoke. Not once.

Mark's best guess was that Mr. T. White had been down for so many years, with so many more to go, that any zest for life had been squeezed out of him. Mark ran into several long-timers at Edgefield who had been all over the system and had run into Mr. T. White at this facility or that. They knew Mr. T. White's story and confirmed that he had another decade to go.

The blank, lifeless expression on Mr. T. White's face matches that of many other inmates with numbingly long sentences. No one at Edgefield had ever seen Mr. T. White get a visit: his family on the outside, whatever was left of it, had long since left him behind. He was a forgotten man.

That lifeless expression on Mr. T. White's face remains a haunting image. Thousands like him, after decades of incarceration, have no family, no money, and many years of incarceration remaining. For such inmates, every day brings the same thing: Nothing to look forward to but more time.

Mr. T. White received no visitors. He had no calls to make, no letters to write, and no mail to receive. He was alone; he was incarcerated; he was warehoused. The sadness in his face reflects the sadness in his heart and goes beyond anything mere words can express. When a prison sentence is twenty, thirty, or forty years, where is there room for "rehabilitation?" Its sheer length engenders only hopelessness.

Most Americans cannot bear the thought of the pain of such prisoners as Mr. T. White. Our country has been on an imprisonment binge for decades, one so massive it defies comprehension. Supreme Court Justice Anthony Kennedy, a Reagan appointee, addressed the seriousness of the issue in the *ABA Justice Kennedy Commission* report.

Justice Kennedy and the members of his commission, including former Pardon Attorney Margaret Colgate Love, courageously challenged the American Bar Association to question, not merely the wisdom of mandatory minimum sentences, but the entire purpose of incarceration and the legal profession's lack of understanding of our nation's prison problem.

Justice Kennedy expressed concerns about:

- the sheer number of people locked up in the United States as compared to other civilized nations;
- the disproportionate impact of incarceration on minorities;
- the costs and length of incarceration;
- the federal sentencing guidelines and mandatory minimum sentences;
- the importance of judicial discretion in sentencing;
- the atrophy of the pardon power; and
- the dehumanizing experience of prison and the importance of rehabilitation as a punishment goal.

The bottom line, Justice Kennedy concluded, is that "our resources are misspent, our punishments too severe, our sentences too long."

Mark may appear to be less interested in talking about the broad malfunctioning of our prison system than he was during his incarceration phase, but that is because, like anyone who has been incarcerated and gets out, he has had a lot of catching up to do. Even though it's been nearly three years since his release, Mark has too much on his plate just putting humpty-dumpy back together again, trying to get his own life back in order.

Once the Edgefield Camp adopted the Residential Drug Abuse Program, inmates with longer criminal histories entered the program and made their way to Edgefield. For this reason, Mark came into contact with many more inmates who had long sentences than he had at any prior period of his incarceration phase. Since most of his time was spent interacting with these men—eating, working out, working on a job assignment, and sitting in his dorm cube—they often talked about the injustice of their cases or the tragic family problems that their incarceration created. Rarely, if ever, did the conversation turn to dreams for the future.

Why? Because, for most of them, that future was too distant to have any real meaning. Not only had too much of their lives already been consumed by prison; too much was still to go. Mark understood their unspeakable longing for family and friends because he had that same longing. Yet he was one of the fortunate few. He had a wife and children who lined up at six in the morning in front of the prison to see him on every single day that visitations were permitted. Most inmates, especially those with sentences as long as Mr. T. White's, aren't so lucky. Most end up in the dustbin of anonymity, out of sight, out of mind.

The Edgefield Camp's pristine status as a minimum went out the window once Edgefield became an RDAP facility. Inmates refer to this program as either "the drug program" or the "DAP program." Inmates accepted into this program have a proven track record of success: it helps keep ex-offenders off drugs and alcohol once they get out. Numerous facilities throughout the federal prison system have adopted the program. Edgefield became one of those facilities during Mark's third year there.

However, the DAP program also brings with it closer monitoring, overcrowding, and an overall deterioration of quality of life. For example, a different set of rules applies to program participants. This includes frequent on-the-spot breathalyzer and urinalysis testing. An inmate not in the DAP program could be out on the jogging track, and a hack will pull up on him and force him to take a breathalyzer test. Because the hacks aren't sure who is in the program and who isn't, they increase supervision and such random testing across all inmates.

Thus, the environment at Edgefield declined rapidly. Ginger and Mark believed that, after more than four years in one place and with the introduction of the drug program to Edgefield, a move to another facility would be appropriate and timely.

There was one catch: it is extremely difficult at the unit team level within a camp to obtain a transfer for what appears to these administrators as no reason. Given that, Mark's transfer had to occur at a higher level. Ginger hired a post-conviction and criminal defense lawyer out of Washington D.C., who reached out to high-level contacts within the prison bureau in both Washington and Atlanta.

Atlanta is the regional office that oversees any designations to the Pensacola Camp, which is the one Mark and Ginger selected as their top choice. They did so for several reasons. First, it was widely considered to be the best minimum camp in the entire BOP system. Second, Mark had already been in conversations for over two years with Paul A. Willis, Chairman of Cypress Systems. Willis committed to hiring Mark upon his release from prison. Cypress is based in Fresno, California, so having a second office in Florida would be wise. Florida has lower payroll taxes than California, no state income tax, and a lower wage base for hourly employees.

Third, more than four years in any one prison facility is too long. Their youngest son, Alex, was also eager to move because he was not fond of Aiken or its school system. He saw better educational opportunities in Florida.

Fourth, the proximity to Ginger's sister in Greenville was not as easy as originally thought. A three-hour drive each way makes it too long to go down and come back on the same day. Ginger's sister and her family could just as easily fly to Pensacola as drive from Greenville to Edgefield, South Carolina.

The Edgefield Administrator supported the transfer when contacted, so for Mark and Ginger it was "Pensacola, Here We Come!"

PART THREE—THE PRISON YEARS
CHAPTER FOURTEEN

PENSACOLA CAMP

**"A man who has committed a mistake and
doesn't correct it is committing another mistake."**

CONFUCIUS

On Mark's forty-sixth birthday, May 1st of 2003, he set out for new horizons, commencing now his second travel furlough since he had been down. This one would take him from the Edgefield Camp to the Pensacola Camp. Mark relished yet another opportunity to pass through the outside world in civilian clothing and feel normal, however briefly.

The Pensacola Camp of the late 1990s and early 2000s had the best of everything: the best food, best learning center, best chapel, nicest "hacks" (prison guards), and best visitors' center. One of his sweetest memories of his first day at Pensacola was going through chow line and seeing chocolate milk. He hadn't had chocolate milk in over four years, and suddenly there was all he could drink.

Both inmates currently at the Pensacola Camp and taxpayers alike may scream at such revelations. Inmates worry that they could lose those chocolate-milk privileges if taxpayers read this and complain to their Congressman about "coddling convicted felons." However, a primary goal of Minimum Camps is rehabilitation, not punishment. Camps are intended to reacquaint inmates who may have been down a very long time with life as it will somewhat resemble once they get out. As such, the harsh physical environment that characterizes many Mediums and Lows in the federal system is replaced with a more open environment and one that offers many more educational and self-improvement opportunities. You seldom meet at a camp an inmate who has worked his way down from a Max or a Super Max. That's because there is one absolute condition to being allowed the privilege of doing some of your time at a camp: you had to be totally clean of any weapons charges. For so many inmates in Maxes and Super-Maxes, weapons were an integral part of their criminal activity before they were incarcerated, so they will never, ever see the light of day at a minimum camp.

Another point is that minimum camps like Pensacola may look pleasant enough, but the unseen reality is that prison is still prison, and the 4 PM count is still the 4 PM count. Furthermore, the Pensacola Camp has since become an RDAP facility, so many of the amenities described here have already been removed.

With those qualifiers now stated, it is true that in 2003-2004—the "good old days" to nostalgic ex-offenders who are now comfortably readjusted to the outside world—Pensacola was more like a college campus than a prison. With no walls and a low guard-to-inmate ratio, we enjoyed an aerobics center with state-of-the-art equipment; a well-appointed outdoor covered breezeway "weight pile" (weight-lifting area); a separate brick building that housed an outstanding art studio, with easels and capacious lockers for one's art supplies; a superb carpentry/arts-and-crafts building with every woodworking and leather-crafts tool imaginable.

Further down toward the ball fields and the jogging track was a music building, which had complete drum sets, many guitars both electrical and acoustical, a baby grand piano, amps, and just about any other musical instrument you can think of. Just beyond the music building were several well-manicured soccer and softball fields, with a half-mile outdoor jogging track on the perimeter and outdoor basketball courts. Just across the short access road from the music building was an excellent library with a separate large law library. Across the way were study cubicles, a yoga room, and an upstairs recreational area where you could catch the evening news, enjoy a few rounds of bridge, or play some noisy table tennis. A half mile or so in the other direction was a regulation-size indoor basketball court where the famous boxer Roy Williams, a Pensacola native, came weekly to play competitive full-court basketball games with playoffs and rankings. There were some good athletes at the Pensacola Camp, and they put Roy through his paces, helping the famous boxer build his aerobic capacity for his next championship match. The big-screen movie theater at Pensacola was arguably as good as the one in town.

The Pensacola Camp was paradise compared to almost any other facility within the vast Bureau of Prisons system. According to Mark, nothing else came close, not even Edgefield when it was brand new.

Mark's initial surprise that Pensacola served chocolate milk was completely trumped by the high quality and broad selection of the food in general at Pensacola. The salad bar had six different types of salad and a selection of eight different dressings. What is interesting is that, on a per-inmate basis, the food budget for every Minimum Camp throughout the system was the same—$2.72 per inmate per day as of January of 2004. That begs the question, how is it that Pensacola had such good fare while Edgefield's food was so disgusting that inmates there preferred to make their own Prison Nachos than eat the food in the Edgefield chow hall?

The answer seems to lie in the experience, care, and shrewdness of the food supervisor at Pensacola. All food supervisors throughout the system are given some freedom to make special purchases both on the internet and with local vendors. Shrewd bidding and a heads' up and caring attitude on the part of the supervisor can make all the difference in the quality of a Minimum Camp's fare.

Then there is the food supervisor's ability to control inventory shrinkage. When it comes to food, the generally pervasive sentiment among guards and civilian supervisors is that inmates will lie, cheat, or steal to get food back to their cube. Based on the number of onions, green peppers, and tomatoes uncovered during the periodic unannounced camp shakedowns, there may be some truth to that sentiment. If a food supervisor was trusting—or dumb—enough to leave a walk-in refrigerator inside the chilled salad prep room unlocked, even accidentally, he would have a run on onions, tomatoes, and green peppers. Hungry inmates can move like stealth ninja operators when word gets out that a refrigerator is unlocked. They rob that refrigerator blind until either one of two things happens: the onions, peppers, and tomatoes are gone, or the supervisor wises up and locks it.

Back in the living units, one onion fetched one dollar; ditto for tomatoes, a buck a tomato, and something like yellow bell peppers might even bring in a buck-fifty. For this reason, only inmates deemed honest and trustworthy by the food supervisor obtained kitchen duty, particularly salad prep duty. An inmate's commissary account balance might get checked: if the inmate had a high-enough balance in his commissary account, he might be deemed well-enough off not to need to supplement his income by selling smuggled onions, peppers, and tomatoes for cash or commissary credits. Some inmates made it into the kitchen because they had been chefs on the outside.

The only way, however, to keep the traffic in the produce refrigerator down to a loud roar was to keep it locked. This forced the salad-prep crew to come get the supervisor every time one of them needed to slice onions, peppers, or tomatoes for an upcoming meal. Then while the food supervisor was back unlocking the produce refrigerator door, other inmates going through the chow line would start stuffing chicken breasts down their shirts.

After years of being scammed like this by inmates, most supervisors at most Minimums stopped caring how well the inmates ate. They grew callous, and their mindset often morphed into one of, "Let them eat garbage. After all, they're only inmates."

Mr. D., the food supervisor at the Pensacola camp, was a notable exception. He had substantial experience and training in food service, including a degree in hotel and food management from the prestigious hotel & food management college, Johnson & Wales, in Rhode Island. He also had significant institutional experience before he joined the BOP. He had also been an athlete, so he understood better than most the need for a healthy balanced diet. He also took pride in the quality of the product his chow hall turned out. If he knew a regional warden or other prison official was coming to Pensacola, you could be sure the inmates would get steak and potatoes that night. Mr. D. delivered a lot of bang for the buck—or better said, a lot of great food for two bucks, seventy two cents per inmate per day.

GINGER'S VISITS TO THE PENSACOLA CAMP

Ginger never missed a visiting day during Mark's entire four years at the Pensacola Camp, and Alex only Fridays, because Friday evening visits were Mark and Ginger's private "night out." Friday visits were from 5 PM to 8 PM. Every Saturday and Sunday morning, without fail, by 6:30AM, Ginger and Alex would already be in the car line at the front entrance to the Saufley Naval Air Station that houses the Pensacola Camp. The visiting room didn't open until 8:30 AM.

The reason Ginger was always first in line is that she herself woke up at 3:30 AM and roused Alex by 4:30 AM, some mornings with difficulty, so they could be out of the house and on the road before six to be at the front gate no later than 6:30 AM. The weekend drill was always the same. Up real early, out the door fast, and get in line in her Ford until the gate guard got the all-clear to let the visiting families through. Had Ginger got to the entrance at, say, 7:30 AM, still a full hour before opening time, she could be so far back in the queue that it could delay her processing through the checkpoint by as much as an hour and a half. That was unacceptable because it would have meant an hour and a half less time with Mark.

That's how it was at the Pensacola Camp. Each camp is slightly different. Broadly speaking, however, the BOP has a visitation policy that each inmate and each family of each inmate must follow. First, the inmate had to get you on his inmate's approved-visitor list. If you had any sort of prior record yourself, you were probably disqualified. The BOP has a standing policy of not permitting ex-offenders to visit current offenders.

After you got notification in the mail that you made it onto the inmate's approved visitor's list, you had to show up with specific ID, and you had to wear appropriate clothing. Many an uninformed scantily-clad woman has been turned away by the hacks clearing visitors to enter the visiting area. She either went back to her car and put on more appropriate clothing, or she would not be seeing her inmate that day.

Female visitors who came more than once quickly learned to bring a clear plastic, see-through purse only. Otherwise, the hacks made you take the purse back to your car and not bring it in, which would cause you to lose your place in line, which could create a long delay. Once you get inside the door to the visitors center, you had to sign in and undergo a discreet and respectful pat-down. Ginger had all of this down cold. She became so familiar to the hacks at Pensacola that they often just took a quick glance at her purse, got her to sign in, and waved her through.

Nonetheless, only after these formalities were completed would the visiting room guard page Mark over the loudspeaker system: "Whitacre! Mark Whitacre! You have a visitor!" Some of the hacks were crueler than others and could mumble a name over the loudspeaker. If the inmate wasn't attentive, he could miss hearing his name get called out.

Mark's was the most called-out name in the history of life in prison, at least when I was there with him. And he was always ready. He'd be waiting in the required garb for receiving visitors—clean white t-shirt and green prison-issue pants—and briskly walk over past the chapel into the inmate-only side entrance as soon as his name was called out. The inmate side entrance had a small ante-room where usually two hacks but sometimes one made Mark sign in, leave his prison ID card, and get a superficial pat-down before entering the larger visitors' center where Ginger and Alex would be waiting.

Ginger and Alex visited Mark with such consistency every single weekend over so many years that the hacks on duty in the visitors' center got to know them and develop so much trust in Mark that they would often—not always, but with increasing frequency as the weeks and months went by—simply wave Mark through without so much as patting him down. If Mark had wanted to, if he hadn't been such a model inmate, he could have smuggled in or out all manner of contraband.

The Bureau had its list of "usual suspects" contraband, but contraband could also be anything the warden said it was. Each warden also had discretion as to how often he would have his facility shaken down for contraband. The frequency of shakedowns accelerated after an inmate might have gotten caught the week before with contraband. Inmates caught with contraband got shipped out with great speed and efficiency.

The two most sought-after items of contraband for our fellow inmates at the Pensacola Camp were, first, prepaid cell phones with the ID numbers scratched off and second, performance-enhancing steroids. Mark never went near either one of these items or any other contraband for that matter. Cell phones were obviously desirable yet illegal items to have in a prison: they gave any inmate willing to take the risk an unmonitored lifeline to the outside world.

Steroids are in demand in prisons because there is a huge weight-lifting sub-culture among the incarcerated male prison population. Most inmates who lift, which equals most inmates who had been down for any length of time, were seriously into their training out on the weight pile. They wanted to get "buff" or "cut." Steroids were the quickest route to buff-ness or cut-ness, but they also constituted serious contraband. It was one thing to get caught with a girly magazine under your pillow. That might get you a Warning Shot, a minor disciplinary write-up, but if you got caught with a cell phone or steroids, or if you tested positive for steroids as part of the camp's random drug-testing program, you were gone. You got shipped both out and up, meaning out of that prison environment and up at least one level from a Minimum to a Low.

Mark had no time for such nonsense. If he smelled trouble, he would just turn and high-tail it. He did not want to give even the appearance of compromising his pristine, shot-less record.

By the time Mark transferred from Edgefield to Pensacola, he was ready to begin a serious weight-lifting regimen. He bulked up, but unlike some, he took no short-cuts. Instead, he relied on a legal high-protein diet from the chow hall to build muscle mass. The entire forty-two months (3 ½ years) he was at Pensacola he never got a single Shot. In fact, the entire 102 months (8 ½ years) he was down he never got a single Shot.

Ginger & Mark at Pensacola Camp, 25th Wedding Anniversary
(June 16, 2004)

It is ironic in hindsight that the one guy at the Pensacola Camp who could have smuggled ten cell phones in every weekend never did. He played strictly by prison rules. Weight-lifters on the outside have used steroids or other performance-enhancing drugs on a regular basis for years. On the inside, that was a big no-no, so it never even came up for discussion as far as Mark was concerned.

That doesn't mean that Mark himself didn't get buff. He got plenty buff over the years, particularly after he got to Pensacola with its superb weight-pile. He made it a point to eat lots of protein. That's one reason he took a job in food service when it came open: greater access to protein. It wasn't entirely illegal to walk into one of the walk-in refrigerators in the back of the kitchen and stuff 4 or 5 hardboiled eggs into your pockets. Mr. D. might have made a special egg purchase that week, in which case he didn't have a problem with an inmate who worked in food service taking more than two. That was one of the perks that came with working in the kitchen.

Mark also got back into the chow line for extra helpings of meat once everybody had been served and Mr. D. gave the go-ahead. He never stole food. He preferred to buy extra pouches of tuna at the commissary. *Always above-board. Never sneaky. Don't cut corners.* Younger and bolder inmates who worked in food service but also worked out, often brought as many as eight extra pieces of chicken back to their cube. They'd chow down protein all night and be ready for their work out the next morning.

Weight-lifting was part of the transformational behavior that Mark incorporated into his daily life as an inmate. He upped the consistency and regularity of his workouts at Pensacola and developed a disciplined work-out regimen that he maintains to this day. On Mondays he did upper body. On Tuesdays lower body. Wednesdays were reserved for a precision-hit workout on the arms. Thursdays he did abs and crunches; Fridays he might do a light weight workout and then go over to the rec room and take a yoga class to improve his almost non-existent flexibility—and get ready for Ginger's visit that evening. This consistent regimen he developed at the Pensacola Camp took Mark to a much higher level of strength and fitness than he had ever known before prison life.

Seeing how Mark had transformed his body helped encourage his two sons to transform theirs. They started pumping iron at home and in gyms before Mark got out. The boys really ramped it up once their father got out. While still in prison, however, he had become their personal trainer, their remote personal trainer, accessible only on weekend visits, when they could fine-tune their workout programs.

Mark was and remains today a tremendous role-model for all three of his children. That's how families stay together: Adjust to the situation. For example, Mark and Alex discussed for endless hours in the visitors' room—much to Ginger's joy and amusement—the minutiae of their respective workout programs. This strengthened not just muscles, but also the father-son bond.

Then as soon as Mark got out of the halfway house, he and his sons put in place one of the most complete workout centers a home could have. Father and sons became each other's spotters on the bench press, and father became head weight-lifting consultant and gave them the benefit of all he had learned about body-building and weight-lifting while down those many years. For Alex in particular, the father-son bond and positive self-image he developed from getting fit with his Dad has been one of the greatest confidence boosters in his life. His Dad was unquestionably the single most important influence in converting Alex from a sedentary lifestyle during most of his father's years in prison to a fitness lifestyle now that they are able to spend time working out together.

Mark reflected during many of our walk-and-talks on the concept of doing "hard" time. I really didn't understand the concept of "hard" time. Mark said that doing hard time comes down to the harsh realization that, if you receive a long sentence and you get to prison, you know that even after years have elapsed, you still have many years to go. Did Mark do hard time? His answer would be, "I'll tell you flat out, Bud, Ginger did even harder time." Indeed, the collateral consequences of his criminal conviction had affected her at least as much as it had him. He understood how she soldiered on those many years of his incarceration. He felt the pain of that deeply the entire eight-and-a-half years he was down. He resolutely and repeatedly reaffirmed how impossible it would have been for him to get through those years without Ginger's unqualified support.

As for their children, all three were devastated. Tanya and Bill had a slight adjustment advantage over Alex because they were nineteen and eighteen, respectively, when their father entered prison. Tanya was already in college. She came out on the other side and is now a successful teacher in Chapel Hill, North Carolina. Bill was only three months from finishing high school when his father was taken away from him, but he was resilient enough to deal with it. Today, he is living, working, and thriving in Pensacola.

None was more impacted than Alex, their youngest, who was only six when his father went undercover, twelve when he was removed from society—and from him. Being so young, Alex had difficulty assimilating what was happening. Ultimately, however, he demonstrated amazing resiliency. Thus, in the end, he was both the least and most affected of the three children by what happened. Least because he was so much younger than his brother and sister and thus sufficiently flexible to bounce back from the tragedy. Most because, with his father out of the picture for such a long time, he lost the balance and advantages young boys from a more traditional two-parent environment take for granted, such as the positive reinforcement that only a father can give. He was twenty-one when his father was finally released from prison. It is a tribute to the entire family, but especially to Alex himself, that he got through his teen years with minimal emotional scarring.

Alex has come out the other side of the entire experience as an independent, determined, and well-adjusted young man. As Paul A. Willis said in a letter recommending Alex for graduate school, "[He] is a young man of impeccable character, strong leadership skills, clear life vision, and a proven life experience that . . . [has built] a positive drive to better himself and a humble passion to help others."

Mark & Ginger at Pensacola Camp 2 Weeks Prior To Release
(December 2006)

THE FINAL DAY

At 8 AM on December 21st, 2006, Ginger pulled her white Ford Escape SUV up to R&D. That morning Mark had donned the civilian clothes that she mailed to him several weeks earlier. Those get held in R&D pending his Walk-Around and clearance for release. Ginger had to throw away the slacks he had worn when he entered prison almost nine years earlier because Mark had gone from a flabby 44 inch waist to a tight 36-inch waist and was all muscle now. He had tried the clothes on several days in advance.

His departure was bittersweet. Many of his fellow inmates were lined up on the sidewalk watching their good friend Mark Whitacre finally get out of that place. Ginger had instructions to report to the Pensacola halfway house, run by Keeton Corrections, a civilian sub-contractor, within half an hour. It was a ten-minute drive straight down the road.

One thing Mark knew as Ginger drove past the Saufley guardhouse for the last time was that in prison he had created a new life, a life worth living to the fullest. He reflected back on the young man who began this sentence nine years ago and found it difficult in many respects to connect to that prior Mark Whitacre. When he stood in front of the judge and took his 108 month sentence for fraud, he was about as confused, broken, and defeated as a man could be. Rebuilding had been a big task, but it was one that had numerous helping hands along the way, none greater or more loving than Ginger's. He also had developed a completely different body, built up through sheer dint of willpower and steel-hard determination.

Ginger drove, and Mark slipped into the passenger's side. He reached over and touched her arm lovingly. She turned and looked at the tears streaming down his eyes. Then they were laughing and crying at the same time, smiling and giggling and still in disbelief that the long journey was finally over. Mark looked back, wondering if a guard would come running out and blow a whistle and yell for them to stop, but as she accelerated away, his anxieties and disbelief that he was actually free also went away.

Mark looked over at the love of his life.

"You don't have to worry anymore, Ging," Mark said. "You're safe now."

PART FOUR

THE POST-PRISON YEARS

Ginger & Mark Anaheim, California (March 2009)

PART FOUR—THE POST-PRISON YEARS

CHAPTER FIFTEEN

VOCATION BECOMES AVOCATION

"The vocation of every man and woman is to serve other people."

LEO TOLSTOY

While Mark was languishing in prison in South Carolina, a bold businessman on the other side of the continent believed there existed a huge yet untapped potential to relieve human suffering by using a chemical substance called selenium to help reduce the incidence of cancer. Selenium is a trace non-metal that is chemically related to sulfur; it has the chemical symbol Se and the atomic number 34. Selenium was recognized as an essential nutrient only four decades ago, but since that time scientific evidence had been mounting that properly constituted selenium supplementation in the human diet packs powerful antioxidant properties, specifically in relation to the reduction in the incidence of certain forms of cancer.

That businessman with a vision and a mission was one Paul A. Willis.

PAUL A. WILLIS & THE HIRING OF MARK WHITACRE

Dr. Gerald F. Combs Jr. had been working closely with Cypress. He knew Willis needed to assemble a first-rate team to meet its objectives. The world-renowned expert suggested a young selenium scientist with impressive credentials, a man who not only specialized in selenium but had extensive global managerial experience as well. Combs made it clear to Willis that he could think of no better fit with Cypress than this particular man. The only catch, Combs added, was that the young scientist happened to be in prison and was not scheduled for release for another five years, 2006 at the earliest.

Because of his extensive volunteer work ministering to inmates in California, the fact of Mark's incarceration bothered Willis not at all. He knew the routine and contacted Mark to ask to be put on Mark's visitors' list. Once he got on the approved list, Willis flew from California to South Carolina in April of 2001 and met Mark and his family in the visitors center at Edgefield Camp.

The two men clicked from the get-go. So did their wives, Susan and Ginger. Aside from a strong background and common interest in the health benefits of High Selenium Yeast, the two men shared many personal and religious values. Both believed that one's work should be consistent with one's values, that one's vocation should reflect one's avocation, and that work and life should be integrated and devoted to service to God.

Over those years from 2001 to 2006, while Mark sat in prison first at the Edgefield Camp, then at the Pensacola Camp, they maintained an active written correspondence and a regular visiting schedule. This gave rise to a high level of trust, goodwill, and common ground between Mark and Paul.

Susan & Paul Willis Anaheim, California (March 2009)

MARK WHITACRE: GETTING "BACK TO MY ROOTS"

Mark makes clear in his essay "Back to My Roots" on his website *www.markwhitacre.com* that all aspects of his life are now in alignment. In fact, Cypress Systems Inc., and what they do is such an integral part of his life that an entire section of this book, beginning on page 239, is devoted to understanding the company, its mission, and its flagship product, SelenoExcell®.

He says

> **At Cypress Systems, I have the opportunity to use both my executive biotechnology experience acquired over two decades and my specialized background with selenium and disease prevention. Although sadly underutilized, selenium has the potential to have the most profound impact upon dietary cancer prevention of any nutrient we know of today. Cancer rates per 100,000 people are about the same as they were 40 years ago. According to the American Cancer Society, 11 million people in America have cancer, one million four hundred thousand new cases will be diagnosed in 2009, and 565,650 Americans are expected to die this year due to cancer. These cancer incidences and death rate due to cancer are unacceptable. Selenium acts as an active component of the important enzyme, glutathione peroxidase, which helps combat free radicals. Free radicals are part of the cause of many chronic diseases including cancer. Selenium plays a vital role in our natural defense system . . .**
> **. . . . It is great to be back to my roots.**

HOPE UNLIMITED FOR CHILDREN

Like Mark and Ginger, Paul and his wife Susan and their three sons don't just talk the talk: they walk the walk in two important ways outside of the office: one, through their JPW3 Outreach Ministries at *http://jpw3.org* and two, through their commitment to a program called Hope Unlimited For Children at *http://hopeunlimited.org* an award-winning program that ministers to the physical, educational, and spiritual needs of Brazil's street children.

Of JPW3, Willis is quoted on their website as saying:

It is not the churches we attend, the bumper stickers on our
cars, or our political persuasion that establishes our identity
as a disciple of Christ, but rather the God-given love that
we show for one another as we live our daily lives.

When I read that bold of a statement placed directly in plain view on
Cypress's website, and involving minimal drilling down in the site to get
to it, I believe I am in the presence of a man who has integrated his work
mission with his life mission in complete devotion to his faith in Jesus
Christ. How many of us can say that we have arranged and integrated
our own lives so wisely?

This was clearly evident in his original naming of Cypress in 1995.
With a personal passion for world outreach and mission, as well as his role
as an Elder of Mission at Trinity Presbyterian Church in Fresno, California,
Paul attended a West Coast mission conference in March 2006.

One particular session at the conference that caught his eye was
called "Business Role in World Missions." The presenter was Steve
Rundle co-author of a book entitled *Great Commission Companies: the
Emerging Role of Business in Missions.* This book clearly outlined the new
paradigm shift in world missions and the strategic role that business and
mission-minded business leaders would play.

For Willis, that session at the conference was transformative. He
grasped the importance of Rundle's mission concept and read everything
else that Rundle had written. He saw clearly how he would integrate his
passion for a Christ-centered world outreach with his other passion, a
business model that was not purely profit-motivated, but motivated by
an over-riding effort to help relieve human suffering.

Rundle quoted theologian R. Paul Stevens, who wrote in his book,
The Other Six Days: Vocation, Work and Ministry in Biblical Perspective:

Mission is the intended occupation and pre-occupation of
the whole people of God, not merely a few of those chosen
representatives or so-called designated missionaries.

Rundle goes on to outline the purpose of his book, as follows:

Our individual callings and gifts may differ, but mission is
nevertheless the central purpose of the entire body of Christ.

This book is for the countless Christian men and women in business who want to do more than watch the game of missions. They want to do more than dole out money to make the game financially viable; they want to be on the playing field. The purpose of this book is to show how it is not only possible today but also necessary for business professionals—and companies owned by Christians—to become more actively involved in missions. Business has a remarkable capacity to touch virtually every person on the face of the planet. Moreover only flesh-and-blood people can build relationships and model the gospel in real-life settings. Business provides such a context for this kind of long-term holistic outreach. Evangelism and discipleship can be integrated into natural workday situations rather than forced to compete with a host of after-work alternatives.

At last, Willis found validation for his own goal of integrating vocation with avocation. Rundle's eloquent presentation of Stevens's insights was a defining moment for Willis.

Willis's passion to integrate his business focus with his missionary work is no more aptly demonstrated than in his efforts as a board member of Hope Unlimited for Children in Brazil. It is mind-boggling to learn that Brazil has an estimated seven million—**seven million!**—street children. These children suffer every imaginable form of abuse, neglect, violence, and exploitation. It is hard for the average middle-class American to comprehend the existence of such a huge number of homeless children withering on the streets of Brazil. A number that large, involving an age group that young, constitutes a humanitarian crisis of epic proportions.

The average lifespan of these Brazilian street children is three to four years. This tragedy cannot go unanswered. Using a religious, Christ-centered model, Hope helps these children undergo personal transformation in order to become equipped to live successful and productive lives.

GINGER GETS INVOLVED

Early in the 2008-2009 school year, Ginger caught the vision of Hope Unlimited and realized that she could establish a classroom correspondence between her kindergarten class in Pensacola, Florida, and the young children of Hope in Campinas Brazil. With the help of two Brazilian co-workers at her school, Ginger used pictures and translated words to open the eyes of the children in her classroom.

Ginger showed her young students that there are children in the world and specifically in Brazil who have struggles and challenges that go beyond those of children the same age here in the United States. Ginger also gave her students a taste of the cultural differences between her group in Pensacola and a group the same age living thousands of miles away. The two groups of children exchanged photo albums and greeting notes and letters. Ginger's whole school pitched in and sent school supplies by the box load to Brazil. Ginger has thereby planted a small seed in young and impressionable minds that they can grow and develop with hope toward the future.

A BRIGHT FUTURE

Paul A. Willis, Mark Whitacre, and Cypress Systems Inc. are a potent combination, one that represents a powerful force for good in the world. Whitacre and Willis will never measure their lives by how much money they make. They will measure their lives by the extent to which they have contributed to a brighter future for mankind and fulfill God's eternal purpose for their respective lives. They believe that you don't simply turn out the lights in your office, close the door behind you, and truncate your work life off from your personal life. They believe that you cannot on the one hand live a life placing faith above all else and on the other go off and work in a place that is not infused with that faith. It would be like spending your week-end at a peace rally and then going to a job Monday morning in a munitions factory.

Perhaps Willis and Whitacre will prove that nice guys *can* finish first. Unlike many people, they have aimed well, meaning they have found a worthy cause to work toward, one in which they can apply all the worldly wisdom they have gained from years in the business world and point that in a direction that serves God's ultimate purpose. These men hold fast to the words of Jesus in Matthew "Do not store up treasures here on earth, where they can be eaten by moths and get rusty, and where thieves break in and steal. Store your treasures in heaven, where they will never become moth-eaten or rusty and where they will be safe from thieves. Wherever your treasure is, there your heart and thoughts will also be." (6:19-21).

Jim Elliot, the great missionary to Ecuador, said "he is no fool who gives up what he cannot keep to gain what he cannot lose." Mark and Ginger could not have possibly imagined back in their Cornell years—when every waking hour revolved around research on the importance to human health of a trace mineral called selenium—that life would come full circle and land him a job that matched his scientific roots in selenium research with his and Ginger's personal belief system. Today, a quarter-century after having completed his selenium research and moved into new areas that unfortunately included prison, Mark was blessed to be given a second chance

Was the chain of events that brought Willis and Whitacre together—by way of Cornell, Ralston Purina (where both worked at the same time but never knew each other), Evonik, ADM, and prison—mere happenstance?

Not on your life.

Their shared faith in God brought them together no less than their interest in selenium. These two men share an unshakeable belief in the goodness of a Heavenly Father who has the ability to weave His purpose and plan into the fiber of their daily lives. It is nothing short of a miracle that somewhere in the middle of these two men's cheerful approach to hard work, there is something that others call "luck" but Mark and Paul call being within the plan of God.

PART FOUR—THE POST-PRISON YEARS
CHAPTER SIXTEEN

ACCEPTING RESPONSIBILITY, REALLY

> "Three conditions are necessary for Penance: [1] contrition,
> which is sorrow for sin, together with a purpose of amendment;
> [2] confession of sins without any omissions; and [3] satisfaction
> by means of good works."

> St. Thomas Aquinas
> Theologian (1225-1274)

Prison is nothing if not a place to reflect. Mark Whitacre had almost nine long years to reflect, not just on what went wrong at ADM, but on what he had accomplished in his life—and what not; on what he wanted to do when he got out—and what not. He has said that when you accept God as the final Arbiter of all things and match that with a long stint in prison, you have a potent combination for learning what is perhaps life's most difficult lesson: That we must all, without exception, accept responsibility for what we have done and who we have become.

I asked him, does that mean we should, when under compulsion, confess to crimes we didn't commit? Based on my understanding of Mark's meaning of accepting responsibility, really, the answer is yes. If you sit with him or hear him speak, you get one overriding impression: the man does not quibble. He says simply and unequivocally, guilty as charged. Next?

In an effort to make sure I understood what his message is, I probed deeper. We have discussed at great length his relative innocence or guilt and the relative innocence or guilt of many people charged with felony crimes. What about Barry Schenk's *The Innocence Project*, I asked? What about Ron Williamson, the man portrayed in John Grisham's brilliant first work of non-fiction, *The Innocent Man*? Williamson received a wrongful murder conviction and spent twelve years on death row before he was exonerated. What about the Duke University lacrosse case and the over-zealous prosecutor behind it? And what about the many thousands of other instances of miscarriages of justice?

There's a saying "everyone in prison is innocent," meaning everyone you meet in prison will give you a thousand reasons why he shouldn't be there. Fully eighty percent of the people Mark and I met at Pensacola insisted that they were innocent. Neither Mark nor I made any such claim, but when you sit and listen to a fellow inmate tell his story—or rather his version of his story—you actually do walk away in most cases with the feeling that the guy got a raw deal.

As for Mark himself, he just doesn't go in that direction. He thinks it's the wrong direction. His former FBI handlers—Dean Paisley, Brian Shepard, and Robert Herndon—now make the case that he is a national hero. Obviously, I know his case extremely well and argue his innocence for him and to him.

It usually starts with a comment from him about accepting responsibility, and I say, "What are you talking about, man? If anybody was innocent, it was you." I go on with how he got a raw deal and had to spend the prime years of his professional and personal life incarcerated and separated from his family. This is a man who spent nearly a decade in prison, not fifteen months like me.

Then we'd circle the tarmac one more time and I'd really warm to playing Devil's Advocate. I'd check off all the mitigating factors: You were only thirty-two when you joined ADM. You were surrounded by battle-hardened veterans. You were making moment-by-moment decisions in a dog-eat-dog business not exactly known for having high ethical standards. Your bosses saw and exploited your naïveté and eagerness to please. You don't have the "short-cut" mentality usually associated with criminals. You deferred financial gain in the early years by investing almost a decade in your education—waiting until you got the degree you wanted for the job you wanted, an approach suggesting you are not a man who takes short-cuts. You cracked under the pressure of it much later than anyone else probably would have. You were railroaded by The Chairman's ability to pull rank in Washington. After ticking off a few more mitigating circumstances, I'd sum it up with, let's face it, dude, if anybody got a raw deal, you did. So what's with this guilty stuff?

Mark brushes all my protestations of his innocence away with a sweep of the hand. Ultimately, he says, only two things matter: One, know when to say no to certain business practices. "I didn't do that." And two, understand when you're in management that your decisions have extended consequences affecting many thousands of people. "I lost track of that too."

So he really does seem to have moved beyond any discussion of mitigating circumstances. He delivers a consistent message, with no hedging. In ADM's own backyard, in a May 2008 letter responding to Tim Cain, the respected *Decatur Herald & Review* reporter:

> **I was certainly no hero in the ADM case. I want to be very clear about that. I wish I would have done what I did for the FBI for all of the right reasons. But I simply did not.**
>
> **I made some horrific decisions and broke some serious federal laws. ADM plays no role in those decisions. They were decisions of my own making. My not thinking clearly because of the pressure of working undercover for the FBI was no excuse.**

> *Decatur Herald & Review*
> Letter from Mark Whitacre
> Published on 5/26/2008

I asked Mark about his mindset at the time of his firing of attorney Jim Epstein back in 1995. I pointed out that, at the time, his belief in his innocence was so deeply held that he fired the guy rather than plead out to a felony.

"Mark, you hired a good criminal defense lawyer, empowered him to negotiate the most favorable deal possible for you, got "the deal of the century", and then fired Epstein when confronted with the requirement that you plead out to a felony. Had you done that then, you would have gotten three to five with mitigating circumstances bringing it down to, most likely, no more than six months in prison. His answer is, "I wasn't *there* yet." *There* meaning at that place of accepting full responsibility in the larger sense. "And besides," he adds, "I was off my rocker at the time."

Mark and Ginger maintain contact with many people still in prison, as well as many out now whom they befriended over the years in prison visitors' centers or chapel at Pensacola. Based on my observation of how the Whitacres approach those offenders or ex-offenders who refuse to admit their guilt, they stress gently—not over-bearingly but gently—that obtaining the "right" or "proper" or "just" outcome in their case is far less important than learning the larger "Christian lesson of accepting

Mark Whitacre in San Diego, California
(September 2008)

responsibility, no matter how strong the mitigating circumstances might be, no matter how "funky around the edges" the question of guilt or innocence is. Accepting responsibility means responding to your situation or allegation in such a way that you relinquish your own perception about those allegations. You accept the perception of others as having validity. You don't dig in your heels. Instead, you believe that, even in our failures and mistakes, God still works through your hardship, criminal conviction, and incarceration to teach you a higher lesson. This principal is clearly demonstrated in Romans 8:28: *"And we know that God causes all things to work together for good to those who love God, to those who are called according to His purpose."*

> And we know that God causes all things to work together for good to those who love God, to those who are called according to His purpose.
>
> ROMANS 8:28

Even in our personal failures God still works His good and perfect plan in our lives to bring us to a better place and a deeper walk with Him.

Not everyone agrees with that approach, but Mark and Ginger have taken the ultimate leap of faith and moved beyond any quibbling about their innocence. They show by example, not words. What they mean to others today as role models echoes back to what they meant to their high school classmates as role models. They still try to set an example not by their words but by their actions.

Mark is not interested in talking about his innocence. It is irrelevant to him. He lives a life today with Ginger that is full of hope and personal freedom. They are both alive; they are not half-dead like so many ex-offenders who got hammered by the criminal justice system. He stresses that the best way to get through that is to face life honestly. The Book of Proverbs says: *"A false balance is abomination to the Lord: but a just weight is his delight"* (11:1).

> He who is faithful in a very little is faithful also in much; and he who is dishonest in a very little is dishonest also in much.
>
> LUKE 16:10

The Bible demands basic uprightness and honesty. When a person starts quibbling, that person is most likely making minor lapses in the truth. Mark no longer excuses minor lapses in the truth. He says that Jesus warned, "*He who is faithful in a very little is faithful also in much; and he who is dishonest in a very little is dishonest also in much*" (Luke 16:10).

> A false balance is abomination to the Lord: but a just weight is his delight.
>
> PROVERBS 11:1

Part of Mark's fundamental requirement for total honesty involves accepting responsibility for one's crimes. If you feel you didn't commit any, then go back and re-examine whether or not you are being honest with yourself.

Former FBI supervisor Dean Paisley calls Mark a national hero and continues to work tirelessly for his executive clemency. While Mark profoundly appreciates Paisley's sense of righteous indignation about his case, Mark believes it is far more important to set a good example in the present than to dwell in the past.

He spoke as recently as April 15, 2009, to a group of FBI agents now under Robert Herndon's supervision. Herndon is still active in the Bureau since his days as one of Mark's handlers, with increased responsibility as a supervising agent in the Kansas City office. Mark stood in front of these agents and apologized for his actions. It is safe to assume that no person whom the FBI helped put away for nearly a decade has ever come back and apologized to them. Most people would instead demand an apology from the FBI, not give one.

On a level more directly related to his case, Mark has reached out to former agent Brian Shepard, whom Mark tried to discredit in the heat of the undercover operation, and apologize. He continues to apologize to his other handler, Robert Herndon. Mark has apologized to them—and to Paisley—for the difficulty he caused them by his deceptive behavior during the ADM years. He adds that, today, he hopes he would be wise enough to never work in a place that didn't set the right example.

In fact, Mark points out that a workplace atmosphere encouraging the right example by its actions is far more important than a workplace with compliance manuals and compliance officers, although those may also be necessary. Cypress has no compliance officers—Mark and his CEO, Paul A. Willis, consider *themselves* to be Cypress's chief compliance officers. And it happens by employees observing the conduct of their lives, not by rules in a compliance manual.

For example, if, as is true, both Mark and Paul are inclined toward temperance, moderation, and frugality, they live it. They don't talk it or scold others who don't follow in their path. If an employee cares to ask them, they are certainly not shy to say that they are driven by principles of moral conduct as spelled out in the Bible. Mark prefers to walk the walk, not so much talk the talk. As such, he is restrained in his criticism of people who may do things that lead to trouble. If he sees an employee or a friend who might be better off, say, drinking less alcohol or spending less money on cigarettes, he will not confront the person. He knows it is much more effective to live by example than to admonish by word.

If he saw an employee or colleague in his industry cutting corners, he would not confront that individual unless the actions were egregious. Rather, he would wait for an opportunity when the person asks him about the appropriateness of some corner-cutting action. Then he might simply suggest that that person use the "what-would-your-children-think" approach. Similar to the test Warren Buffett told employees of Salomon Inc. when he stepped in to become chairman in the middle of a crisis, Mark would say, ask yourself before you make any business decision whether or not you would be willing to have that decision immediately explained to your children in language they could understand and then be willing to encourage your children to make the same decision. If the answer is yes, then you are probably making an ethical decision.

The sooner a person charged with a crime gets over quibbling about the details, *even if there is some truth to them*, the sooner that person will begin to heal. Because the charge of a criminal conviction, whether right or wrong, is irreversible. Mark is one of the least shy men imaginable. If he learns that an ex-con who might have become a friend somewhere along the way has started "backsliding," meaning letting the natural human tendency toward resentment bubble over and block their efforts toward living more successfully, he will share with them—yet again—his personal credo of taking full responsibility for your actions, regardless of mitigating circumstances.

As for how Mark lives his life now, he likes things black or white. When I remind him that life is not, in fact, black or white—there's a huge field of gray out there—he counters this by saying what he now says in speeches: when your values are clear, your decisions are easy. When your values are not clear, your decisions are hard. This position is so crystal-clear for him today in contrast to what it was fifteen years ago that he finds black or white more readily obtainable.

Compared to fifteen years ago, he understands today that the rules of life are the rules of life: you tell the truth in every instance; you apply yourself with all you've got to your business; and you speak no ill of other men. As for number one, telling the truth, he is quick to remind that he did not tell the truth when he made up the sabotage story at ADM that started the whole mess. That little white lie is what started the ball rolling. As for number two, applying yourself to your work, although he did apply himself strenuously at ADM, the means did not justify the ends. Today, unlike then, there is no friction between what he does and what he believes. His work is consistent with his value system. Vocation and avocation do indeed match for him; life is one seamless whole bent toward serving others and being honest with God. As for number three, speaking no ill of others, he believes that it is important to be honest with others but now knows that being honest with them does not have to mean speaking ill of anyone, including his former bosses and including "fair-weather friends," those who loved him when he was on top but who did not support him when he was in trouble. Instead, his view is that he cannot change what others think of him and that, for each friend he lost, he has gained five. He also thinks that it is more important to share honestly his own failures than to talk about the failures of others. That would be to speak ill of them.

The definition of *responsibility* generally boils down to the application of the Golden Rule and the statement by Jesus to "Do unto others as you would have them do unto you." Whether you are an individual or a company—Mark Whitacre or Cypress Systems—the Golden Rule applies to both individuals and corporations.

While he admonishes in speeches to future managers to always do the right thing, he acknowledges that there may be situations where what is the right thing is not always clear. For example, he has mentioned that there are competitors in his current industry who exaggerate the effectiveness of their product. His policy is to stay away from directly criticizing them and to focus instead on the facts and scientific data that supports his company's claim. This disproves in a more convincing manner, with hard proof, the claims of the exaggerators. Let the numbers do the talking. Says Mark, "What someone else does is none of my concern. What I do is what matters to me, and I just stay away from those people."

Mark's position today may not be shared by another famous whistleblower, Jeffrey Wigand, the individual who courageously put a halt to the insertion of known carcinogens into tobacco. Wigand, like Mark, waged a one-man battle and lost. Wigand lost to Big Tobacco; Mark lost to Big Agriculture. Both brought great benefit to society for their actions—but great chaos to their own lives. Actor Russell Crowe portrayed Wigand in a 1999 film *The Insider* directed by Michael Mann that captured Wigand's battle against Big Tobacco and was itself based on an unforgettable article in *Vanity Fair* (May 1996) entitled "The Man

Who Knew Too Much," written by Marie Brenner. Both captured the
price paid by a whistleblower exposed.

———————

While the parallels between Mark's and Wigand's case are uncanny,
there is one big difference in their two outcomes: Mark kept his marriage
intact and made it stronger, whereas Wigand lost his marriage as part
of the collateral damage of being a whistleblower. While much of that
difference may have to do with Ginger's strength of character, Mark does
not impugn Wigand's wife for leaving her husband. It is just a factual
statement that the two men had different outcomes on the domestic
front.

Mark today would simply walk away from whistleblowing against
such a powerful entity as ADM. Wigand, by contrast, when asked, said
he absolutely would do it again. Mark's bottom line is, do what's best for
my family. Knowing what he knows about how harsh retaliation against
whistleblowers can be, he would just walk away rather than become
the sacrificial lamb he became. Once safe, he would then speak out to
Congress, the FDA, or other relevant authority.

———————

Human nature is complex and can exhibit both selfish and generous
traits at the same time. Mark was performing both a selfish act
(embezzlement) and a generous, pro-social one (exposing wrongdoing by
wearing a wire) at the same time. Mark thinks that, in corporate America
today, stronger protections are in place for whistleblowers. There is greater
opportunity in corporations for employees to call an anonymous 800
number within the company to report wrongdoing. Today, therefore, he
hopes that one should not have to choose between sacrificing oneself or
walking away. There is a middle ground where the offending company
can be exposed without the one doing the exposing getting hurt.

This is what makes the Whitacre story so compelling. The essential
message is don't quibble, be honest with yourself, take responsibility for
your actions, refuse to blame others, forgive your enemies, and get rid of
any crutches that prevent you from growing and moving forward. Tell
the truth, and don't work for a company that cuts corners, no matter how

attractive the pay. The truth becomes much clearer when your values are clear. Says Mark, "Walk daily with Jesus Christ, who is Himself the Truth, and you can't go wrong. And if you go wrong, admit it."

Mark may not fit the hero mold, but he is honest. And for the crime of embezzlement that he *did* commit, he has accepted full responsibility. Really.

PART FOUR—THE POST-PRISON YEARS
CHAPTER SEVENTEEN

MARK & GINGER: MATURE

"The true index of a man's character is the health of his wife."

CYRIL CONNOLLY

Mark & Ginger Anaheim, California (March 2009)

Ginger Lynn Whitacre, the selfless and devoted wife of the man she has known and loved since she was thirteen, will prompt you to re-evaluate your notions of how to deal with life's bumps, problems, and vicissitudes. She will also remind us—by example rather than talk—that God is the source of all true healing. With healing comes maturity, and to mature fully, one must first and foremost mature spiritually.

She is the same unpretentious, down-to-earth, mild-mannered woman she was at age twenty, thirty, and forty. And she still discharges her duties as teacher, wife, and mother with the same good humor and abiding faith in God that she had in those prior decades, but now there is a ripeness to her outlook that comes only with spiritual maturity.

We can, I think, distill what got her through the past fifteen difficult years down to three bedrock principles, or "action steps":

1. **Pray, and try it using a positive image of the outcome.** The ancient Greeks said, "Whatever you ask for in prayer, believe that you can receive it and it will be yours." The Bible says, *"You can pray for anything, and if you believe, you will have it."* (Mark 11:24-25).

2. **Mature, and mature spiritually first.** The other types of maturity, emotional and physical, will not really mean anything without spiritual maturity at its core. For Ginger, great adversity is what helped her mature spiritually. Her husband went to prison when they were both just passing through forty and when their youngest was not even a teenager. At forty, we seldom think about the golden years, the final third of our lives. Today, however, both Ginger and Mark are in their fifties, and they now reflect more often on those golden years. They do not fear growing old. Rather, they look forward to it. They have matured spiritually such that they welcome growing old together and delight in its anticipation. They will be years of service, years of giving back, years of helping others.

3. **Live in the present.** You seldom hear Ginger or Mark dwell on the past or even think about how horrific Mark's years in prison were. Mark and Ginger are looking forward, not backward. They are thankful for what they have *right now*. They do not complain

about what they lost in the past. Nor do they fantasize about the future. They plan for the future but live in the present.

Many people fear growing old and speak of the final years disparagingly. Not Mark and Ginger. Aside from their use of the free-radical scavenging capabilities of selenium and other antioxidants to help retard the aging process, they have matured spiritually to where they approach old age hopefully and expectantly. They look forward to doing good works and serving others into their seventies, eighties, and nineties. They expect to live, together and in service to God and their fellow man, to a ripe old age. Ginger lives her love. She does not merely talk about it, although she is not reluctant to tell her husband, children, family, and friends how much she loves them. She takes great pains to follow through on promises made. You will never find her making a promise and not keeping it. The thoughtful care she selflessly provides to her intense husband, her far-flung children, and her tender students is joyous to behold.

Ginger would be the last to claim she's perfect. She lives in the present—principle number three above—but there are still times when, like all of us, she agonizes over mistakes she has made.

And her stamina and patience do have their limits. For example, if her husband starts to veer off course from the correct order of the Four F's that FBI Supervisor Robert Herndon spelled out—Faith, Family, Fitness, Firm, in that order—she will put her foot down.

Yet there is little question in my mind and most certainly none in Mark's, that, were it not for Ginger, he would not be alive today. I have read her many healing letters sent to him while he was in prison. They rise above the level of notes that say simply "hang in there, honey." Those letters were meant to tell him unequivocally that nobody will succeed in keeping her from holding them together—not the Chairman, not the DC Prosecutors, not the doubters and naysayers, and most certainly not the United States Bureau of Prisons. She will always be in his corner. If those of us who have been incarcerated or are incarcerated today had such support, the walls of prison would be no walls at all. *Who can find a virtuous and capable wife? She is worth more than precious rubies. Her husband can trust her, and she will greatly enrich his life. She will not hinder him but help him all her life* (Proverbs 31:10-11).

Mark and Ginger calculated how much time in days, months, and ultimately years, she spent in prisons, that is, in prison visitors' centers. It amounts to three and a half years. That's three times the length of my entire sentence. Then you add to that the countless hours she spent waiting in car lines, writing letters to Members of Congress or the President or the DOJ, or contacting people by telephone in pursuit of her husband's release. Just the time spent in car lines adds up easily to another six months.

———————

Today Mark and Ginger have a thirty-six year history together that is unprecedented in its richness and depth. All the money in the world cannot buy what they have. As for principle #3 above, they do indeed live in the here and now. They have no interest in rehashing past hurts, opening old wounds. With that deep reservoir of goodwill—built up over nearly four decades—they have a level of trust, acceptance, understanding, and forgiveness for each other that is truly awe-inspiring. Today they live with pure joy in an atmosphere of hope, love, and great optimism about the future. They have that cheerful heart that is like medicine, as expressed in Proverbs.

Given his tendency to work incredibly long, hard hours, Mark is doing an excellent job of self-correction. He returns time again to the four F's. Ginger, perhaps because she is a teacher, knows that Mark cannot simply unlearn habit patterns so deeply ingrained that they go back to Ohio State. There is a theory about learning that says the way to learn a thing is to "hear or feel" it two hundred times. *Two hundred times.*

Understood in that context, she does not expect her husband to change at once, after years and years of hundred-hour work weeks and almost nine years of incarceration during which time he worked so hard that he attained four more advanced degrees. When he starts to revert to total immersion in his work, she patiently brings him back, perhaps by making him take her for a walk on the beach or help her with some yard work. By the same token, she appreciates it when he himself, unprompted, takes steps to put faith and family to the front of the line, before fitness and firm. She expects him to get a little lost sometimes, and either she brings him back or he brings himself back.

———————

As for their many acts of quiet or anonymous charity, I will give you but one example. Over the course of their six years living in Moweaqua,

Mark and Ginger had purchased four residential properties in that town for income and appreciation. Their tenants were decent local townsfolk. For the Whitacres, such investments were a diversification move as part of their overall financial plan.

One day they learned that one of their tenants had a high school daughter who had, tragically, just been in an automobile accident that caused her permanent paralysis from the neck down. As soon as the news reached them, Mark and Ginger rushed over to the woman's house to offer their condolences. The distraught mother, their tenant, clearly was beyond functionality at that point. Immediately—and without prompting or fanfare—they suspended her rent payments for at least a year, telling her not even to think about it until the status of her daughter's injury became clearer.

Such acts of generosity were done silently by the Whitacres. Moweaquans had known about them for years, so the townsfolk were skeptical of a public relations machine that tried to portray a man who had given so much back to his community as suddenly an avaricious fraudster. Perhaps he was a Robin Hood, stealing from the rich to give to the poor, or perhaps, in fact, he was an honest man who had simply gotten caught up in something bigger than he was able to control. At the time of the price-fixing scandal, when Mark was being smeared elsewhere, the local paper ran articles supportive of the Whitacres. Today they still receive regular e-mails, cards, and letters from their friends in Moweaqua. No bridges have been burned.

Nor have Mark and Ginger forgotten their brethren who have suffered from the emotional and economic slam of incarceration. When Mark was incarcerated, Ginger became an inspiration and mother hen to many of the wives whose husbands were in prison. She helped many of the younger wives in particular. Many prison-widowed wives with young children are suddenly thrust into the unknown world of single motherhood. They end up being the sole provider and often need a small financial boost, fifty dollar here or a hundred dollars there, just to put food on the table or get a tank of gas. Ginger pops something in the mail to them. No fanfare, no headlines, no nothing.

Ginger has helped many women with husbands in prison get over rough spots. She remembers like it was yesterday when she was in exactly their place. When Mark first entered prison in March of 1998, she was left with three children, reduced earnings capacity relative to Mark's prior income, and the remains of his 401-K, which at the time were entirely inadequate. College tuition for their eldest daughter alone eclipsed Ginger's entire annual salary as a schoolteacher.

KENNETH L. ADAMS

Just as Ginger from time to time appears like a small angel for women desperate to make ends meet while their husbands are in prison, so did such an angel appear for her, like an apparition appearing out of the mist. That angel came in the form of a letter from a Washington, D.C. based attorney. The letter she got one day looked like any other on legal letterhead; she and Mark had received many of those over the years. Fortunately, she didn't throw this one out because it contained a substantial check. The attorney's name was one Mr. Kenneth L. Adams. He represented a number of large companies as class-action plaintiffs against Archer Daniels for civil antitrust violations. Adams and the plaintiffs knew the important role Mark played in exposing the lysine and citric acid cartels that led to large financial settlements in favor of Mr. Adams's clients.

Neither Adams nor the plaintiffs who received the settlements were under any obligation to share their recovered overcharging with the Whitacres. Yet Adams and the plaintiffs put checks in the mail to Ginger, in thanks for what her husband had done. There was no legal obligation to give the Whitacres a penny. Nobody was forcing Adams to make these payments; he did it solely because it was the right thing to do.

Before Ken Adams began sending her small percentages of each of the settlements that came in, money was the scarcest commodity of all. It was because of Ken Adams that the Whitacres were able to put their children through college. It was because of Ken Adams that she was able to live in Aiken and Pensacola. It was because of Ken Adams that she was able to put gas in the car! The family could not have otherwise survived and lived near whatever institution was incarcerating Mark.

PAUL A. WILLIS

While Mark and Ginger owe a profound debt of gratitude to Ken Adams and those plaintiffs for voluntarily sharing monies recovered from the old Archer Daniels in class action settlements, they are just as fortunate in another respect: Paul A. Willis.

Here is a man who gave Mark a job—a serious, high-ranking job—the minute Mark got out of prison. Most ex-offenders, even highly educated white-collar ex-offenders, face nearly insurmountable obstacles when it comes to finding employment upon release from incarceration. Most employers are understandably reluctant to hire someone with a criminal record. In the words of former U.S Pardon Attorney Margaret Colgate Love, "And yet, even as more and more people are acquiring a criminal record, relief from the lingering disabilities and stigma of conviction has never seemed more elusive." Mark and Ginger are doing their part to provide some of that relief.

Mark cannot change the past; he can only change himself. As the great statesman Charles Malik put it: "Success is not fame, wealth, or power. Faith is seeking, knowing, loving, and obeying God. If you seek, you will know. If you know, you will love. If you love, you will obey."

Genuine success is the spiritual process of developing a mature and constructive personality. Despite the ability of prison to warp the personalities of both the one incarcerated and those closest to the one incarcerated, neither Mark nor Ginger—nor their children—has fallen into that trap. One thing is as certain as death and taxes: Mark and Ginger will never get a divorce.

One thing is as certain as death and taxes: Mark and Ginger Whitacre will never get a divorce. The Whitacre family is now on a trajectory of accomplishing, with the help of a loving God, their highest hopes.

The Whitacre story is now complete except for one thing. A Presidential Pardon. Although the family has explicitly stated that, since Mark's release from prison, they no longer place as much emphasis on obtaining executive clemency, many supporters think otherwise. To the family, only one pardon matters and that is God's pardon.

Important supporters, most notably Dean Paisley, believe strongly that a pardon is necessary in terms of sending a larger message to future whistleblowers.

PART FOUR—THE POST-PRISON YEARS
CHAPTER EIGHTEEN

THE WHITACRE PARDON PETITION

"Why not pardon my sin and take away my guilt?"

JOB 7:20

The Whitacre family's pursuit of executive clemency started in 2000 when Mark got unexpected legal mail while incarcerated at Edgefield Minimum. Their efforts continued unabated until his release from prison in December of 2006. Now that he is out, however, executive clemency has taken a back seat to getting on with life. Nonetheless, granting executive clemency to Mark Whitacre at this time would send an important positive signal to future whistleblowers. As such, it would carry high symbolic importance.

For that reason, members of the FBI, prominent politicians, clergymen, and hundreds of private citizens have urged Mark and Ginger not to brush aside the pursuit of executive clemency, so on March 6, 2008, Mark flew to Washington, DC, with Dean Paisley, the former FBI supervisor of the price-fixing case, in an effort to rally support on Capitol Hill and at the Department of Justice for a full pardon from the former President George W. Bush. As far back as early 2001, then-Pardon Attorney Roger Adams at the Department of Justice recommended Mark's application for consideration by the White House, but the Bush Administration took no action, and, like the former Bush Administration, the new Obama

Administration has signaled it is going to require all petitioners to have been out of prison for at least five years before becoming eligible for a full pardon. For Whitacre, that means December of 2011.

THE HISTORY AND MEANING OF PARDONS

The presidential power of the pardon made it into the Constitution because our Founding Fathers were both deeply religious and recently arrived from England. Their vesting of the president with pardon power is based on the royal Prerogative of English Kings, but in fact has deeper roots in the Christian concept of forgiveness.

In Christian theology, a *pardon* is extended to man by God through Jesus. It is an act of forgiveness for all worldly transgressions. Divine pardons involve both atonement and forgiveness and derive directly from God's pardoning of sin through death by crucifixion of Jesus Christ. When Jesus said on the cross, "Father, forgive them, for they know not what they do," God listened and said, OK, for your suffering, Son, I will make that available to those sinners on earth who atone for their sins and pledge never to sin again. In Christianity, the prospect of being pardoned gives each living person the opportunity for spiritual regeneration, or rebirth. To be born again is to go from spiritual death to spiritual life. The specific language in the Bible is at John 3:3: *"Jesus replied, 'I assure you, unless you are born again, you can never see the Kingdom of God.'"* Thus a religious pardon must involve repentance and rebirth.

A presidential pardon, by contrast, can be exercised in whatever manner the president deems appropriate. It is one of the few absolute powers left to presidents, one of the last vestiges of royal prerogative in an age when other presidential powers have gotten increasingly diluted since FDR was president. Every sitting president has the ability to override the justice system, free anyone he wants, and return a person to the state of legal innocence he had before he ever committed his crime.

The president doesn't have to justify his actions to Congress, you, me, or anyone. His pardon of any person cannot be challenged or overturned by any other branch of the government. It is at the president's sole discretion. The pardon is untouchable by Congress; it would take a constitutional amendment to make any change in the pardon power.

Executive clemency is an issue most people don't think about until a controversial pardon or commutation hits the news. Such controversy was stirred up when President George H.W. Bush—Bush One—pardoned former Secretary of Defense Casper Weinberger for arms sales to Iran in what became known as the Iran Contra Affair. That was followed by the controversy surrounding Bush Two's commutation of Scooter Libby. Another one involved the Clinton pardon of Marc Rich on the last day of his Presidency. Many remember how Gerald Ford's swift pardon of Nixon was accompanied by the observation, "our nation's long nightmare is over." Before Bush Two's departure from office, pundits were handicapping whether Bush Two, who had already commuted Scooter Libby's sentence, would grant Libby a full pardon. He did not.

THE WHITACRE CLEMENCY JOURNEY

Mark's clemency journey started in early 2000 while he was still an inmate at the Edgefield Camp. He had two years down and nearly seven to go. Neither Mark nor Ginger initiated the executive-clemency process. They believe a silent angel acting alone talked to someone in the Justice Department and jump-started the process. In late January 2000, Mark got called to see a case manager, who handed him an envelope containing a blank executive clemency application and a generic cover letter that explained how to complete it. At the time Mark had barely heard about executive clemency, let alone considered it a serious option while still in prison. He automatically assumed that pardons were only granted to people who had been out of prison for at least five years.

Little did Mark know that his FBI handlers started to fight for his pardon. While Shepard and Paisley both worked on his pardon after they retired, the younger Agent Herndon was still active with the Bureau yet took no small risk by pushing buttons at DOJ, FBI, and Antitrust in seeking permission to send his pardon letter in support of Mark's pardon.

Herndon risked losing friends and allies, not to mention the respect of his colleagues in the Bureau. He was even told that he could get suspended or fired from the Bureau if he supported Mark too strongly, because he was repeatedly told not to go against the wishes of the Antitrust Division prosecutors. Nonetheless, Herndon called the Pardon Attorney at DOJ, who understood that he was at cross-currents with the Antitrust Division.

Herndon did it because supporting Mark's pardon petition was the right thing to do, and he risked job security by doing so. When one steps back and looks at the actions of Paisley, Shepard, and particularly Herndon, who, unlike the other two, was still active with the Bureau and not retired, it took compassion and courage to support Mark's pardon petition.

———————

Mark wasted no time completing the application and, within a week, had it in the mail to the Pardon Attorney at the Department of Justice in Washington, D.C. The postmark was February 6th, 2000. He and Ginger were elated at the thought of commutation. Over numerous visiting hours in those following weeks, they pondered who the silent angel might be. They had their surmises and hunches, but nothing concrete. It had to have been someone who knew about both Mark's case and the pardon process. They developed a short list of names, but never tried to contact any of them, reasoning that the silent angel, whoever he or she was, might have valid reasons for wanting to remain anonymous.

Several short months after Mark's filing, former FBI agent Dean Paisley paid Mark a visit in Edgefield. Ginger was present; she was always present when Edgefield visiting hours allowed it. Paisley had been the FBI's Supervisor in Charge of Operation Harvest King and had retired from the FBI in April 1994, well before Mark got sentenced to prison. Paisley had been with the Bureau twenty-five years. After retirement, he took a job for several years as the head of security at Walt Disney World in Orlando and now has his own private investigation agency in Springfield, Illinois. Could he have been the Silent Angel? Paisley certainly had detailed knowledge of Mark's case, and, during his long FBI career, had in the early nineteen-eighties been in charge of background checks for those petitioning the Pardon Attorney for executive clemency.

Although Whitacre and Paisley had exchanged correspondence, it had been years since they'd seen each other. Paisley walked into the visitor's room wearing his trademark big smile and carrying in a special case a big **white** Stetson hat for Mark. He handed the white Stetson to Mark ceremoniously and told him what he had told him many times in the past, during the years they worked together on Harvest King:

"You are the good guy, Mark, and the good guys wear the white hats. They were the bad guys, so let the bad guys wear the black hats." And with literal "hat in hand," Paisley graciously added, "Mark, someone should have been here long ago to thank you for your service to our country."

The prison guards would not actually allow Paisley to give Mark the hat. Ginger took it home at day's end for safekeeping. To this day, it occupies a prominent place on their mantel, and Paisley's symbolic act of good will meant a great deal to the Whitacres. If Paisley was the Silent Angel, he never let on, and they never asked.

Paisley's perspective on the pardon process remains an anchor for Mark and Ginger to this day. Many hundreds of pardon requests are rejected each year, and Bush II rejected 9,000 pardon petitions in his first seven years. However, Mark's petition remained alive, with the hurdle seeming to be the five-year wait rule. He and Ginger attribute that in no small measure to Paisley's indefatigable efforts on Mark's behalf. Paisley wrote many letters to both the Pardon Attorney's Office and the White House. He brings clarity and legitimacy to the widely held belief that Mark has been the victim of injustice. As Paisley said in one of his letters, "Mark was abandoned by the very agency that he had so ably assisted."

In another letter to the Department of Justice, Paisley said:

> **Mr. Whitacre was the only source of information [in the ADM case] and his cooperation was paramount to the success of the case. Through training and direction given him by the case agents, Mark performed admirably, collecting pertinent information, both technical and non-technical, which supported numerous counts of violation of federal law. Without his continued willingness to assist the FBI, this case would not have been able to be brought to a logical conclusion.**

> **I personally have a great deal of respect for Mr. Whitacre. He sacrificed his career, reputation, family, and his own stability to assist the government in what is now considered the biggest and most important antitrust case ever brought to justice.**

> **Although he violated the terms of his agreement with the U.S. government, that violation was not related to the**

antitrust matter and his eventual prosecution in the antitrust case was highly discretionary and, I believe, wrong.

Mr. Whitacre received a harsher sentence than the ADM executives who organized and controlled the antitrust case.

Dean Paisley
FBI Supervising Agent (ret)

Thanks to Paisley's encouragement and knowledge of the process, they thought they could fast-track either a commutation or a pardon that same year, 2000. Clinton would be leaving office at the end of the year after his second term. Paisley tried to warn the Whitacres that the process usually takes years, but it was widely known that Clinton was working up a long list of folks to pardon on his last day in office. So with Clinton close to going out, the Whitacres' hope sprang eternal.

In the interim, Paisley made it clear that they would have to do a great deal more than just complete the application. They needed to mobilize key players, including plaintiffs and plaintiffs' attorneys. They needed as many signed Character Affidavits as possible. They needed people from all walks of life who knew Mark to send strong supporting letters to the Pardon Attorney.

Getting that support was made easier by a *Dateline NBC* interview that aired on primetime television on the NBC network on September 10th, 2000. The interview was timed to coincide with the release of *The Informant*, written by *New York Times* journalist, Kurt Eichenwald, who covered the case for the business section of the *Times*.

In advance of the *Dateline NBC* airing, a large crew from NBC, after getting all the necessary permissions, descended on the South Carolina prison camp at Edgefield and spent many hours interviewing Mark inside the compound. In addition, Robert Herndon, who is still an FBI agent operating out of Kansas City and was one of Mark's three FBI handlers, was interviewed on camera, as was the author of *The Informant*, Kurt Eichenwald.

Ginger had no interest in being part of the *Dateline* brouhaha. She had grown suspicious of the media's manipulation of the entire ADM case, and reliving in front of millions of viewers the painful process that landed her husband in prison was of no interest. After much urging and cajoling by the producer, however, she finally agreed to be interviewed. She did so primarily because she thought it might give Mark's clemency petition a boost.

The interviewer, Chris Hansen, asked many difficult questions of Mark in prison and of Ginger in their living room in Aiken. As difficult as it was for both of them, the explanations and honest answers they gave seemed to have helped listeners understand what immense pressure Mark was under and how it created the mental state that so badly clouded his judgment. Ginger told their side of the story in her typical straightforward manner, explaining that a series of disasters occurred, one after another, that proved, if proof were needed, that the FBI had been forced to abandon her husband due to pressure coming from the DC prosecutor's office, that a check had been bounced in the Bank of Justice. She explained how unbearable it was to watch her husband melt down as she stood by, not merely helpless to prevent it, but feeling like she was in large measure its cause.

The flurry of publicity surrounding the interview, and particularly the publication of the Eichenwald and Lieber books, added balance to the debate. But the fact remained that her husband was sitting in prison—with seven years to go at the time of that interview—while two of the perpetrators, Mick Andreas and Terry Wilson, were within months of completing their much shorter sentences.

No wife wants her husband to become a sensation for the reasons Mark became one. He had become a symbol of retaliation against whistleblowers and of betrayal of trust by the government he served. In my view, he also helped save millions of consumers millions of dollars. Ultimately, the cleansing hose of his wife's moral stance cleared the way for consumers to get a fair deal, although the legend that the fifteen-year ordeal made of Mark almost destroyed him. And anyone who knows him will tell you that he has the skin of a rhinoceros.

They were fortunate in one respect: their strong belief in God, their family values, and their increasing closeness all grew stronger the longer Mark was in prison. There is data to suggest that many people who receive long prison sentences cease to have any real existence, even to their families, after about three years. Three years seems to be the magic cut-off point. Longer than that means oblivion; shorter than that means only that you may have a fighting chance that your spouse and children will be waiting for you when you get out. The scenario has been repeated many times: an incarcerated husband with a long sentence calls home one day from one of those dreadful wall phones in prison. A strange male voice comes on and gruffly barks, "She doesn't want to talk to you anymore. The divorce papers are in the mail." Click. Such a scenario was not even a remote possibility with Mark and Ginger. If he was doing time, Ginger was doing time right alongside him, both literally in visitors' centers and figuratively speaking.

A key element in fast-tracking Mark's commutation effort would be convincing the Oval Office that Mark's mental state was severely impaired at the time he committed his crimes. Ginger knew her husband. She was the one there to see him crumble one day at a time. She had maintained from Day One that Mark's actions reflected—not greed and deceit—but short-term impairment of judgment. The forensic psychiatrists at Springfield Medical supported her contention. And a former prosecutor who had worked out of the Chicago office of the U.S. Attorney's office, and who himself was involved in bringing the case against ADM and Mark, supported Mark's pardon on that basis in a September 2000 NPR radio interview and later (2004) with a very strong support letter for executive clemency.

───────────────

To the point of a recommendation from the Pardon Attorney's office to the President, Ginger focused intense effort on developing overwhelming support for Mark's commutation or pardon. That meant rallying close friends, family, religious leaders, Congressmen, a judge, and other elected representatives to support the petition. Ginger explained to anyone who would listen, until she was hoarse, that Mark changed the future of how the Sherman Antitrust Act would be applied to cartels. Before Mark, the government never had an inside look at how price-fixing crimes occurred. To illustrate, a key component of fixing the price of something at an artificially high level is controlling the *volumes* produced. Once producers agree to control the volumes, scarcity happens. When scarcity happens, prices go up. When prices go up, it costs the end user. When prices go up due to the creation of artificial scarcity resulting from collusion among producers, a crime has occurred, at least in this country.

ADM manufactured essential food additives used in poultry and animal food. They also manufactured or processed some of our mainstay dietary staples. When a price-fixing cartel is successful, virtually every American household pays a hidden surcharge to the production cartel by paying more for their groceries than they otherwise would because of the overcharge on the ingredients. Because such price-fixing is secretive and nearly impossible to uncover, only someone inside the organization is able to capture such shenanigans and the curmudgeons behind them for public exposure.

Mark did exactly that, making the case for clemency very strong: if the court of last resort, our government, doesn't stand up for the whistleblower, who will? What corporate executive in his right mind, after seeing what happened to Mark Whitacre, would turn government informant and risk the retaliation that was visited on Mark, his wife, and their children?

———————

These major indicators of Mark's mental condition formed the platform for Mark's original petition for executive clemency in 2000. After the *Dateline NBC* program, Ginger succeeded in obtaining well over one hundred support letters, which were sent to the Pardon Attorney's office. These came from diverse sources across a broad swath of their shared past and included letters from all three FBI agents who worked on Harvest King, one former prosecutor of the case, Chuck Colson of Prison Ministries, Ken Adams (lead counsel in class action lawsuits brought against ADM), Jim Lieber, author of the excellent *Rats in the Grain*, Art Schmidt, the Whitacre's neighbor from his Ralston Purina days, John Ashcroft, former professors from college and grad school including Dr. Combs, friends, cousins, immediate family members, two prosecutors from the Justice Department of Canada, employees who were still at Archer Daniels, employees from their Evonik (Degussa) days in Germany, and baseball legend Harmon Killebrew, among many others.

Paul A. Willis, Founder, Chairman & CEO of Cypress Systems, Inc., wrote:

I strongly believe that the Pardon Office now has a low-risk opportunity to exercise the time-tested American value of doing the right thing when the situation is warranted.

Mark has incurred almost half of his sentence; he has paid back the majority of moneys at question; he has expressed complete and continuing remorse; he has reached out to help others during his incarceration; and finally, he has exhibited all the characteristics of someone who has been rehabilitated and can be successfully released back into society to function as a productive, responsible, and fully contributing social member. Respectfully, I believe that the Government (whose purpose is to act on behalf of its citizens) can no longer expect to gain more by continuing or prolonging the long-term incarceration of Mark Whitacre.

Paul A. Willis
Letter to Pardon Attorney
October, 2001

Excerpts from a letter by Kenneth L. Adams, an attorney who represented companies that were victimized by the price-fixing cartels exposed by Mark:

Without Mr. Whitacre's cooperation neither the government nor my clients ever would have known about the lysine and citric acid cartels. Without his active assistance, tape recording cartel meetings and phone conversations inside ADM for 2 ½ years, the government never would have been able to convict the cartel members. Thanks to Mr. Whitacre, the government was able to obtain guilty pleas and record fines. Thanks to Mr. Whitacre, the government secured high profile convictions of major corporate price fixers, sending a powerful message to the other international companies which hopefully will make them think twice before conspiring to fix prices. Thanks to Mr. Whitacre, American purchasers of lysine and citric acid who were illegally overcharged . . . recouped tens of millions of dollars in civil damages from ADM and its co-conspirators.

As it turned out, Mr. Whitacre (like many government informants) was not a saint but a lawbreaker in his own right. He was charged, convicted, and jailed for his wrongdoing. But he received no consideration at all for the critical role he played in blowing the whistle on two massive global cartels. As a result, he has been punished far more severely than the criminals he exposed. Not only is that unfair, it undermines the interests of justice."

> Kenneth L. Adams
> Letter to Pardon Attorney
> August 21, 2000

Ginger herself, in one of many letters sent to the White House, to senators, and to the Pardon Attorney at DOJ, wrote the following:

Most importantly, granting Mark Whitacre clemency (pardon or commutation to time served) would be a positive signal for potential whistleblowers at Enron—or any other company—to come forward even though they themselves may have broken some laws as Mark did.

> Ginger Whitacre
> Letter to Senator Fritz Hollings
> February 25, 2002

Other allies of the Whitacres wrote letters in support of not just commutation but a full and immediate pardon. Baseball Hall of Famer Harmon Killebrew wrote to Bush Two:

Dear President Bush:

In all my 22 years of professional baseball and my 25 years of post career activities, I have met and socialized with most of the living former and current Presidents of the United States, and I have never written to ask for a political consideration. The following matter has moved me emotionally, and I feel that I need to ask for your help in this worthy cause . . . . I would like your help in . . . considering Mark Whitacre's active participation for pardon consideration . . . Please give this your utmost immediate consideration and help . . . .

Harmon Killebrew
Letter to President George Bush
November 19, 2001

Many other people wrote letters. Several more must be mentioned. The Whitacres neighbor from their years in St. Louis came to their defense with the energy and outrage of a man half his age. Arthur "Art" Schmidt's letter is one of the most heart-felt and eloquent in its simplicity. He wrote this:

I am an 82-year-old man. I have no axe to grind and nothing to gain. But the evil injustice heaped on Mark Whitacre has overwhelmed me for the last five years. The greatest Whistle Blower this country has ever seen wastes away in prison with an unfair sentence. He risked his life to provide evidence the FBI required. Today, FBI agents and others involved in the case come forward to testify to the injustice received by Mark Whitacre. The Federal Pardon Attorney's innumerable letters in the files verify this fact. Why would any Whistle Blower come forward when he can expect to be treated unfairly by our justice system?

With much Humilty and Respect,

Arthur R. Schmidt
Letter to White House
July 17, 2002

Art Schmidt, now almost ninety, continues to work indefatigably to help Mark obtain a presidential pardon.

After the Pardon Attorney recommended Mark's petition to the President, those who wrote the President on the Whitacres behalf got encouraging replies from the White House stating that Mark's case was being seriously considered. There have been many meetings and conversations over the years, each one giving the Whitacres hope that a pardon was just around the corner. One such instance was when, at Ginger's request, a conference call was arranged that included then-Pardon Attorney Roger Adams and Associate Pardon Attorney Sam Morrison, and her. She had assembled a lengthy document spelling out in great detail all pertinent issues relating to the case and the pardon. While the conference call substantially assisted Justice in gaining a better understanding of why Mark's commutation and pardon were fully justified, nothing happened.

The Whitacres persevered, trying many alternatives, including the use of well-placed lawyers and lobbyists, including the hiring of an attorney, David Schertler. Before going into private practice, Schertler had spent years at the DOJ. In private practice, Schertler most recently represented Ben Glisan for his role in the Enron scheme. With Schertler's help, they felt certain that they were in line for a Bush pardon at Christmas 2001, Christmas being the traditional season of presidential forgiveness. Bush gave no pardons in 2001; his first being not until Christmas in 2002.

The family employed the services of the affable and effective Steve Kupka, a respected lobbyist and now the managing partner of the Washington, D.C., office of Kansas City-based law firm, Husch Blackwell Sanders. Mr. Kupka's contacts and knowledge of governmental affairs greatly assisted the Whitacres in keeping their petition for commutation (with possibility of full pardon) visible with the White House Counsel's office and the Department of Justice.

However, nobody surmised the extent to which Bush Two would let, as pardon attorney specialist Margaret Love put it, the power of the pardon atrophy. After the pardon feast that Clinton had engaged in right before his departure, Bush Two entered office with too much negative overhang from the Clinton pardon scandal. In fact, Bush entered office amid congressional hearings and a federal investigation of Clinton's last minute pardon of Marc Rich. This led to Bush's hard-line stance on pardons. At his first presidential news conference, on February 22, 2001, Bush Two said he would "be different." Of pardons, he said: "I'll have the highest of high standards."

Bush Two ended up granting only a small handful of pardons, and those he did grant were very non-controversial cases, such as a man who had received probation thirty years earlier for making moonshine and a minister sentenced to two years in the 1950's for not reporting for military induction. However, even at the end of Bush Two's administration, he ended up handing out fewer pardons than almost any other president. Bush's stinginess cannot be attributed to backlash from Clinton's final grants of dubious pardons. Bush Two may have been overly concerned that someone he pardoned would be released and then commit another crime. Clearly, that was not a risk in Mark's case. Whatever Bush Two's reasons, the plain truth is that he woefully under-utilized his one true power, the power of the pardon. Without it, there's no safety net in the system to rectify injustices such as that perpetrated against the many innocent people who are in prison today.

Today, some two and a half years after Mark completed his full sentence and more than seven years after his petition was recommended to the president by the Pardon Attorney, still no action has been taken. There has been a change of administrations, and the new President has a great deal on his plate besides pardoning white-collar ex-offenders.

Before Bush Two left office, and as recently as March of 2008, even the former FBI agent whom Mark had turned against wrote a letter supporting a pardon. Agent Brian Shepard wrote:

> **I am writing this letter in support of Mark Whitacre regarding his request for a pardon stemming from the charge that he violated the Sherman Antitrust Act. As the FBI case agent from the inception to the conclusion of the investigation involving the Archer Daniels Midland Company (ADM). I had almost daily contacts supervising his efforts for the FBI.**
>
> **. . . . Because of my first hand knowledge and close relationship directing Whitacre throughout the price fixing investigation at ADM, granting him a pardon at this time is the proper decision to make morally, ethically, and logically.**

Brian D. Shepard
Letter "To Whom It May Concern"
(Hand delivered by former Supervisory Agent Dean Paisley)
March 3, 2008

In a letter from Chuck Colson, founder of Prison Ministries, and a man who has worked tirelessly for more than thirty years with thousands of prisoners, wrote:

> . . . . [Whitacre] has been an active participant in Christian programming [in prison], and . . . is a responsible citizen looking to do some good with the rest of his life.

> . . . . I think that we put too many non-dangerous people in prison and for much too long a time. I can't imagine what would be accomplished by keeping Mr. Whitacre longer than he has already served, either for him, for the federal budget, or for the public welfare.

> I hope that your office will favorably consider this petition.

Charles W. Colson
Letter to White House
(Hand delivered to White House Counsel)
August 6, 2004

While a pardon is no longer front and center for Mark and Ginger as they move forward with their lives and good works, it matters to my sense of justice—and to that of many others—that something be done.

President Obama has a large number of intractable problems on his plate, pushing the urgency of granting pardons further down his list of to-do items. Nonetheless, I believe the time is here for Obama to rectify the many injustices that have occurred to many Americans now doing time or who did time and are out, but are still carrying the stigma of convicted felon.

As a friend of the family, I address you directly, Mr. President, and I speak for many hundreds of people, including the FBI, who know the Whitacre family. We all pray for your wisdom and ask you to *"Please pardon Mark Whitacre!"*

CHRONOLOGY

May 1, 1957	*Mark Edward Whitacre* born Wilmington, Ohio
August 15, 1958	*Ginger Lynn Gilbert* born Middletown, Ohio
May 1975	Mark Whitacre graduates high school, Morrow, Ohio
May 1976	Ginger Gilbert graduates high school one year later, Morrow, Ohio
June 16, 1979	Mark Whitacre and Ginger Gilbert marry, South Lebanon, Ohio
December 1979	Mark graduates Ohio State, Columbus, Ohio
December 1982	Mark defends dissertation and completes all requirements for award of his PhD, Cornell University, Ithaca, NY
January 1, 1983	Mark starts in R&D with Ralston Purina Company (now part of Nestlé group), St. Louis, Missouri
May 1983	Mark receives PhD, Cornell University, Ithaca, NY
Jan 1983-June 1984	Mark employed by Ralston Purina Company (now Nestlé Purina PetCare), St. Louis, Missouri
July 1984-October 1989	Mark employed by Evonik Chemical USA (formerly Degussa USA), Teterboro, New Jersey

March 1985-Oct 1988	Mark dispatched to Evonik's World Headquarters, Hanau, West Germany
December, 1984	Mark and Ginger adopt biological brother and sister, *Tanya M. Whitacre* and *William A. Whitacre* when they were five and seven years, respectively
December 14, 1985	Ginger gives birth to son, *Alexander R. Whitacre*, in Hanau, Germany. Mark working for Evonik
1989-1995	Mark employed by ADM, Decatur, Illinois
October, 1992	Mark is named Corporate Vice President/Officer of ADM, Decatur, Illinois
November 5, 1992	Mark begins undercover work for FBI against ADM, Decatur, Illinois
June 27, 1995	Mark exposed as informant
August 9, 1995	Mark officially fired from ADM
September 4, 1995	Mark lead story in *Fortune Magazine* and on cover
Aug 1995-Dec 1997	Mark CEO of Chapel Hill, NC biotechnology company
March 4, 1998	Mark pleads guilty to fraud and immediately begins serving a ten-year-and-eight-month prison sentence
June 1998	Bill, Mark and Ginger's middle child and younger biological brother of Tanya, graduates Chapel Hill High School, North Carolina, several months after Mark goes to prison
1998-Present	Ginger teaches elementary school, first in Aiken County, South Carolina, then in Escambia County, Florida
May 2000	Tanya, Mark and Ginger's eldest and biological sister to Bill, graduates college, East Carolina University, Greenville, North Carolina; Mark remains incarcerated
January 2004	Alex, youngest child of Mark and Ginger, finishes high school and starts at University of West Florida (UWF)

June 16, 2004	Mark and Ginger celebrate 25th wedding anniversary in visiting room at Federal Prison Camp Pensacola
December 21, 2006	Mark released to halfway house & home confinement, residing in Pensacola, Florida
December 22, 2006	Mark starts with Cypress Systems, Inc. of Fresno, California and opens branch office in Pensacola, Florida
February 2007	Ginger named 2007 Teacher of the Year by Warrington Elementary School, Pensacola, Florida; Mark attends
June 13, 2007	Mark released from halfway house and home confinement; traveling permitted
March 6, 2008	Mark flies to Washington DC with retired FBI agent Paisley to lobby Capitol Hill and Department of Justice for presidential pardon from Bush, gives first public speech since release (to Young Presidents Organization of Washington DC)
March 25, 2008	Mark promoted to Chief Operating Officer & President of Operations, Cypress Systems, Inc.
April 6, 2008	FBI Supervisor Paisley (retired) first praises Mark publicly as "national hero" to several media outlets
May 2008	Filming begins for *The Informant,* directed by Steven Soderbergh (director of *Traffic, Erin Brokovich, Ocean's Eleven, Twelve, and Thirteen, etc.);* Matt Damon plays Mark Whitacre
October 2008	*The Informant* (2009 film) goes into post-production
December 2008	Alex graduates UWF, Mark, out of prison since 12/2006, attends graduation
March 2009	Documentary *Undercover: Mark Whitacre, Operation Harvest King* airs on Investigation Discovery Channel
October 9, 2009	USA premiere of *The Informant* (2009 film)

CYPRESS SYSTEMS INC.
&
THE IMPORTANCE OF SELENIUM

A BRIEF HISTORY OF CYPRESS SYSTEMS INC.

In June of 1996, Willis led a buyout of the specialty yeast division of Fleischmann's Yeast Company. He renamed the entity Cypress Systems Inc., and in July of 1996, incorporated Cypress in California, relocating its corporate headquarters to Fresno. When asked why he named the company Cypress, he replies "We are a California company, and "Cypress" sounded appropriate based on the famed *Lone Cypress Tree* that is located on 17-Mile Drive in Monterey, California on the scenic road through Pebble Beach." That is only part of the reason Willis named the company Cypress. The other part is that **CYPRESS** is an acronym for **C**hrist-**Y**our-**P**rovider-**R**edeemer-**E**manuel-**S**avior-**S**anctifier, and Willis is a deeply religious man who is, among other things an Elder of Mission at Trinity Presbyterian Church in Fresno.

See "About Us" at *http://www.cypsystems.com.*

Upon forming Cypress, Willis retained as his Director of Fermentation Dr. Lon Baugh, who in 1979 pioneered and co-developed the production protocol for mineralized yeast with Dr. Henry Peppler. At the time, Dr. Baugh was Vice President of Production at Dixie Yeast in Gastonia, North Carolina, and Dr. Peppler was Director of Research at Universal Foods Red Star Yeast.

In 1983, a dapper, bow-tie wearing scientist named Dr. Gerald F. Combs, Jr., of Cornell University, and his colleague, Dr. Larry Clark, who is now deceased, of both Cornell and the University of Arizona Cancer

Center, began conducting several important clinical trials involving selenium. Both scientists had been conducting research for years on the possible anti-carcinogenic effects of selenium. They selected Dr. Baugh's High Selenium Yeast as the intervention agent in an important decade-long planned clinical trial conducted by the National Cancer Institute.

This "Gold Standard" cancer-prevention trial has been commonly referred to as the Nutritional Prevention of Cancer Trial or simply the NPC Trial. It is also sometimes known as the "Clark & Combs trial." The objective of the NPC Trial was to test the effects of selenium supplementation on the prevention of skin cancer. Although the trial showed no effect on skin cancer it was unblinded early because it demonstrated a forty-five to sixty-three percent reduction in colon, lung and prostate cancer. These dramatic results of the NPC Trial were published in the December 1996 issue of the Journal of American Medical Association (JAMA). Cypress continues to use Dr. Baugh's original protocol to produce its High Selenium Yeast, which is trademarked as SelenoExcell® High Selenium Yeast.

As a result of much of this early work, the Food and Drug Administration (FDA) finally in 2003 gave a Qualified Health Claim related to the cancer-prevention benefits of selenium, which reads:

> **(1) Selenium may reduce the risk of certain cancers.** Some scientific evidence suggests that consumption of selenium may reduce the risk of certain forms of cancer. However, FDA has determined that this evidence is limited and not conclusive.

> **(2) Selenium may produce anticarcinogenic effects in the body.** Some scientific evidence suggests that consumption of selenium may produce anticarcinogenic effects in the body. However, FDA has determined that this evidence is limited and not conclusive.

What is unique about this claim is the second part. No other nutrient has ever been acknowledged by the FDA to have anticarcinogenic effects. Cypress is committed to on-going rigorous scientific trials that might someday justify a Public Health Claim for the cancer-preventive role of selenium and SelenoExcell®.

WHAT IS SELENIUM?

Selenium is a trace element found to a varying extent in soil. It enters the human diet through plants such as whole grains and the meat of animals that graze on vegetation containing selenium. Selenium naturally occurs in foods such as seafood, garlic, eggs, and mushrooms.

HOW CAN SELENIUM HELP FIGHT DISEASE OR PREVENT CANCER?

It is believed that selenium helps fight diseases including cancer by neutralizing harmful elements called "free radicals," which are unstable molecules that damage cells. Selenium has been shown to have strong antioxidant properties. Antioxidants are minerals and vitamins that can inhibit the formation of free radicals before they are able to cause damage by breaking down the molecules of the cells. It is estimated that between fifty and one hundred different selenium-containing proteins exist in the human body, including those that build heart muscle, red blood cells, and sperm. It is also thought that selenium has other anticarcinogenic properties that go beyond just grounding the harmful free radicals.

On a global scale much of today's farming soil and resulting food products are nutrient-depleted. Thus, it is important to supplement the human diet with proper dosages of the food form of yeast-based selenium. Research indicates that in many parts of the world even a well-balanced diet does not supply enough selenium.

There are numerous forms of selenium. It has been well proven that the natural food form of organically bound selenium found in Cypress's SelenoExcell® product is the most effective in helping to suppress free radicals. The salt form of selenium, known as sodium selenite, has been shown to have far less bioavailability than the organically bound form. Bioavailability refers to how readily and efficiently the body can utilize a specific nutrient. When referred to in connection with selenium, organic forms of selenium are used by the body better than inorganic salt forms, thus making the organic forms more bioavailable. The organically bound form of selenium found in Cypress High Selenium Yeast contains multiple organic selenium compounds which are believed to have a synergistic effect and possibly contribute to the product's cancer prevention benefits. There are other forms of synthetic organic selenium compounds such as selenomethionine which are a single amino acid (methionine) that has a selenium molecule attached to it.

THE SELECT TRIAL

The National Cancer Institute released in October of 2008 the results of its SELECT Prostate Cancer Prevention Trial. "SELECT" stands for the "Selenium and Vitamin E Cancer Prevention Trial." SELECT was the largest-ever prostate cancer prevention trial conducted and was undertaken because previous studies suggested that selenium and Vitamin E (alone or in combination) might reduce the risk of developing prostate cancer by sixty percent and thirty percent, respectively, but only a large clinical trial such as SELECT would be able to confirm those findings.

The SELECT Trial was terminated early because it found no effects of either selenomethionine or vitamin E on the incidence of prostate cancer. The SELECT Trial did not use the standardized high selenium yeast. The trial added clarity that what selenium form is used does matter.

Willis has publicly stated that he was disappointed that the SELECT Trial did not use high selenium yeast. In 1998, Cypress signed a Clinical Trial Agreement with the National Cancer Institute in order to reconfirm previous clinical results that were obtained using high selenium yeast. According to Mark, high selenium yeast is different from selenomethionine because it contains *several different forms of organically bound selenium* as well as selenomethionine. Cypress suspects that the advantage of SelenoExcell® High Selenium Yeast lies in its content of *multiple forms of selenium,* including some forms that are more direct acting in anticarcinogenesis.

CYPRESS SYSTEM'S MISSION

Cypress's primary mission, as stated at its website *http://www. cypsystems.com* is to advance the prevention—not the treatment—of cancer through selenium supplementation and to address related health problems through an overall health stewardship program. The company maintains corporate and personal stewardship in three primary areas: (a) nutrition, health, and fitness; (b) environmental resources; and (c) outreach to others. Cypress also pursues a business strategy to establish itself as the premier manufacturer of specialty fermentation minerals such as selenium, chromium, and zinc.

As part of the Cypress mission, a primary platform for Mark Whitacre as an "agent of change" is the Excell Health Campaign. Located at *http://www.excellhealthcampaign.com*, the campaign's goal is to be a resource and tool to educate consumers. This campaign is intended to help people develop their own health regimen so as to prevent cancer and other chronic diseases such as diabetes and heart disease.

NICKNAMES OF PRISONS
WHITACRE ATTENDED & DATES

Nickname in this Book	Prison/Jail Name Location	Whitacre's Dates At Location
"Decatur Jail"	Macon County Jail Decatur, Illinois	March 1998
"Springfield Medical"	Medical Center for Federal Prisoners (MCFP Springfield) Springfield, Missouri	March 1998– May 1998
"Butner Low"	Federal Correction Institute Butner (FCI Butner) Butner, North Carolina	June 1998 (1st Stay) & July–August (2nd Stay)
"MCC Chicago"	Metropolitan Correction Center (MCC) Chicago, Illinois	July 9-21, 1998
"Atlanta Holdover"	United States Penitentiary, Atlanta (USP Atlanta) Atlanta, Georgia	Aug-Oct 1998

"Oklahoma Transfer"	*Federal Transfer Center Oklahoma (FTC Oklahoma) Oklahoma City, Oklahoma*	*Oct–Nov 1998*
"Yazoo"	*Federal Correction Institute Yazoo (FCI—Low, Yazoo) Yazoo City, Mississippi*	*Nov 1998–March 1999*
"Edgefield Camp"	*Federal Prison Camp Edgefield (FPC Edgefield) Edgefield, South Carolina*	*March 1999–May 2003 (4 Years & 2 Months)*
"Pensacola Camp"	*Federal Prison Camp Pensacola (FPC Pensacola) Pensacola, Florida*	*May 2003–December 2006 (3 Years & 7 Months)*

GLOSSARY
OF
PRISON SLANG

There are many sources on the internet for learning the language of life on the inside. One of the *least* reliable is *The Correctional Officer's Guide to Prison Slang*. This manual for guards is something of a joke. They contain many slang words that are no longer in use except by the guards themselves. Two *reliable* slang sources are *Inside Prison* and *Felonious Ramblings*.

If you are unlucky enough to "go away to cooking school" (go to prison), you don't want to arrive there a complete "fish" (not wise to prison life). Hire a consultant and memorize a list more extensive than the one below.

Several reality television shows, particularly *Prison Break*, use accurate prison slang. Some slang words are used to keep the uninitiated or the correctional officers in the dark while two inmates converse.

The list below is limited to terms Whitacre or the author came across while doing time.

Term	Explanation
Ad-Seg	Administrative Segregation. Means you are in the "hole" (solitary confinement) because you are being investigated. You stay there until the investigation is complete. Is different from "PC" (Protective Custody), which is also a euphemism for going to the hole, but PC is for protection against getting shanked by other inmates.
Hack	Guard or Corrections Officer.
Cop-Out/Kite	In a broad sense, a Cop-Out is any written correspondence, such as a request for a bunk change or medical or dental services. A Kite is usually "dropped" or left anonymously with the warden. If you want to change from an upper bunk to a lower bunk, get a new job assignment, etc., you "put in a cop-out." If you snitched on others to curry favor with the hacks, you "dropped a kite on someone" to your administrative supervisor. In higher security prisons, a kite can also be a note passed between inmates, usually of the nature of illicit information, such as a cryptic written order to kill another inmate.
Shot	A disciplinary action. When you "get a shot," you get a negative write-up that goes in your "jacket" or permanent record.
Baby's Momma	The unwed mother of an incarcerated male, as in "My baby's momma is comin' to see me next week."

Bunkie	Your bunkmate, either above or below you. In dormitory-style minimum camps, lower bunks against a wall are the most coveted, as are compatible bunkies.
Cellie	Your cellmate.
Cube	Cubicle. A six-bunk mini-area in an open dormitory-style minimum prison camp. See sketch of Whitacre's cube on page 255.
Snitch	Anyone who rats somebody out for something. Snitches exist not only in prisons, but also in courtrooms and police stations.
Dry Snitch	Someone who rats another person out by speaking loudly in front of an officer. This is an indirect form of snitching and is sometimes unintentional, many times quite intentional.
Shakedown	A search of a particular inmate's cell or of the entire prison facility if it's a minimum camp. At higher security levels, it usually refers to a cell search. Shakedowns come randomly, although they also come as a specific result of someone dropping a kite on someone else. For example, if you know that another inmate you work with mowing lawns has a cell phone (serious contraband) stashed in the woods, and if you know that the hack watching the work detail will punish the entire work crew if that one

	inmate gets caught, you have to decide whether to drop a kite on that inmate or risk getting a serious shot yourself. Both options are unpalatable.
Weight Pile (Iron Pile)	The weightlifting equipment or workout area of a prison, often in the prison yard or under a breezeway on the compound.
Shipped Out	If a prisoner "ships out" on his own, he may be transferring to another facility (e.g., to one that has the RDAP drug program). If, however, a prisoner "got shipped out," he was removed from the facility for committing an infraction or found using contraband and got taken away to receive additional charges and get transferred to a usually more unpleasant federal facility.
DAP or RDAP Program	The 500-hour Drug Abuse Program or Residential Drug Abuse Program. If successfully completed, an inmate with a history of drug or alcohol abuse gets a one-year reduction in his prison sentence.
Shank	A homemade knife. Sometimes also called a "shiv." These are easily obtainable in prisons and frequently used.
Wolf Ticket	Speaking aggressively to someone without intending to back it up. "He's selling wolf tickets" means he's talking a big story but won't actually do anything about it.

U.A.	Urinalysis. Usually conducted randomly and often in the middle of the night. It is required protocol in all federal prison facilities.
"Good Lookin' Out"	A phrase used to show appreciation to someone who helped you out.
Punk	A homosexual. On the outside, a punk means some sort of young tough. In prison, "punk" never means that; it only means the man is a (usually passive) homosexual.
Your Jacket	Your prison file. The file that contains all the information on a prisoner, usually held in the office of your Unit Case Manager.
My Bad	Means "my mistake" or "I'm to blame." Now an all-too-prevalent expression on the outside as well. I find the expression distasteful and suggestive of a limited vocabulary. Whatever happened to "so sorry"?
She's Clean	Refers to an attractive female. May also refer to one whom the prisoner believes has no sexually transmitted diseases.
Dawg	Slang for "my close acquaintance of an African-American ethnic origin" as in "Waddup Dawg?" The Caucasian version might be "dude."
Pack Out	Gather all your worldly possessions and have them mailed to another facility you may get to much later.

Buck Rodger Time	A release date so far off that the prisoner cannot imagine release.
Running A Store	A prisoner is "running a store" when he is selling goods or services, often contraband, out of his locker as a result of bartering commissary items by virtue of winning at card games played illegally in the middle of the night.
Commissary/Canteen	Items sold legally by the Bureau of Prisons. Some prison facilities have commissary privileges twice a week, some daily, some once a week. You have to have money in your commissary account to be able to buy these "luxury" items.
Psych Tip	Faking psychological symptoms in order to get drugs from the clinic.
Pill Line	The line outside the clinic that inmates who take medication stand in, usually twice a day. Sometimes called Med Line.
Jody	A man on the outside whom your girlfriend or wife may use to pay the bills while you are down.
Cadillac	Having a single bunk and the greater privacy that comes by not having the annoying presence of a bunkie.
Grandma's	Gang headquarters. As in "Carlos needs to see you at Grandma's right away."

Self-Report	A recently admitted prisoner who is allowed to show up at Receiving & Discharge on his or her own.
Cell Soldier	A person who talks tough when the cells are locked but is timid when others can get to him and fight him or shank him in the day room.
On Paper	Being out of prison and on supervised release. Derives from the fact that you must complete and submit a written monthly financial and personal report to your probation officer. "How much paper you got?" means "How many months or years of supervised release do you have?"
To Be "Short"	To be close to your release date, as in "Yeah, he's short, so he don't care no more."
Bit	A short prison sentence, as in "I got a three-year bit." Opposite of a jolt.
Jolt	A long prison sentence, as in "He got a life jolt." Opposite of a bit. In the context of this book, the author got a "bit" while Whitacre got a "jolt."
Diaper Sniper	Child molester
Robocop	The type of guard or hack who writes up every infraction (gives you a "Shot"), no matter how small.

THE LOOK & FEEL OF A PRISON CAMP

Sketch of Mark Whitacre's Prison Cubicle, Pensacola Federal Prison Camp

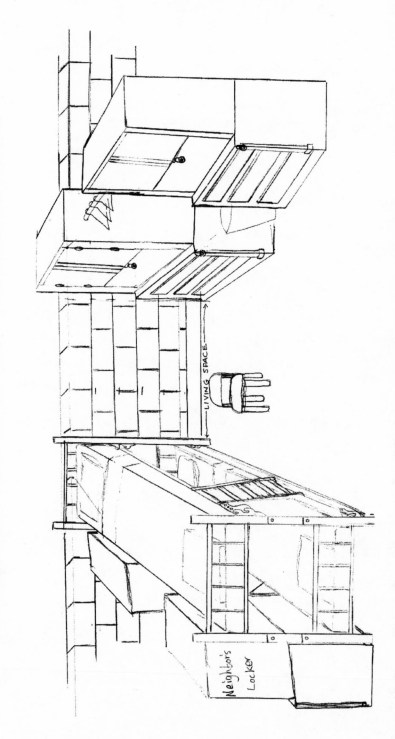

NOTES

FOREWORD BY PAUL WILLIS

1. For complete information about Cypress Systems Inc., go to *http://cypsystems.com*.
2. Biblical quotes selected by Willis are from Jeremiah 29:11 and Jeremiah 18:6, respectively. Jim Elliot's quote is from Elizabeth Elliot, ***Through Gates of Splendor*** (1956). See also *http://www.elizabethelliot.org*
3. Willis's reference to Martin Luther shows how significant Luther's great religious revolt was in the sixteenth century. Luther himself asserted that he had "never seen a Bible until he was twenty years of age" and until after he found peace in the monastic life. His disputes with the Catholic Church grew from there and went on to become particularly focused on the Pope. Luther in his reformist mode believed that the Bible was the only source of faith and that it contained the inspiration of God and that therefore its reading is invested with a quasi-sacramental character. He also put forth that human nature was corrupted by original sin and that man, accordingly, was deprived of free will, meaning, whatever man does, be it good or bad, is not his own work, but God's. Luther also believed that through faith alone man is saved and can confidently believe that God will pardon him. Luther also believed that the "priesthood" is universal and that every Christian may assume it and said that a body of specially trained and ordained men to dispense the mysteries of God is needless and a usurpation of God's power. He meant to include the Pope as being a human who has usurped the power of God. Luther's most famous

remark as recorded in history was when he stood before the Diet of Worms and said, "Here I stand. I cannot do otherwise. So help me, God. Amen." Luther also translated the New Testament into German, and the invention of the printing press gave his translation a huge boost by allowing the multiplication of copies of his translated Bible.

3. For a more detailed discussion of the company founded by Paul Willis, see the appendix starting on page 239, *Cypress Systems Inc and the Importance of Selenium.*

INTRODUCTION—THE ARRIVAL

1. A detailed synopsis of the 2009 Warner Bros. film, *The Informant*, including user comments and a list of outside reviews, is available at *http://www.imdb.com/title/tt1130080/synopsis.*

2. The documentary TV program, *Undercover: Operation Harvest King* first aired on **Investigation Discovery** on March 10, 2009. There have been multiple re-runs since then.

3. See *Fortune* Magazine, September 4, 1995, cover story.

4. To further elaborate, the Warner Bros. movie, *The Informant*, is based on Kurt Eichenwald's book of the same name. Matt Damon stars as Mark Whitacre. The screenplay was written by Scott Z. Burns, who also wrote the screenplay for *Bourne Ultimatum. The Informant* is directed by Steven Soderbergh and has a scheduled USA release date of October 9, 2009, with an international rollout planned shortly thereafter. See *http://www.imdb.com/title/tt1130080/*

5. "Hometown Stands by Fallen Star." *The Cincinnati Post*, Saturday, August 26, 1995. Article written by Dan Horn (Horn 1995).

6. In terms of visitor-count to Whitacre's website, see *http://www. markwhitacre.com/*

7. For inmates who qualify, the "good-conduct" credit allows fifty-four days to be removed from one's sentence for each year served. Thus, Mark served, net, eight-and-a-half years. I was fortunate enough to earn it as well, and served only fifteen months of an eighteen-month sentence.

8. For details of how the Nigerian fraud operates, see *http://www. snopes.com/crime/fraud/nigeria.asp.* See also Lieber's discussion of the embezzlement on pp. 306-307 of *Rats* and Eichenwald's discussion on pp. 431-436 in *The Informant* where he mentions the "'Nigerian Advance Fee Fraud' also known as the '419 Fraud' after the relevant portion of the Nigerian penal code." Et seq.

9. In a radio interview on Tuesday, April 14, 2009, on KMBZ News Radio 980 in Kansas City on the Darla Jaye Show, Whitacre and FBI Supervisory Agent Robert Herndon were on the show together. During that interview, Herndon discussed the Lou Peters award, his pardon push on Mark's behalf, and the approval of a monthly stipend in the amount of $17,500 per month in the event that Mark got dismissed. See *http://www.kmbz.com/ pages/2589230.php?*.

CHAPTER ONE—*TWO GOOD KIDS*

1. The village of Morrow is named after Governor Jeremiah Morrow, ninth Governor of Ohio, who served from 1822 to 1826. Given its modest population of only 1,200, Morrow even today doesn't qualify as a town, but only a village. According to the most recent (2000) census, more than half the residents are married couples with an average of three children. They live in approximately 500 housing units, and the racial mix of Morrow is about ninety-eight percent Caucasian and less than two percent Hispanic, African-American, or native American. The male/female ratio of Morrow is 83 men per 100 women as of the last census. This compares with a national average of 96 males for every 100 females and suggests the average age of Morrow may be a little older, as men tend to die younger than women.

2. The full lyrics to the song "To Morrow" are available at *http://www. musicsonglyrics.com/K/kingstontriolyrics/kingstontriotomorrowlyrics. htm*

3. Mark described first seeing Ginger in one of many telephone conversations and in several subsequent e-mails in April of 2009.

4. Lebanon, Ohio, is home town to, among others, astronaut Neil Armstrong, actor Woody Harrelson, and Medal of Honor winner Gordon Ray "Bird Dog" Roberts.

5. The excerpt of the letter from Ginger to Mark is taken from private correspondence between them. Letter dated June 14, 2001.

6. The information regarding these aspects of the Whitacres is redacted from telephone conversations and confirming e-mails between Mark Whitacre and the author dated March 17, 2009.

7. Frisch's Big Boy Restaurants started in 1946 with one drive-in located in nearby Cincinnati. The chain is still thriving in 2009. See *http:// frischs.com*.

8. International Order of the Rainbow for Girls (IORG) information is available on their website at *www.gorainbow.org*.
9. Goiter is an enlargement of the thyroid gland and is often caused by a deficiency of iodine. Although the disease is rare today since the introduction of iodized salt, it was a serious disease at the time Mark's grandfather died of it.

CHAPTER TWO—*WHIZ KID*

1. "Whiz Kid" is defined in the dictionary as "an exceptionally intelligent, innovatively clever, and precociously successful young person." By that definition, Mark was the very embodiment of the term. From his early years growing up in Morrow, Ohio, through the double-major undergraduate years at Ohio State, continuing into his intense research phase during the graduate years at Cornell, right up through the early years at ADM, where, in 1989 at the tender age of thirty-five, he became the youngest corporate officer in the company's history, the most apt moniker applied to Mark was Whiz Kid. The original Whiz Kids were ten U.S. Army Air Force veterans of World War II who, just after the war in 1946, became Ford Motor Company executives. During the war, all ten were part of an operation known as Statistical Control. After the war ended, they offered their services to Henry Ford II, but only as a group. Take all ten of them or none. Henry Ford II had recently taken over the company from his grandfather and was badly in need of management help, so he accepted the offer. These Whiz Kids took Ford to new heights. Most prominent among them was Robert McNamara, who eventually became Ford Motor president, then controversial Secretary of Defense, and later, president of the World Bank.
2. Dr. Gerald F. Combs Jr. became emeritus at Cornell University after 29 years on the Nutritional Sciences faculty. From 2002 to the present, he has been Director, Human Nutrition Research Center at the U.S. Department of Agriculture (USDA) facility in Grand Forks, North Dakota. He is still active in selenium research, among many other activities.
3. Mark Whitacre received the following degrees following his graduation from Little Miami High School in Morrow, Ohio: (1) a Bachelor of Science (BS) from Ohio State University (Animal Nutrition); (2) a Masters in Science (MS) from Ohio State University

(Animal Nutrition); (3) a PhD from Cornell University (Nutritional Biochemistry); (4) a Masters in Business Administration (MBA) from Kensington University; (5) a *Juris Doctor* (law degree) from Kensington University; and during prison (6) a second JD from Northwestern California University School of Law; (7) an LLM (Masters in Law) from Northwestern California University School of Law; (8) a PhD in Psychology from Kensington; and (9) a PhD in Economics from Kensington

4. Using the Consumer Price Index to calculate the relative value of a dollar, $350 in 1980 would be $881 in 2009 dollars. That's a very hefty utility bill indeed.

5. Dr. Carl Sagan was the (now deceased) astronomer and author best known for his groundbreaking TV series "Cosmos" and his pioneering work on the possibility of life on other planets.

6. For interested readers, Mark's research involved measuring the enzyme levels for glutathionine peroxidase, which converts hydrogen peroxide into water and oxygen. Hydrogen peroxide is toxic to the body. Mark found that selenium, a trace mineral, was an anti-oxidant that could help prevent pancreatic degeneration. His rigorous scientific proof of this action was considered an important breakthrough in selenium research and was published in successive articles in scientific journals, in particular the *Journal of Nutrition*. All four of Mark's academic treatises on the subject are available at *http://www.markwhitacre.com/education.html*.

7. Lab costs were substantial due mainly to the inclusion of several electron microscopes which use a focused beam of electrons instead of diode lights to image the specimen with high resolution to gain information as to its structure and composition. New ones cost in excess of $10,000, sometimes much more.

8. The justification of human behavior quote by Benjamin Franklin is found in *The Autobiography of Benjamin Franklin*, p 38.

CHAPTER THREE—*RISING STAR*

1. In the Ralston R&D Department, Mark's focus was on conducting controlled animal nutrition studies to improve the nutrient uptake of certain proteins and amino acids and increasing their bioavailability for specific animals in order to stimulate growth.

2. Today (2009) the Deutsche Mark has been replaced by the Euro, which is the common currency of members of the European Community. England still uses the Pound Sterling. Switzerland still uses the Swiss Franc.

3. For rich discussions of the history of antitrust, see Eichenwald pp. 56-58 (Eichenwald 2000) and Lieber's entire chapter "The Rise and Fall and Rise of Antitrust." pp. 101-117 (Lieber 2000).

4. For an excellent background discussion of Terry Wilson, see Lieber, p. 141.

For an excellent discussion of the ascension of Dwayne Andreas to power and his ties to the international intelligence community, see Eichenwald, pp. 19-29. For an excellent history of the Archer Daniels Midland Company from the earliest years, see Lieber, pp. 71-79.

5. The most complete discussion of the evolution of "competition law," known in the United States as "antitrust law" that I found was in Wikipedia under *http://en.wikipedia.org/wiki/Antitrust.* That entry contains an excellent discussion of the history of laws governing competition, including Roman legislation going back two millennia, Middle Age laws to control monopolies going back to the Norman Conquest, Renaissance developments in competition law, up to today's antitrust legal precedents, including an extended discussion of the Sherman Act of 1890 and the Clayton Act of 1914.

6. Rockefeller and Standard Oil were the reasons antitrust legislation took such a foothold in the United States. Antitrust laws were minimized in the 1980s under the influence of the "Chicago School" of economic theory, which blamed such laws for the loss of U.S. supremacy in the world economy. The Wikipedia article even discusses anti-monopoly law as it exists today in China, Japan, the European Community. The article also discusses in depth the theory behind the competing doctrines of *laissez-faire* as espoused by John Stuart Mill and Adam Smith's position on antitrust laws as espoused in his *Wealth of Nations.* Modern economic theory regarding antitrust law was heavily influenced by Paul Samuelson, the author of the most successful economics text of the twentieth century. Samuelson advocated a general market *laissez-faire* policy but backed the American government's antitrust policies. In the U.S., the Antitrust Criminal Penalty Enhancement and Reform Act of 2004 arose largely because of Whitacre's unmasking the practice at Archer Daniels Midland. This law raises the maximum

prison term for price fixing from three to ten years, and the maximum fine from $10 million to $100 million.

7. The basic problem that Whitacre brought to the attention of legislators and legal scholars alike is that, when firms hold large market share, consumers almost invariably pay higher prices and get lower quality products than they do if the markets are competitive. The debate over antitrust law will no doubt continue for many years, but without Mark Whitacre's willingness to give law enforcement and lawmakers a true glimpse at how it is done, antitrust law would not be as highly evolved as it is today.

CHAPTER FOUR—*AUSPICIOUS BEGINNINGS*

1. For an excellent description of Dwayne Andreas when he was at the peak of his power, see the *Fortune* Magazine article of October 8, 1990, by Ronald Henkoff entitled "Oh How the Money Grows at ADM: Dwayne Andreas—the king of corn, beans, and clout—cultivates friends in high places and reaps record profits for Archer Daniels Midland." The article can also be found at *http://www.money.cnn.com/ magazine/fortune/fortune_archive/1995/09/04/205874/index.htm.*

CHAPTER FIVE—*GOING UNDERCOVER*

1. For a discussion of different types of corporate whistleblowing—self-appointed do-gooders with financial motive—see article entitled "The Dark Side of Whisteblowing," *Forbes* Magazine, March 14, 2005, pp. 90-98. In that case, the government paid the whistleblower $126 million, whereas Whitacre did not get any money for his whistleblowing and as of May 2009 has received no compensation from any government entity.

2. Read both (Eichenwald 2000) and (Lieber 2000) for more detailed and elaborate descriptions of Mark Whitacre's undercover activities.

CHAPTER SIX—*LEADING TWO LIVES: WIRED & DANGEROUS*

1. Regarding the comment, "grand juries are virtually unknown today outside the United States . . .", many people in America do not understand their purpose. A grand jury is nothing more

than a group of average citizens brought into a courtroom strictly to decide whether there is sufficient evidence of a crime for the prosecution to proceed with. Most grand juries have twenty to twenty-four members, a simple majority of whom must agree on a decision. Grand juries meet in secret, without the accused party or his lawyer present, and listen to one-sided evidence presented by a prosecutor against persons suspected of a crime. No judge is present at grand juries, and no defense lawyers are present to give the other side of the story. If the grand jury decides, after hearing just one side of the case, that sufficient evidence exists, they permit the issuance of a formal charge, called an indictment. Grand juries today are virtually unknown outside the United States. England abandoned grand juries in 1933. Australia abolished them in 1958 and New Zealand in 1961. Canada abolished the practice in the 1970s. Even in the United States, only approximately half the states in the U.S. still employ the grand jury system.

2. Most jurisdictions have replaced grand juries with Preliminary Hearings, at which a judge hears evidence from only the prosecution's side concerning the alleged offenses and makes a decision on whether the prosecution can proceed. Federal grand juries must involve charges of "capital or infamous crimes" that are under federal, as opposed to state, jurisdiction. Such charges must be presented under the Fifth Amendment to the Constitution.

   Critics argue that grand juries as conducted by our federal government are unjust because the defendant is not represented by counsel and does not have the right to call witnesses. Intended originally to serve as a check-and-a-balance against prosecutorial abuse, the grand jury instead presents an opportunity for a prosecutor to compel testimony that does nothing more than permit them to build the case they will present at the final trial.

CHAPTER SEVEN—*WHISTLEBLOWER EXPOSED.*

1. The report mentioning Whitacre as a possible heir to the position of general operating manager of the whole company was written by food analyst Bonnie Wittenburg. Wittenburg later moved to American Express Financial Advisors in Minneapolis, which was spun off and became Ameriprise.

2. For a detailed discussion of David and Carol Hoech's ongoing battle against ADM, see Lieber starting at page twenty-four and continuing through page thirty-two. Lieber lucidly discusses the complicated reasons why prosecutors wanted to give David Hoech immunity in order to elicit testimony from him that would be damaging to Whitacre. See also Lieber, pages fifty-two through fifty-five, especially on page fifty-five where David Hoech filed an ethics complaint for prosecutorial misconduct. See also Eichenwald page 141 and pp. 558-559 where he says David Hoech continued his letter writing after Whitacre went to prison. He says Hoech accused the government of selling Whitacre out by cutting a deal with the company Whitacre had informed on.

3. Eichenwald's book contains an excellent discussion of the evolution of the article and interview with Whitacre by Scott Kilman that appeared on the front page of the *Wall Street Journal* can be found on pp. 331-332 and its aftermath on pp. 401-402. (Eichenwald 2000)

CHAPTER EIGHT—*THE MELTDOWN*

1. Mr. Ian Howes is a successful Raleigh-Durham, North Carolina, based English businessman and entrepreneur who graduated from the University of Warwick, located in Coventry, West Midlands, England. Warwick is considered one of England's leading universities and has been successful at commercializing its academic research. Howes is also a Chartered Accountant. He was formerly CFO and Vice President of Corporate Development for Erimos Pharmaceuticals. Mr. Howes in May 2009 organized a Christian Business Men's Community (CBMC) breakfast gathering during which Mark Whitacre on National Prayer Day, May 7, 2009, had the opportunity to give his testimony.

2. Regarding Whitacre's first suicide attempt, see Eichenwald, pp.382-391 (Eichenwald 2000) and Lieber pp. 14-16. (Lieber 2000). According to these and other sources, while attempting suicide early the morning of August 9, 1995, Mark was saved by his Moweaqua estate groundskeeper, Rusty Williams. Eichenwald indicated that, after calls placed by Ginger to Mark's Chicago attorney Epstein, Mark was taken to a mental-health professional in Chicago (3 hours to the north) to see a psychiatrist named Dr. Derek Miller. After a

week there, he was diagnosed as manic-depressive. Lieber said that the suicide attempt was seen by some as an admission of guilt to theft. Questions also arose about whether Whitacre had faked the gassing in order to arouse sympathy, obtain better treatment from the government, or even get ADM off his back. Lieber indicated that the facts of the event were strange enough to stimulate a series of articles in the *Echo,* an obscure journal for forensic psychiatrists. Eichenwald's version seemed to stress a link between the suicide attempt and recent revelations of his embezzlement activity.

3. According to notes regarding Mark's conversations with his psychiatrist, Dr. Derek Miller, Whitacre, shortly after firing Epstein, told Miller that he believed Epstein worked for the Russians.

4. Lithium is a chemical element that, in its carbonate or salt form, is useful as a mood-stabilizing drug. It was at the time of Mark's first suicide attempt and is still today used as the primary drug treatment for bipolar disorder because it is the only known drug to treat both manic and depressive phases. Bipolar is so called because one end of the emotional "pole" is a very high manic phase, while the other end of the emotional "pole" is a very low depressive phase. Many well-known people have taken or still take lithium, including Ted Turner of CNN fame, Jack Welch of GE fame, the actress Patty Duke, TV icon Mike Wallace of 60 Minutes, and NBC news personality Jane Pauley. She wrote a book about her personal struggle with bipolar disorder entitled *Skywriting: Out of the Blue.* She spoke openly in interviews about being treated.

5. RDAP = Residential Drug Abuse Program. Sometimes also referred to as the "DAP Program," the program is designed by the United States Bureau of Prisons for those inmates who have had a serious drug or alcohol abuse problem. An inmate may volunteer for the RDAP program and, if he or she meets the criteria for a drug use disorder as defined by the American Psychiatric Association's Diagnostic and Statistical Manual, that inmate enters a one-year program at a facility that runs the RDAP program and, upon successful completion, *gets a one-year reduction in his or her sentence.* An inmate must be recommended by his case manager for the RDAP program and approved by his or her drug abuse program coordinator. In my experience, many inmates game the system in order to qualify for the RDAP program by either exaggerating

the extent of their drug "abuse" or getting a lawyer who knows the system well enough to make sure that drug or alcohol abuse is included in the inmate's Pre-Sentencing Report (PSR). RDAP is really just telling us that prison sentences are in most cases too long. I believe more reasonable (shorter) sentences would be preferable to this back-door solution to long prison sentences. No inmate can be blamed for wanting to shorten their sentence by a year. If all that is necessary is that you exaggerate the extent of your prior drug or alcohol problem, why not? What constitutes "abuse" is a matter subject to wide interpretation.

6. "Shank" in prison can be either a noun or a verb. The noun "shank" is a term similar to "shiv" that refers to any makeshift sharp knife that can be used as a weapon. The verb "shank" means to use that weapon to stab another inmate. Inmates are extremely creative when it comes to constructing shanks out of various materials.

7. A shank can be formed from pieces of stray glass found in a prison recreation yard, from the metal shanks in prison-issued boots (hence the term), or from a thin razor blade that gets sandwiched between two wooden tongue depressors taken from the medical room.

CHAPTER NINE—*INMATE #07543-424*

1. Whitacre's fraud sentencing by Judge Harold Baker is extremely well-covered in both Eichenwald's *Informant* and Lieber's *Rats In The Grain*. For additional background, go to *http://www.commondreams. org/views/080800-101.htm* which has an interview with Lieber. Also go to the NPR episode that aired on September 15, 2000 at *http:// www.thislife.org/Radio_Episode.aspx?sched=837*.

CHAPTER TEN—*SPRINGFIELD MEDICAL*

1. Published in 1962, the book *One Flew Over the Cuckoo's Nest* was an immediate success. In 1975 it was made into a film with the same name directed by Milos Forman and starring Jack Nicholson. The film won five Academy Awards.

2. The practice of gouging inmates for phone costs is widespread in both federal and state prison facilities. The state of New York and its prison system share in the revenues generated by the phone company

that is awarded the contract. They collect about $20 million a year by accepting 57% of the phone company's revenues from calls made by prisoners. Prison phone calls can greatly contribute to a prisoner's rehabilitation.

CHAPTER ELEVEN—*MCC CHICAGO: URBAN WARFARE*

1. An excellent description of MCC Chicago is based on information obtained from a. Mark Whitacre himself, b. the Bureau of Prisons website under "facility locator," and c. the Wikipedia article at *http:// en.wikipedia.org/wiki/Metropolitan_Correctional_Center,_Chicago*. See also the website *http://mcc-chicago.com* part of a website managed by a former inmate named Michael Santos, who had a twenty-one year journey through imprisonment and whose main website is at *http:// michaelsantos.net*.

CHAPTER TWELVE—*DIESEL THERAPY TO YAZOO*

1. Yazoo City is forty miles northwest of Jackson and is known as the "gateway to the Delta" for its location on the transition between the two great landforms peculiar to Mississippi's land geography. Yazoo City has a population of about 15,000, not counting the inmates at the Yazoo prison complex, and Haley Barbour, the current governor of Mississippi, is from there and has a home on Wolf Lake, a lake just north of Yazoo City.

2. Writer and Editor Willie Morris immortalized Yazoo City in his works of prose with his trademark reflections on the American South, particularly the Mississippi Delta. He attended my alma mater, the University of Texas at Austin where he became the editor of *The Daily Texan*. He became a Rhodes Scholar and returned to become editor of *The Texas Observer*, a liberal Texas magazine. His books *North Toward Home* and *My Dog Skip* became best-sellers, the latter having been made into a movie starring Kevin Bacon, Diane Lane, and Luke Wilson.

3. John Grisham audited Morris's classes when Morris became writer-in-residence at the University of Mississippi in Oxford, Mississippi, where he encouraged a new generation of writers.

CHAPTER THIRTEEN—*EDGEFIELD CAMP*

1. Author James Lieber interviewed Whitacre at the Edgefield Camp on May 22-23, 1999, and again on July 30, 1999, at which time he also met with Ginger Whitacre and their three children. Lieber's account of these experiences and interviews has a more objective and neutral POV. He gives Whitacre's explanation of events involving the ADM case and balances it with his own observations. Lieber's exposition begins on page 297 of *Rats* and continues through page 309.

2. The recipe for Prison Nachos: a. dice 4 onions and 4 tomatoes b. heat 4 or 5 jalapena "squeeze-cheese" bottles (bought at commissary) in the microwave ovens c. mix the contents of 4 noodle soup flavoring packets with the onions and tomatoes d. take the contents of 9 bags of large nacho chips (bought at commissary) and place them in two double-lined plastic garbage bags. e. crush one strip bag of saltine crackers and pour them into the garbage bags (to absorb moisture) f. add the mixture of cheese, onions, and tomatoes to the double-lined garbage bags full of nacho chips g. shake the garbage bag until the nachos are fully covered h. divvy up and EAT!

3. American Bar Association, Justice Kennedy Commission, *Reports with Recommendations to the ABA House of Delegates,* August 2004, pp.13-14.

4. Margaret Colgate Love, "The Debt that Can Never Be Paid: Report Card on Collateral Consequences of Conviction." *Criminal Justice Magazine,* Fall 2006.

CHAPTER FOURTEEN—*PENSACOLA CAMP*

1. Most of the background description about the Pensacola Camp comes from first-hand experience of the author, who attended FPC Pensacola from January 2003 to March 2004.

2. The comment about Alex's good character is excerpted from a recommendation letter dated August 14, 2008, by Paul A. Willis, Chairman, President & CEO of Cypress Systems Inc. addressed "To Whom It May Concern."

CHAPTER FIFTEEN—*VOCATION BECOMES AVOCATION*

1. Steve Rundle and Tom Steffen, *Great Commission Companies, The Emerging Role of Business In Missions* (Downers Grove: InterVarsity Press, 2003), p 13, 16
2. R. Paul Stevens, *The Other Six Days: Vocation, Work, and Ministry in Biblical Perspective* (Grand Rapids: Eerdmans, 1999), p 208.

CHAPTER SIXTEEN—*ACCEPTING RESPONSIBILITY, REALLY*

1. There are a number of parallels between Mark Whitacre and Dr. Jeffrey S. Wigand. The latter, presumably before Mark's case, became known as "the ultimate whistleblower" when, on February 4, 1996, he exposed his company's (Brown & Williamson Tobacco Company's) practice of deliberately chemically altering their nicotine to create an even greater nicotine addiction to their tobacco products. B&W did not recall their tobacco products from the market and retaliated massively against Wigand. He was fired from the company on March 24, 1993, and harassed for most of the rest of his life. He went on to teach high school chemistry in Louisville, Kentucky, and was eventually named Teacher of the Year by the state of Kentucky. However, he was financially ruined and emotionally greatly damaged.
2. In the realm of personal and business ethics, Mark takes a very practical view not unlike that of Warren Buffett. Both boil things down to "don't do anything you wouldn't want to be on the front page of your hometown newspaper." The specific reference in this chapter is to Warren Buffett and his advice to the employees at Salomon Inc. after he became chairman in the wake of the Treasury bid scandal. See "Salomon Inc.: A report by the chairman on the company's standing and outlook," as reported by *The New York Times*, Thursday, October 29, 1991.
3. The Innocence Project is a national litigation and public policy organization dedicated to exonerating wrongfully convicted people through DNA testing and reforming the criminal justice system to prevent future injustice. See *http://innocenceproject.org*
4. Tim Cain is a business journalist for the *Decatur Herald Review*. To read the complete article, go to *http://www.herald-review.com/blogs/timcain/?p=1061*

5. Mark's full admission of guilt is in his essay entitled "An Ethics Lesson For Tomorrow's Business Leaders" which is located at *http://www.markwhitacre.com/businessethics.html*.

CHAPTER SEVENTEEN—*MARK & GINGER: MATURE*

1. Compared to their focus on the Cornell years, Ginger and Mark barely think about prison anymore. Despite its great length and many hardships, the harsher aspects of prison have quickly receded from their memory. As a family, yes, they acknowledge it as part of their shared history, but around the house it's almost as if prison never happened. The poet Maya Angelou once said, "History, despite its wrenching pain, cannot be unlived, but if faced with courage, need not be lived again."

CHAPTER EIGHTEEN—*THE WHITACRE PARDON PETITION*

1. Article II, Section 2 of the United States Constitution gives the executive officer of the United States the power to pardon. The wording is sweeping." .... [The President] shall have Power to Grant Reprieves and Pardons for Offenses against the United States, except in Cases of Impeachment."
2. On September 15, 2000, National Public Radio's Ira Glass, the host and producer of *This American Life* ran a full-hour broadcast entitled "The Fix Is In," with Mark Whitacre. Glass and his production crew traveled to the Edgefield, South Carolina, Prison Camp and set up the interview in the Edgefield visiting room during non-visiting hours.
3. Apparently Scott Z. Burns, who wrote the screenplay for the Soderbergh/Damon movie, *The Informant*, was driving down the highway one day when the program came on his radio. Burns became so mesmerized by the cinematic possibilities for the story that he pulled over on the spot to listen to the rest of the program. Thus was planted the seed for the making of the movie. In a recent in-depth interview with Steven Soderbergh (May 13, 2009), he mentions this as the genesis for the movie again *http://www.comingsoon.net/news/movienews/.php?id=55125*. In that same interview, Soderbergh referred to Whitacre during his undercover years in the 1990s as "Willy Loman on acid."

4. Presidential power has declined steadily since Washington first took office, including the President's power to conduct foreign policy, the veto power, and the power to declare war. An excellent book discussing this is by James M. Scott, entitled *After the End*, published by Duke University Press in 1998.

5. Clinton was challenged by members of Congress for pardoning Rich after he accepted a reported $450,000 donation to his presidential library from Rich's ex-wife. The donation left the strong impression that the pardon was bought. Rich was in Switzerland in 1983 when he was indicted by Rudy Guiliani for tax evasion and making illegal oil deals with Iran during the embargo. He still lives in Switzerland today and is ranked 242nd on the Forbes 400 List of the wealthiest people. Interestingly, Rich was represented from 1985 until 2000 by none other than Scooter Libby.

6. Commutation versus pardon: commuting is the act of reducing a sentence. A President has the ability to commute a sentence before it's even begun, such as Bush II did with Libby. A full pardon can do the same thing; it can also reduce a sentence. But more commonly a pardon is granted after a person serves his prison sentence. And unlike a commutation, a pardon absolves the person of his status as a convicted criminal and restores his civil liberties.

7. President Gerald Ford is widely considered to have lost the 1976 election by pardoning his predecessor, President Richard M. Nixon.

8. Anything that is not prison issue is not permitted and considered contraband.

ACKNOWLEDGMENTS

Writing this book from the Whitacre family perspective has been a unique challenge. Mark and Ginger Whitacre understood this intuitively and, for that, I owe them my deepest gratitude. It is insufficient merely to say that primary thanks go to them and their children for enabling this book to happen. They inspire me by their integrity and compassion for all people, particularly those in prison.

I have been influenced by many teachers. One in particular, however, stands head and shoulders above the rest: the late Margaret "Peg" Feldman. Miss Feldman was my tenth grade English teacher, and she told me when I was young that I was a gifted writer. I leave it to the reader to determine the accuracy of her observation. I wish to acknowledge and honor her memory and her influence on me as a great teacher of English and writing.

I gratefully acknowledge the authors of the two books that paved the way for this one: Kurt Eichenwald, author of *The Informant,* and Jim Lieber, author of *Rats in the Grain*. Both are far better writers than I will ever be. Years of writing business news under a deadline (Eichenwald) and legal briefs (Lieber) put them in a league of their own. Without Eichenwald's book, there would be no movie, and without Lieber's book, many details about the case and its aftermath would not be so readily available. I urge readers of this book to also read theirs.

Bill Rice, a friend of many years whom I first met when he was teaching writing at Harvard College, provided so many insights on so many levels at so many stages of this book, that I cannot adequately thank him. Bill understands more about the art, not merely the craft, of writing, than I ever will.

I could not have stood up under the demands of bringing this book to completion without the support of my brother Rusty. Not only did he proofread and edit like a master, he offered unflagging encouragement on a daily basis. I also wish to extend special thanks to Jack Fultz, Roy and Elena Segers and their baby daughter Madeleine, Darrell Williams, Denise Carlson for her professional indexing skills, Steve Gardner for his understanding, and to the "friend I never met."

Many other people, too numerous to mention, have also given generously of their time commenting on the book. I appreciate their contributions.

Any faults in the text or errors in the work, either of omission or commission, are my sole responsibility.

Finally, I reserve my deepest appreciation and greatest thanks to one person above all others, my daughter Hannah. She is the inspiration for all that has meaning in my life. She is a never-ending source of wonder to me and reminds me that laughter, song, dance, learning, and music are expressions of love, and that unconditional love is the greatest love of all. Hannah, you are my greatest love of all.

LIST OF INTERIOR IMAGES

All Images Courtesy Whitacre Family Collection Unless Otherwise Noted

INDEX

Please note: The acronym "MW" refers to Mark Edward Whitacre. The acronym "GW" refers to Ginger Lynn Gilbert Whitacre. Page numbers in italics indicate photographs or illustrations.

A